Y0-BWD-319

Annuals

Other Publications:

THE SEAFARERS

THE ENCYCLOPEDIA OF COLLECTIBLES

WORLD WAR II

THE GREAT CITIES

HOME REPAIR AND IMPROVEMENT

THE WORLD'S WILD PLACES

THE TIME-LIFE LIBRARY OF BOATING

HUMAN BEHAVIOR

THE ART OF SEWING

THE OLD WEST

THE EMERGENCE OF MAN

THE AMERICAN WILDERNESS

LIFE LIBRARY OF PHOTOGRAPHY

THIS FABULOUS CENTURY

FOODS OF THE WORLD

TIME-LIFE LIBRARY OF AMERICA

TIME-LIFE LIBRARY OF ART

GREAT AGES OF MAN

LIFE SCIENCE LIBRARY

THE LIFE HISTORY OF THE UNITED STATES

TIME READING PROGRAM

LIFE NATURE LIBRARY

LIFE WORLD LIBRARY

FAMILY LIBRARY:
    HOW THINGS WORK IN YOUR HOME
    THE TIME-LIFE BOOK OF THE FAMILY CAR
    THE TIME-LIFE FAMILY LEGAL GUIDE
    THE TIME-LIFE BOOK OF FAMILY FINANCE

Annuals

by

James Underwood Crockett

and

the Editors of TIME-LIFE BOOKS

Watercolor Illustrations by

Allianora Rosse

TIME-LIFE BOOKS, ALEXANDRIA, VIRGINIA

Time-Life Books Inc.
is a wholly owned subsidiary of
TIME INCORPORATED

FOUNDER: Henry R. Luce 1898-1967

Editor-in-Chief: Hedley Donovan
Chairman of the Board: Andrew Heiskell
President: James R. Shepley
Vice Chairmen: Roy E. Larsen, Arthur Temple
Corporate Editors: Ralph Graves, Henry Anatole Grunwald

TIME-LIFE BOOKS INC.

MANAGING EDITOR: Jerry Korn
Executive Editor: David Maness
Assistant Managing Editors: Dale M. Brown, Martin Mann,
John Paul Porter
Art Director: Tom Suzuki
Chief of Research: David L. Harrison
Director of Photography: Robert G. Mason
Planning Director: Thomas Flaherty (acting)
Senior Text Editor: Diana Hirsh
Assistant Art Director: Arnold C. Holeywell
Assistant Chief of Research: Carolyn L. Sackett
Assistant Director of Photography: Dolores A. Littles

CHAIRMAN: Joan D. Manley
President: John D. McSweeney
Executive Vice Presidents: Carl G. Jaeger,
John Steven Maxwell, David J. Walsh
Vice Presidents: Peter G. Barnes (Comptroller),
Nicholas Benton (Public Relations), John L. Canova (Sales),
Herbert Sorkin (Production), Paul R. Stewart (Promotion)
Personnel Director: Beatrice T. Dobie
Consumer Affairs Director: Carol Flaumenhaft

THE TIME-LIFE ENCYCLOPEDIA OF GARDENING

EDITORIAL STAFF FOR ANNUALS
EDITOR: Robert M. Jones
Assistant Editor: Marian Gordon Goldman
Text Editor: Betsy Frankel
Picture Editor: Jane Scholl
Designer: Leonard Wolfe
Staff Writers: Lee Greene, Lucille Schulberg
Chief Researcher: Joan Mebane
Researchers: Muriel Clarke, Evelyn Constable,
Margo Dryden, Elizabeth Evans, Helen Fennell,
Helen Greenway, Villette Harris, Mary Kay Moran,
Louise Samuels, Toby Solovioff
Design Assistant: Mervyn Clay
Staff Illustrator: Vincent Lewis

EDITORIAL PRODUCTION
Production Editor: Douglas B. Graham
Operations Manager: Gennaro C. Esposito
Assistant Production Editor: Feliciano Madrid
Quality Control: Robert L. Young (director),
James J. Cox (assistant), Michael G. Wight (associate)
Art Coordinator: Anne B. Landry
Copy Staff: Susan B. Galloway (chief), Heidi Sanford,
Patricia Miller, Florence Keith, Celia Beattie
Picture Department: Barbara S. Simon
Traffic: Jeanne Potter

CORRESPONDENTS: Elisabeth Kraemer (Bonn); Margot
Hapgood, Dorothy Bacon (London); Susan Jonas, Lucy T.
Voulgaris (New York); Maria Vincenza Aloisi, Josephine du
Brusle (Paris); Ann Natanson (Rome). Valuable assistance
was also provided by Holland McCombs (Dallas); Sally
O'Quin (Los Angeles); Carolyn T. Chubet, Miriam Hsia
(New York); Jane Estes (Seattle).

THE AUTHOR: James Underwood Crockett, a graduate of the University of Massachusetts, received an Honorary Doctor of Science degree from that University and has been cited by the American Association of Nurserymen and the American Horticultural Society. He has worked with plants in California, New York, Texas and New England. He is the author of books on greenhouse, indoor and window-sill gardening, and has written a monthly column for *Horticulture* magazine and a monthly bulletin, *Flowery Talks,* for retail florists. His weekly television program, *Crockett's Victory Garden,* has been seen by more than three million viewers on 125 public broadcasting stations throughout the United States.

THE ILLUSTRATOR: Allianora Rosse, who provided the 98 delicate, precise watercolors of flowering shrubs beginning on page 92, is a specialist in flower painting. Trained at the Art Academy of The Hague in the Netherlands, Miss Rosse worked for 16 years as staff artist for *Flower Grower* magazine. Her illustrations of shrubs, trees and flowers have appeared in many gardening books.

GENERAL CONSULTANTS: Donald Wyman, Horticulturist Emeritus, Arnold Arboretum of Harvard University. Staff of the Brooklyn Botanic Garden; Robert S. Tomson, Assistant Director; Edmond O. Moulin, Horticulturist; George A. Kalmbacher, Consultant Taxonomist; George H. Spalding, Botanical Information Consultant, Los Angeles State and County Arboreta. (Regional consultants are listed on page 171.)

THE COVER: Golden California poppies soak up sun. Originally a yellowish Pacific Coast wild flower, the California poppy is now grown the country over in shades of yellow, red, orange and pink, as well as white.

CONTENTS

Living color the summer long 1

If you ask people who like to grow annuals why they grow them, they may give you a dozen different reasons. They will say that they like them for cut flowers, or for the color they add to the garden, or because they are so easy to grow, or because annuals make it possible for them to have a new garden every year. They're right, of course. But my real reason for growing annuals is this: It does my heart good to start a tiny seed and produce a full-grown plant in a single season, and to reflect, as I gather armfuls of flowers for the house, that even the rankest amateur can grow flowers just as beautiful. I grow annuals for the sheer joy of growing them. And I suspect that deep down this is why other people grow them too.

A good part of this pleasure comes from the flowers themselves, which bloom continuously. Unlike other plants, which store up energy in their roots and rise from those roots again, annuals live and die in one season. To perpetuate their kind they produce seeds, great quantities of them—as much as 50 per cent of an annual's dry weight may be in seeds at the end of a season. To produce many seeds they must produce many flowers. And if those flowers are cut before the seeds can form, the plant tries again and again, in an effort to make up the loss while there is still time. The more you cut an annual, the more it blooms; it is like having your cake and eating it too. If you give a plant good soil, water and room to flourish, the results can be spectacular. My oldest daughter, Carol, when she was eight, received a single petunia plant upon completing a year of Sunday school. She tended it carefully and kept away competition from weeds, grass and nearby overhanging plants. On one day in August of that year I counted no less than 300 blossoms and buds on the single plant!

Along with the joy they bring, annuals can be extremely useful and practical flowers to grow. Because they are themselves temporary, they are ideal for temporary plantings around rented homes and summer cottages. For the same reason they are welcome fill-ins in the garden where permanent plantings have not yet

Bright summer color splashes a garden planted with annuals. Pansies, petunias and dwarf snapdragons are clustered at lower right, white feverfew at left, and tall yellow, pink and orange snapdragons at the rear.

grown large enough to be effective. Because their root systems are small, most annuals are easily moved about the garden if lifted with a big spadeful of soil; experienced gardeners often plant late-blooming varieties in spare pockets in their vegetable gardens, where they will be ready for transplanting into the flower garden as other flowers fade. Many gardeners also plant annuals in pots and other portable containers so they can shift them around at will, to provide color where it is needed; an unusual pot, like a strawberry jar, brimming with bright-colored annuals can be a real summertime conversation piece on a patio. And finally, annuals can provide almost instant screening; there are a number of fast-growing, prolifically flowering annual vines that can turn an eyesore view into a pleasing vista in a matter of a few weeks.

CHOOSING RIGHT VARIETIES
There are hundreds of species of annuals available to the gardener, and thousands of varieties within those species; indeed, the main problem with annuals is deciding which of the many varieties to use. To help you choose which plant to grow where, the photographic essays following show many types of annuals in home settings, and the encyclopedic listing of Chapter 5 provides descriptions of 250 species, and more than 200 of these are illustrated in color. Each encyclopedia entry gives general information about the plant and flower (size, colors, shape); lists requirements for soil, light and climatic conditions; and tells when and how to plant seeds or seedlings in various parts of the United States. A summary chart following the encyclopedia tabulates characteristics of 243 species and varieties, making it easy to pick out flowers of any desired size, color or growth habits. Part of the fun of gardening comes from trying plants one has never grown before. For that reason I strongly suggest that you include each season a few annuals that are new to you. Send for seeds of unfamiliar species and, as they mature, a whole new world of pleasure will open its doors to you.

Because all annuals do not grow at the same rate of speed, the encyclopedia also notes which ones need to be started indoors on window sills or in cold frames (page 87) or greenhouses months before outdoor weather is warm enough for them. A few, such as annual carnations, double-flowering petunias and wax begonias, which take as long as four to six months to go from seed to flower, are ordinarily procured as growing plants in the spring from a commercial greenhouse or garden center. Such plants begin to blossom soon after they are set out and continue until frost.

PLANNING YOUR GARDEN
Because the choice of flowers is so wide, and so many combinations of different varieties are possible, it is important not to plant a garden haphazardly. Before you actually begin, I urge you to use the in-

formation in the encyclopedia and charts to make a plan on paper. It is so much easier to change things on paper than in the garden itself. Also I urge you to be realistic about the size of your garden. One that is small enough to give pleasure without drudgery is far more desirable than one that requires every waking minute to keep it from reverting to wilderness—even a bed of annuals only three feet across permits you to plant various groups of flowers and have them intermingle gracefully.

When planning your garden, don't make the mistake of thinking only of the flowers themselves. They should be considered as part of the whole garden, not as separate entities. They are much more effective when seen against one another or against some other garden feature—a fence, a wall, a hedge. Logically you may want to put taller plants at the back and smaller ones in front, but do not be too rigid about this. A little variety in plant height throughout the beds adds interest to the garden. Choose colors you like, and colors that are pleasing in combination with one another and with the color of your home, but avoid planting too many colors and too many plant varieties; masses of single colors of one plant species are usually much more effective. Match the actual configuration of your flower bed to its surroundings: formal gardens call for precisely symmetrical beds, but in informal gardens the beds are more appealing if they are curved to blend with the shape of permanent plantings. Keep in mind too that the color and texture of foliage, as well as the way flowers grow—in tall spikes, like larkspur and lupine; in clumps, like marigold and browallia—have an important bearing on the overall design of the garden. Generally speaking, it is also an excellent idea to make each group of plants overlap the one beside it, so that blossoms seem to flow into one another rather than stand out as isolated spots of color.

When selecting annuals for your garden, you must of course consider its conditions of climate, sunshine and soil. Most annuals do require direct sun, although there are a handful that bloom in the shade. The majority demand plenty of water, which can come either from the heavens or the garden hose. Very hot weather kills some annuals, but the problem of cold is easy to get around—just grow the plant indoors until frost danger has passed. Soil requirements for most annuals are less stringent than for many other plants; however, you will find that close attention to the soil is worthwhile because it pays a handsome return in quantity and beauty of bloom.

Years ago I had a college professor who objected strenuously whenever any of his students called soil "dirt." To him, and to most serious gardeners, that wonderful material in which plants grow de-

COWSLIP WINE

Experiments in making tasty drinks from flowers are legion, ranging from geranium tea to dandelion wine. The following recipe for a wine made from cowslips, close relatives of the primrose (Primula polyantha, page 147), appeared in 1770 in the "Art of Cookery made Plaine and Easy," written by a Mrs. Glasse: "Take six gallons of water, 12 pounds of sugar, the juice of six lemons, the whites of four eggs. Beat very well, put all together in a kettle, let boil half an hour, skim very well; take a peck of cowslips, if dry ones, half a peck; put them into a tub with the thin peeling of six lemons, then pour on the boiling liquor, and stir them about. . . . Lay the bung loose for two or three days to see if it works, and if it don't, bung it down tight."

GROWING CONDITIONS

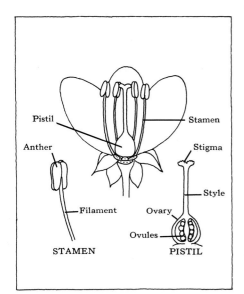

Each bright, delicately shaped blossom on an annual is a miniature factory designed to propagate its species by producing as many seeds as possible during the plant's short life. In a typical flower, shown cutaway above, this reproductive system consists of long, thin male stamens surrounding a jug-shaped female pistil. When the pollen ripens, the anthers at the tips of the stamens open, releasing thousands of pollen grains. Some of these grains, carried by the wind or by insects such as bees that feed on the sweet nectar produced by the flower, are deposited on the fuzzy surface of the stigma atop the pistil; there they form pollen tubes that grow down through the slender column called the style, finally reaching the ovary (shown cutaway in detail, right) and fertilizing the eggs, or ovules, to produce the flower's seeds.

serves the more dignified name of soil. It is easy enough to say that there are many kinds of good soil, for plants differ enough in their requirements that a soil admirably suited for one kind of plant might not be at all what is needed for another species. Nevertheless, a good garden soil has certain characteristic qualities. It should be deep and fertile; it should be well drained; it should have an abundant supply of organic matter so that it can hold moisture; and it should be porous so that air and moisture can get into it. Such a soil is normally inhabited by myriads of soil bacteria, which are constantly breaking down the organic matter in the soil to its basic chemical components and making these components available to plants for their nourishment and growth.

A word you often meet in horticultural literature is *humus,* defined in my dictionary as "a brown or black substance resulting from the partial decay of leaves and other vegetable matter; organic part of soil." Horticulturally speaking, humus is generally thought of as that portion of the organic matter of soil that has decayed to the point where its origin can no longer be determined. As humus continues the process of decay, it releases the nutrients that plants actually assimilate. Needless to say, a soil without humus is a barren soil.

Have you ever wondered just what makes up the soils of our gardens? Usually soil is a mixture of rock particles in various stages of weathering, plus a certain amount of humus. There are certain soils, such as muck soils, which are nearly all organic matter, composed of decayed peat and other vegetation, but ordinary garden soil is made up almost entirely of tiny bits of rock, with much less organic matter than is optimum for good plant growth.

One does not have to be a gardener for long before one is aware that there are two schools of thought regarding the treatment of soil for the best production of plants. One camp holds that all chemical fertilizers are taboo, and some go so far as to say that they are poisonous to our soil. They claim that everything that goes into soil to promote plant growth should be organic in nature. These are the organic gardeners, and they are a multitude. From the number of blue ribbons they win at county fairs, one would be inclined to say that they make a very good case for their cause. The other group might be called the chemical gardeners. They hold that the soil is simply a convenient place for plants to get support so that they can hold themselves upright, and the food that they need should be supplied by chemical formulas. They say that since plants have to have all their food in its basic chemical form before they can assimilate it, why go to the bother of carting heavy manure onto the ground and mixing it in, then waiting for soil bacteria to break it down so that the plants can use it? The discussions between proponents of each view go on and on, and they can become extremely caustic.

I believe that there is ample room for most gardeners in the area between the extremes. It is a commonly accepted fact that organic matter adds more to a soil than its food value, for it improves the physical structure of a soil tremendously, giving it the capacity to hold moisture and making it open and friable so that roots may easily penetrate it and supply the plant with food. On the other hand, chemical fertilizers are invaluable in supplying what might be called quick energy and are regularly used as side dressings to grow crops. The term "side dressing" is given to the practice of adding a surface application of a chemical fertilizer alongside plants to give them an extra boost during their growing period. This is usually cultivated into the top inch or two of soil. Rain or irrigation water carries the nutrients down to the plant roots.

There are three soil characteristics that exert the most influence on the growth of annuals (and other plants): (1) porosity, which determines how quickly water drains away; (2) fertility; and (3) acidity. In most areas of the United States and Canada, all three of these characteristics are fairly simple to alter if necessary —even to the point of providing special conditions for individual beds of flowers if you want to take the trouble.

The texture of soil can be a problem if it is either too "light" —so sandy that moisture drains away very quickly—or so "heavy" with clay that moisture and air cannot penetrate it. The remedy is the same in either case: Add organic matter to attain a soil structure that is open but still retains moisture. The additive most commonly used for this purpose is peat moss, which is sold in bales or bags by garden-supply centers. Peat moss is vegetable matter that has partially decayed in the water of marshes; it retains the original fibrous nature of the plant material from which it came and the fibers help hold water in the soil. Make sure peat moss is moist before use, otherwise it can be unpleasantly loose and dusty to work with. If it is dry, leave it outdoors for a few weeks so rain can dampen it, or hose it down with a fine spray until it feels spongy.

Most soils also need adjustments not only to their texture but also to their acidity. You can find out how much adjustment is necessary by testing with one of the kits sold by garden-supply stores. For a more elaborate analysis, send a soil sample to the nearest office of your county agricultural extension service (listed as such under the heading of the county name in the phone book) or to a commercial laboratory that makes soil tests. Such tests indicate acidity in terms of a number called a pH factor. The pH scale runs from 0, extremely acid, or "sour," to 14, extremely alkaline, or "sweet." For annuals, and indeed for the majority of garden plants,

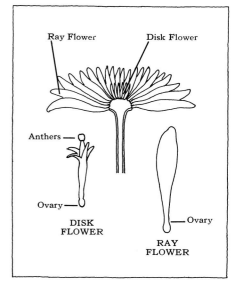

A daisy head, shown cutaway above, is typical of the most highly evolved family of flowers, the composites, which includes such other common annuals as zinnias and chrysanthemums. As the term indicates, a composite is not one flower but many separate flowers living on the same flower head. The tiny flowers crowded together at the center, or disk, are called disk flowers; each has both male anthers and a female ovary (detail, left). Each petal, or ray flower (right) has an ovary at its base, which may be functional or sterile. A composite is designed for highly efficient reproduction: a single bee carrying pollen on its body can pollinate scores of disk flowers in a matter of seconds.

ACID AND ALKALINE SOIL

Many flowers, annuals included, come in both single- and double-flowered varieties. The single-flower type (top drawing), such as a poppy, has one ring of petals and closely resembles the wild flower from which it came. Double flowers (lower drawing) have numerous overlapping rings of petals. Because of their popularity, doubles have been selected for breeding and for crossbreeding to produce new varieties. Semi-doubles are flowers that have more petals than the original wild flower but less than doubles.

the optimum pH reading is between 6.0 and 6.8—in other words, slightly acid. The agricultural tests will indicate what you should do to bring your soil's pH factor into balance, as well as how to improve its texture and fertility.

Lime will sweeten soil that is too acid, and various forms of sulfur will cut down alkalinity. The safest form of lime to use around plants is ground limestone, which is slow-acting and continues its work for years. Slaked or hydrated lime produces very quick effects but it is also very powerful, and most garden authorities agree that it should be used only with great caution. Because limestone acts slowly, it should be incorporated into the soil well before the planting season. In fact the ideal time to apply limestone is in the fall. To raise the pH one-half to one unit, add five pounds of ground limestone for every 100 square feet of light to medium soil; for heavier soils with a lot of organic matter, increase the amount by one third. If fertilizer is also being used, the two should go into the ground at least a week apart, for lime acts to reduce the nutritive value of the nitrogen in the fertilizer.

An alkaline soil can be improved by the use of ground sulfur, iron sulfate or aluminum sulfate. Sulfur acts slowly but is effective for years; iron sulfate and aluminum sulfate are quicker acting but do not last as long. Of the latter two, iron sulfate is preferable because it also adds iron to the soil, encouraging rich, dark foliage. If you use aluminum sulfate, you run some risk of an aluminum build-up in the soil that might be toxic to plants. To lower the pH one half to one unit, add one-half pound of finely ground sulfur, or three pounds of iron sulfate or aluminum sulfate, to each 100 square feet of soil; for heavier soils, increase the rate one third.

ADDING THE VITAL NUTRIENTS

Along with additions of peat moss and lime or sulfur, most soils need extra nutrients for growing plants. It must be applied with caution, however, for too much is as bad as not enough. Many annuals flower most abundantly if the soil is relatively infertile; generous doses of nitrogen-rich fertilizer make such plants concentrate their energies on growing big stems and leaves instead of blossoms. And an excess of fertilizer can actually kill a plant. I once experimented by putting two or three times the recommended amount on some coleus plants. After a while I pulled them up and found their roots burned to short stubs.

The nutrients generally in short supply are three chemical elements: nitrogen, which makes plants lush and green; phosphorus, which stimulates root growth and gives young plants extra energy; and potassium, which promotes vigorous growth so plants are better able to resist disease and cold. All three elements are present in variable amounts in such organic fertilizers as manure and cottonseed meal; bonemeal contains nitrogen and phosphorus; wood ashes are a good source of potassium.

Chemical fertilizers, which contain compounds plants can use directly, act faster. Many gardeners prefer them for this reason and also for their uniformity. Each bag of a so-called "complete" fertilizer contains all three essential elements in a proportion spelled out on the label. This balance of nutrients is specified by a series of three numbers, such as 5-8-7, 10-6-2, 4-8-4, 5-10-5. In each case the first number indicates the percentage of nitrogen, the second the percentage of phosphorus and the third the percentage of potassium (all in the form of various compounds). The remainder of the bag's contents is some sort of inert material, such as sand or ground peanut hulls, which helps to dilute the powerful chemicals and distribute them evenly through the soil.

In my own garden, I use both organic and chemical fertilizers. I do not hesitate to apply chemical fertilizers when I think a plant needs the quick energy of a booster shot. But for a general soil additive it is hard to beat well-rotted barnyard manure even though it usually contains little nitrogen, and the gardener who has access to horse, cow or poultry manure is fortunate indeed. If he is prudent he will keep his source of supply a secret—genuine manure is not easy to come by. (Manure is also sold in dry form in bags at garden stores, but it is generally more expensive.) As an alternative, and a very good one, many gardeners turn to a chemically enriched compost, which is sometimes called synthetic or artificial manure. These terms imply inferiority, yet such compost can be even more valuable than good natural manure. It improves the physical structure of the soil enormously—lightening heavy soil, giving body to light soil. The soil of a plant bed into which two or three inches of compost has been worked makes gardening a joy.

A nutritious compost is made by combining such things as leaves, hay, straw, grass clippings and other plant refuse, then enriching it with small quantities of simple chemicals and permitting the mixture to decay. In preparing a batch, spread the plant ingredients in layers 4 to 10 inches deep, depending on the coarseness or fineness of the material—grass clippings should be 4 inches deep, heavy plant stems, 10 inches. Over each layer sprinkle a mixture of six parts ammonium sulfate, three parts superphosphate and four parts ground limestone, using about a pint of this combination to each two bushels of plant material. (In lieu of these chemicals, you can also use a mixture of 10 parts of an all-purpose chemical fertilizer, such as 5-8-7, to 2½ parts of ground limestone.) If a small amount of barnyard manure is added to each layer, it will seed the pile with bacteria that speed decomposition.

THE LIFESAVING FOXGLOVE

Although the ancients stocked their pharmacopoeia with many herbs and flowers, they overlooked the foxglove; the English herbalist John Gerard observed in 1597 that the plants "are of no use, neither have they any place amongst medicines." Not until the 18th Century was the value of foxglove recognized. Today modern medicine, despite its wide range of synthetic wonder drugs, continues to rely on the foxglove extract, digitalis, for the most widely used medication in the treatment of heart disease.

MAKING ENRICHED COMPOST

Make the pile four to six feet high; it will shrink considerably as it composts. And keep the layers level but dish-shaped, to catch and hold rain water. The easiest way to achieve this is to build the pile inside an enclosure (plain board fencing will serve). The pile should be moistened as it is prepared, and should be kept moist during the period of decay; fork over the entire pile from time to time, so that the dry outer material gets into the center where it will "brew" faster and the whole pile will decompose uniformly. At the end of the brewing period, which takes three to six months, depending on the plant materials used and the warmth and moisture maintained, you should have about two pounds of compost for every pound of plant material—the added weight comes mostly from moisture absorbed during the composting process.

SEEDS: KEY TO QUALITY Yet no matter how carefully you handle fertilizers, choose plant types and treat your soil, a large part of your effort can be wasted unless you use good-quality seeds. Good seeds are first of all fresh seeds. Although we have all marveled at the tales of 1,000-year-old lotus seeds that have sprouted, most seeds in fact lose their vitality in two or three years, and the older they are the less likely they are to germinate. Most reputable seedsmen mark their seed packets with a date indicating the year for which they were produced.

Good seeds are also the result of careful breeding programs, a fact often overlooked by cost-conscious home gardeners who attempt to raise plants from seeds they themselves have grown. On the farms of reputable seedsmen, horticulturists inspect the seed crops regularly, pulling out plants that do not meet a certain standard. Few home gardeners possess the critical eye necessary for such selectivity, or the willingness to destroy plants, however imperfect, that still add a bit of color to the garden. As a result home-saved seeds are likely to represent mixed parentage—those friendly bees visit good plants and poor plants indiscriminately, and the fruits of their labors may reflect the qualities of either one.

Home-saved seeds can also be a disappointment on another score because so many of today's annuals are hybrids. Their seeds do not always breed true, that is, the offspring do not resemble the parents. Hybrid petunias, for example, generate many seeds that will produce sturdy seedlings. But the novice gardener tempted by the prospect of getting more brilliantly colored flowers free will find his hopes dashed, for the flowers on second-generation plants are likely to be the muddy magenta of their semiwild ancestors.

THE HYBRID ARISTOCRATS In sharp contrast to the doubtful progeny of home-grown seeds are the outstanding plants that can be grown from scientifically bred seeds. Perhaps the most noteworthy among these breeding achievements are the big, sturdy and colorful marigolds and petunias yielded by the so-called F_1 hybrid seeds (F derives from "filial," while the subscript 1 stands for first generation). The production of these seeds begins with the selection of two different parent plants; these can be plants of the same species or a different species, but each parent must have been so inbred over many generations that when mated with its own kind it always yields a duplicate of itself. These two parents are mated by a delicate hand process. Seedsmen force open the bud of the chosen seed-producing flower and remove its pollen-bearing stamens, the slender filaments in the middle of the flower *(drawing, page 10)*. Then they dust the stigma, the top of the female organ in the bud, with pollen from the chosen male plant and enclose the bud in a plastic bag to protect it from any further pollination by insect- or wind-borne pollen. The result is F_1 seeds, which combine desirable qualities from both parents and produce plants superior to either. Since F_1 seeds must be regenerated by this complex method every season, they cost more than ordinary seeds.

In efforts to demonstrate the worth of new and improved flowers such as those of the F_1 hybrids, professional seedsmen go to great lengths. Throughout the United States and Canada, for instance, they sponsor a network of trial grounds where new plant varieties are grown alongside standard types to determine whether or not the new ones are superior. Judges in each area score the plants according to their performance under local conditions, and the findings are compiled by a national board of horticulturists. The plants that win approval are designated All-America Selections, and seedsmen list them as such in their catalogues. From year to year the number of All-America Selections may vary, and indeed in some years no plants may be chosen because the judges found no new varieties better than the old ones.

Good seeds ordinarily can be purchased from racks at garden centers, but many gardeners prefer to order them by mail from the seed catalogues of various companies. The range of choice is much greater and through catalogues you can get the more unusual species, flowers that may not be available locally, or compare the qualities of different species at your leisure. For a dedicated gardener, one of the delights of winter is leafing through the bright pages of the seed catalogue with its promise of spring. I began ordering seed catalogues when I was eight years old. I remember lying awake at night for fear that some seedsman would come knocking at the door to ask my parents what this eight-year-old kid thought he was doing, ordering seed catalogues. But you can learn a lot from a seed catalogue. I still read them for information on new flower varieties, for tips on planting and cultivation—and just for fun.

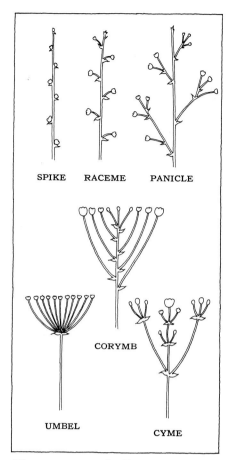

SPIKE RACEME PANICLE

CORYMB

UMBEL CYME

The appearance of a flowering plant in a garden depends not only on the size, shape and color of its blossoms, but on inflorescence, the order of flowering and arrangement of the blooms on their stems. In the spike type of flower (above), which includes such annuals as snapdragons, many blossoms grow tightly along a central stalk. The raceme type, such as larkspur, is similar except that the blooms are borne on their own smaller stalks along the central stalk. In the panicle type, such as babies'-breath, the side stalks branch to bear small clusters of flowers. The umbel type—blue lace flower, for example—has stalks that spread from the very top of the main stalk. In the corymb type, such as candytuft, stalks rise from various points along the main stalk to form a flat-topped cluster. And in the cyme type (sweet William), the main stalk is terminated by a flower, which blooms first, followed by other clusters on the main and side stalks.

The many roles of nonstop blooms

Like jewels, the flowering annuals have one primary purpose: to delight the eye. And like jewels, they delight in many ways, formally or informally, setting off background colors, framing features, calling attention to focal points. But they can also surpass jewels, for as living flowers they appeal to all the senses. The silken shells of petunias or the velvety petals of salpiglossis almost ask to be touched. The pungence of marigolds fills a warm summer day; as the light fails, evening stock freshens the air. A few annuals like basil and scarlet runner beans are cultivated for their taste. And one can even hear the whispering sounds of rabbit-tail or quaking grass when the breeze rustles its slender stalks.

Yet for all their gemlike qualities and delicate gifts to the senses, annuals are very practical. They are surprisingly versatile, sturdy and cheap—the all-purpose plants of gardening. They blossom under a wide range of conditions quickly, brightly and so steadily that their flowers might be called nonstop blooms. They produce great masses of color by themselves, or sharp accents of color for other plantings. In parts of the country where midsummer sun is often hot enough to wilt grass, they thrive if properly watered; planted along the edges of a perennial garden in the spring, they produce fresh color in July and August, just when most perennials are not in bloom. Some varieties are especially adapted to lend summer liveliness to the geometry of formal boxwood gardens; others do the same for informal rock gardens, complementing the perennial alpine varieties often grown there; and still others flourish in the shade of a wall or a dense-foliaged tree where few flowers can grow.

Annuals inherit much of their toughness and versatility from their ancestors, the wild flowers that gave birth to modern garden flowers and that still bloom exuberantly all over the world. And although the annuals grown today have been domesticated into a whole catalogue of sizes, shapes and shades, they retain that same wild determination to be what one writer called "the finishing touch to Nature's handiwork."

On an ivy-covered wall, a basin filled with annual carnations hangs above massed Martha Washington geraniums.

16

Plants that take the edge off edges

Among the places where annuals can be most attractively and usefully employed is along the edges of walks, walls and garden beds, where they screen and soften straight, man-made lines and provide graceful transitions from one outdoor area to another. Whether they blossom out of high pots or low beds, edgings of flowers catch the eye and lead it, framing a view *(left),* pointing toward a front door *(overleaf)* or just drawing attention to their own colorful blooms.

Strategically located, the bright colors of the flowers provide brilliant accents against the background greenery of permanent plantings or the muted colors of wood, slate, adobe or brick. Reds, whites or yellows play nicely against the far-off blue of sky and water. The palette of colors is almost limitless, for annuals come in nearly every shade from near black to pure white. The color schemes are up to the gardener's own eye; even if he makes a color mistake, it is no disaster. Next year the gardener can try new colors, and new kinds of flowers as well.

Cascading white and purple petunias and pink geraniums edge a flagstone walk at Marblehead Neck, Massachusetts. From the walk or the nearby house the flowers make a stunning frame for the harbor view.

Outside a house in New Mexico, plantings soften the edge of a curb and lead the eye—and footsteps—to the front door. At left,

purple and white petunias brim from pots; at right, yellow dwarf marigolds rim a curved bed of juniper and perennial delphinium.

Pink wax begonias provide a low, neat edging for a border on a Long Island lawn (above). Behind them are perennials—fuchsia-colored bee balm and yellow marguerites—and a flowering shrub, blue hydrangea. The wax begonias keep the garden colorful for months, even when the other flowers have faded.

In curves of color, low-lying white wax begonias and pots of pink geraniums soften the line of permanent evergreens and blue hydrangeas in another garden. A huge basket of perennial trailing begonias hangs from the tree at left.

An edging of a single, boldly shaped flower—pink Gertrude geraniums—outlines the length of a curved brick wall on a grassy

terrace in Spokane, Washington. The sweep of flowers unifies the wall and permanent plants with simplicity and elegance.

Summer color in the rocks

Some gardeners believe the only flowers that belong in a rock garden are alpine plants, which are perennials. But annuals make rock gardens, like other gardens, come to life again after the first flush of spring-blooming perennials has faded. Annuals to be used in this way should be carefully selected from among those that are small in size, with limited root systems, and can survive in the tiny, quick-draining pockets of earth between the rocks. The plants should lie low, never much higher than the 12 inches or so of the red salvia shown blooming below.

In the rock garden pictured above, a border is filled with annuals displaying their brilliant colors: white alyssum, blue lobelia and spiky red salvia. The garden also makes use of various perennial flowers and low, rock-covering sedum.

Clumps of godetias—pink, red and white with pink markings inside the flowers—make a bright display on the slope of the rock garden at left. To the left of the godetias are red snapdragons and purple verbena; perennial chrysanthemums and spikes of heather are seen at lower left.

Massed blooms
for a
formal garden

Many of the annuals that supply bright patches of random hues in informal gardens can be used equally well in broad tapestries of color to soften and enliven the geometric design of formal gardens. A formal garden, which provides a pleasant area for strolling in or just looking at, depends on strict pattern, repetition and symmetry for its effect. It generally contains flowers that blossom profusely and are low-growing and compact; such flowers will fill up the spaces between trimmed evergreen borders such as boxwood with uniform masses of color and will not straggle or overlap the precise green edges. Well suited to this use are dwarf varieties of zinnias, marigolds, petunias and ageratum, which have been bred to just such specifications. Alyssum, lobelia, gazania, wax begonias, periwinkle and portulaca are also good choices. Within the strong framework of a formal pattern, like that of the garden at right, the gardener can often achieve a more arresting effect with only two or three kinds of flowers than he could if he planted the same flowers in informal beds.

Annuals enliven permanent plantings in a precisely reconstructed Victorian garden in San Antonio, Texas. White Madagascar periwinkles emphasize the curve of the beds in the foreground. Portulaca in a rainbow of colors fill the squares between paving and clipped boxwood in the background.

Flowers that grow in the shade

Most annuals, being natives of semiarid regions of the world, demand full sunshine in order to survive. But for gardeners who want to grow flowers under trees, or along a wall that cuts out sun, there are a number of plants that flourish in the shade. Many inherit this ability from wild flowers that bloom on the dark floors of dense tropical forests. Three of the most popular are wax begonias, impatiens and coleus (see chart beginning on page 166 for others). Shade-tolerant annuals are best started indoors or bought as growing plants to be set outside.

Two kinds of shade-tolerant annuals, blue ageratum and red impatiens, bloom brightly in front of tall perennial Shasta daisies in the Denver garden above. Set under trees, the flowers get only a few hours of sunlight a day, yet blossom from early summer until fall.

Annuals selected to thrive in the shade of a wall enhance a garden in San Diego, California. At the front are pink wax begonias. Just beyond, bright red cineraria leans out over the brick border beneath dark red impatiens. The red leaves of bloodleaf (Iresine) are seen at center.

Borders: brilliant and functional

The visual impact of great numbers of annuals, massed by themselves without other kinds of plantings, can be so striking that no other reason is needed for planting them. Yet such large beds of flowers can perform useful functions too. Placed to one side of back yards, they can act as cutting gardens; the flowers removed will hardly be missed because the plants generate new blooms so quickly. Laid out in a border around one or more sides of a lawn, wide beds of annuals can define and enhance the central space. Snaked in a curve across an open lawn, as in the picture at right, they separate two parts of a garden—a play area from a formal outdoor living space, for example. A border can also serve as a transition from one kind of outdoor area to another (overleaf).

Many-colored masses of different annuals provide an exciting rainbow effect, but plantings of one or two colors can be equally dramatic—all yellow flowers, yellow and white, red and white, or related colors such as yellow and orange, as seen on the following pages.

A blaze of annuals snakes across a lawn in Massachusetts. The small lavender flowers in front are ageratum. The taller flowers, from right to left, are yellow snapdragons, feathery pink and orange zinnias, pink petunias and golden marigolds, with white and purple petunias added as the pattern repeats.

Orange and yellow marigolds provide a bright splash of color bordering a wall and a rolling field of grass in Connecticut. The

flowers were grown from seeds sown in spring indoors and transplanted to the border. Next to the stone wall are woodland ferns.

How
to grow
annuals 2

Many an eager gardener, anxious to get an early start, begins to dig too soon. He starts cultivating his annual bed before the soil has had a chance to dry out, and instead of loosening and aerating the ground as he should, he makes the wet earth harder and denser. Choosing the right time to begin work is the first task facing anyone who wants attractive banks of pretty flowers. A soil that is ready for digging holds its shape when it is squeezed in the hand, but disintegrates at the flick of the finger.

This test holds everywhere in the country. In those parts of the United States where the ground freezes hard during the winter months, Zones 3 through 7 *(map, page 164),* the time for beginning the gardening cycle comes in the spring, soon after the frost leaves the ground. But in Zones 8, 9 and 10 where the ground does not freeze, a garden can be started in any month of the year. And even in zones of severe frost, gardeners sometimes prepare the soil in the fall and plant hardy seeds—such as poppies, cornflowers, larkspur and nigella—to winter over and germinate in the first warm days of spring. A fall-prepared garden has other benefits. Soil nutrients and conditioners have a chance to blend in more thoroughly. This is especially true if ground limestone, a slow-acting additive, must be spread to neutralize acid soil.

The first step in readying a flower bed—whether you are going to plant seeds or transplant seedlings grown indoors or bought from a garden store—is to dig along the edge with a spade, which makes a clear, sharp outline. Then turn over the soil within the bed with a spading fork—easier to dig in and lift up than the solid-bladed spade. Dig to the full depth of the fork, breaking up the lumps as you go. (For the proper technique, see the drawing on the next page.) Then spread 2 or 3 inches of organic material over the soil. Most commonly used for this purpose is coarse moist peat moss, purchased by the bag or bale from the garden-supply store, but well-rotted manure or compost is better (both supply extra nourishment, and compost from your own pile is free). Over this layer

A young housewife selects petunias already started in pots to provide instant flowers for her garden. Hallmarks of a good ready-to-plant annual are dark foliage and sturdy growth with many branches.

of organic material spread a thin layer of chemical fertilizer.

The kind of fertilizer to be used at this stage is critical. If it contains a high proportion of nitrogen compounds, it will spur the plant to produce luxuriant foliage but few flowers. The right kind is one that is low in nitrogen, for example, 5-10-5 (5 per cent nitrogen compound, 10 per cent phosphoric acid, 5 per cent potash). High-nitrogen fertilizers such as 10-5-10 should be used very sparingly.

Turn the fertilizer and the peat moss, mixing them thoroughly into the soil, and continue to break the lumps; then rake the surface with a steel-toothed rake until it is very fine. Finally add on top of the bed a thin layer of another fertilizer, 20 per cent superphosphate, which encourages root growth and an abundance of flowers; use about three quarters of a pound of superphosphate for every 100 square feet. If the soil has an unusually high content of clay—indicated by a tendency to form a crust after rains—add an additional layer of fine peat moss to prevent crusting. Spread the layer about 1 inch thick and rake it into the top 2 or 3 inches of soil. Moisten the bed, let the water soak in, and rake it again.

SPACING THE PLANTS   Considering how much most gardeners value space in their own personal surroundings, it is surprising how few of them remember that flowers, too, need room to grow. The spectacular blooms in seed

PREPARING AN OUTDOOR SEEDBED

Break up the soil of the seedbed by driving a spading fork into the soil the full depth of its tines; then pull back. If you are right-handed, apply pressure to the fork with your left foot to avoid having to step aside when you pull back on the handle.

Turn over the soil with the fork, removing stones and debris; break up clods by hitting them with the back of the fork. Then cover the soil with 2 or 3 inches of peat moss, compost or manure, followed by a thin layer of low-nitrogen fertilizer.

After thoroughly mixing the soil, peat moss and fertilizer with the spading fork, rake over the seedbed several times until it reaches a fine consistency. Then add a thin layer of superphosphate to stimulate root growth, and rake it in thoroughly.

catalogues are partly the result of the growers' gardening routine, which automatically gives each plant living space to reach its full potential. Home gardeners should also be careful to avoid crowding their plants. The encyclopedia section at the back of this book indicates how far apart each species should be planted—and this distance applies not only to the groups of seeds sown outdoors, but to transplanted seedlings as well.

One simple way to space plants properly is to rule off the garden in a grid based on these optimum distances; e.g., if the mature plants need 8 inches between them, the grid lines should be 8 inches apart. You can make such a grid by marking the intervals with a rule and at each mark laying your hoe handle flat on the ground and pressing it lightly into the soil with your foot to make a line. At each intersection of lines set out a plant or sow a few seeds. The intersecting lines remind you where seeds were planted; anything that sprouts elsewhere must be a weed and can confidently be hoed up. (The weeds generally come up before the seedlings and are usually hard to recognize.) If the bed is to contain more than one kind of flower, demarcate the areas for each by drawing a curved line through the bed with a pointed stick, so the various flowers will blend together attractively.

Pouring seeds into the ground from their little paper envelope sounds like an absurdly simple step. But once you inadvertently dump a whole packet—enough for an entire row—into a single spot, you'll realize there's a trick even to this. The correct technique depends on the size of the seed. Large seeds, like those of nasturtiums, can be poured into the palm of the hand and placed in the soil one by one. Medium-sized seeds, like those of zinnias, can be tapped gently from the seed packet. To do this, slit or tear off the top of the packet and squeeze the two long sides of the packet together between the thumb and forefinger, so that the packet spreads open. Tap the top of the packet with the index finger, and the seeds will slide out of the packet mouth a few at a time. Very fine seeds are more easily handled and evenly distributed by mixing them first with fine sand; both seeds and sand are then sprinkled on the soil at the grid intersections.

The depth to which seeds should be covered also depends on their size—and, to a certain extent, on the time of year. In early spring, when the soil is still cool and damp, seeds need a light covering so that all possible warmth from the sun can reach them; in later spring and summer they need to be sown deeper because the sun quickly dries out the soil and could deprive them of needed moisture. Thus, seeds that are sown $\frac{1}{8}$ to $\frac{1}{4}$ inch deep in the spring—the usual depth for the average-sized seed—should be

THE ROYAL CORNFLOWER
Cornflowers—so called because they thrive in fields of grain—flourished in ancient Egypt, where they were considered fit for royalty. In 1922 when archeologists opened the tomb of Tutankhamen, an Egyptian king of the 14th Century B.C., they found among the gold and alabaster treasures buried with him several garlands of cornflowers. The blossoms were still blue, preserved in the dark and dryness of the sealed chambers in which the Egyptians laid their royal dead.

HOW TO SOW SEEDS

CROSSHATCHING THE BED TO SPACE PLANTS

1. *To set seeds in order to space plants properly and simplify weeding, first mark off the bed in a grid by pressing a hoe handle into the soil. Separate the grid lines by the distance specified for mature plants (Chapter 5).*

2. *Place several seeds at each of the points where the lines intersect. Sow large seeds individually and cover them to the depth called for in the instructions on the seed packet; tap small seeds from the packet and do not cover them. Firm the soil around the seeds.*

3. *Sowing seeds only at the grid intersections makes it easy to identify weeds—anything that sprouts elsewhere must be a weed. When hoeing weeds, clear the area in front of you before working farther into the bed to avoid trampling on young plants.*

4. *When the seedlings produce their first true leaves, thin the bed by removing all but the most robust plant in each clump. Pull out the weak seedlings carefully. Be sure the soil is moist so they can be pulled without disturbing the roots of the remaining plant.*

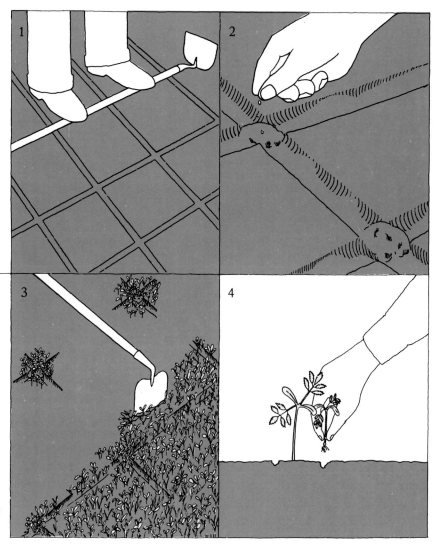

sown ¼ to ½ inch deep later on in the season. There are two exceptions to this rule. Very fine seeds never need covering no matter when they are sown; they cover themselves because they are finer than the soil and slip down into it. The other exception is sweet pea seeds, which are planted in a deep trench according to a special procedure *(page 41)* that is designed to protect their delicate roots from too much of the sun's heat.

Immediately after the seeds are sown, firmly press the soil down on top of them with the heel of your hand or the back of a hoe. Leave a shallow depression to mark the spot; this not only acts as a little reservoir, gathering the water that the seeds need to germinate; it also makes the grid intersections more obvious, clearly distinguishing the seed-bearing spots from the areas that can safely be weeded. Water the seeds gently but thoroughly with a very fine

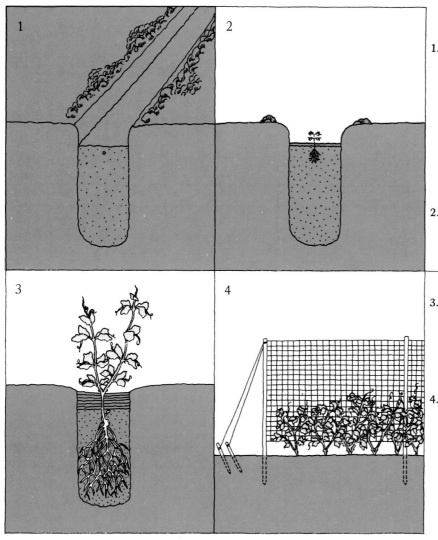

SPECIAL TECHNIQUES FOR GROWING SWEET PEAS

1. *To grow the temperamental sweet pea successfully, first dig a trench 1 foot wide and 2 feet deep with vertical sides. Fill the trench to within 4 inches of the top with a mixture of 40 per cent well-rotted cow manure, 40 per cent loam and 20 per cent sand. (If decayed cow manure is unavailable, compost will do.) Push the seeds ½ inch into the mixture, 2 inches apart.*

2. *When the seedlings are 2 inches tall, pull soil from the sides of the trench, adding ½ inch around stems as support for the plants.*

3. *Pull on another ½ inch of soil for each 2 inches of plant growth, repeating until the trench is filled almost to the level of the ground. Leave a central depression to retain moisture.*

4. *Provide a sturdy support for the climbing plants by setting 6-foot-high stakes of redwood or cedar 6 feet apart and stretching mesh-fiber or plastic netting between the stakes. The sweet peas will climb by winding their tendrils around the netting. Mulch the soil during the dry summer months to keep it moist and cool.*

spray. Make sure they stay moist until they have sprouted. If the garden location is exceptionally sunny, lay a piece of burlap or loose-mesh cheesecloth over the seedbed to prevent evaporation of moisture. Peg down the burlap with sticks or anchor it with stones. This cover serves a dual function: it not only protects the seedlings from drying but also prevents heavy rains from washing away shallow-sown seeds. Be sure to remove the cloth just as soon as the seedlings sprout. Keep checking; if you leave the covering in place too long it will shade the plants and stunt their growth, and you might pull up some of the seedlings with the covering.

The seeds of most annuals take one to two weeks to germinate. After three or four days watch for a set of embryonic seed leaves. Technically these are not true foliage but part of the sprouting

CARING FOR SEEDLINGS

seed; they appear only at this stage, and you will never see anything like them on the plant again. Within a week you should see a second set of leaves directly above the seed leaves. These are true leaves and they should be recognizable as such, for they will be miniature versions of the leaves pictured on the mature plant in the encyclopedia section *(page 89)*. As soon as these first true leaves appear, the sturdiest specimen in each little clump of seedlings should be singled out for preservation. The rest should be pulled out carefully after first making sure the soil is moist so the unwanted plants can be removed without disturbing the roots of the plant that is left to mature.

In another week or so, when the remaining young plants are between 2 and 4 inches tall and have developed several sets of leaves, they are ready for the pruning process called "pinching back." This operation should be performed also on seedlings transplanted into the garden from indoor seedbeds *(Chapter 4)* and on young plants purchased from nurseries. Pinching back removes the top growth of a plant and forces it to develop side branches. It produces a sturdier plant and a heavier crop of flowers—for flowers generally bloom at the end of branches. It is simple to do: using your thumbnail and forefinger, just pinch off and remove the tip of the stem immediately above the top pair of leaves.

MULTIPLYING BLOSSOMS BY PINCHING BACK

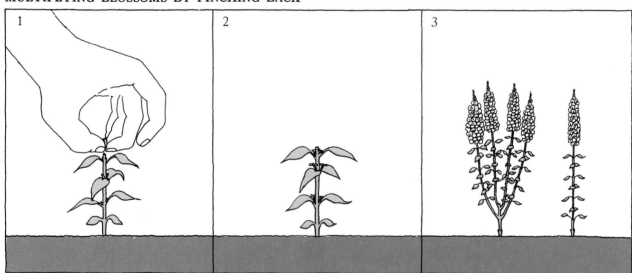

To increase the number of flowers a plant bears, pinch off the tip of the stem above the topmost leaves. This "pinching back" is done when a young plant is 2 to 4 inches tall and has three or four sets of leaves.

Pinching back the plant causes the little buds at the leaf base along the stem to begin developing into branches of their own; their growth is stimulated by energy that would otherwise have gone to the tip.

A plant whose tip has been pinched off *(above, left)* will be bushier and produce a number of flowering branches; an unpinched plant *(above, right)* will produce fewer flowers and may grow only one stem.

The huskiness that pinching back promotes is the key to telling a good plant from a poor one when you buy plants at the nursery. In the beginning, forget about blossoms on most annuals no matter how attractive they may be. Instead, concentrate on the foliage color and growth habit of the plants. Dark leaves and sturdy growth with side branches already evident are far more important than a few blossoms, and make a plant a much better buy. All too often plants already in bloom in flats and pots have tall, unbranched stems with few leaves at the bottom, and the leaves are often yellowish in color. Such plants, if purchased, should be pinched back to force the development of side branches.

When they have reached about a third of their total growth, tall-growing plants like cosmos and delphiniums need bracing against heavy winds and rain. And certain other plants with weak stems or a sprawling habit of growth—clarkias are a good example—benefit from some sort of prop. The ideal support for a weak-stemmed plant of short to medium height is a branch of twiggy brush pushed into the ground alongside it (*drawing below*). The brush should be about 4 to 6 inches shorter than the ultimate height of the plant so that the plant will eventually grow over it and hide it.

Tall plants need supporting stakes of bamboo or reed large

STAKING AND SUPPORTING

SUPPORTS TO KEEP FLOWERS UPRIGHT

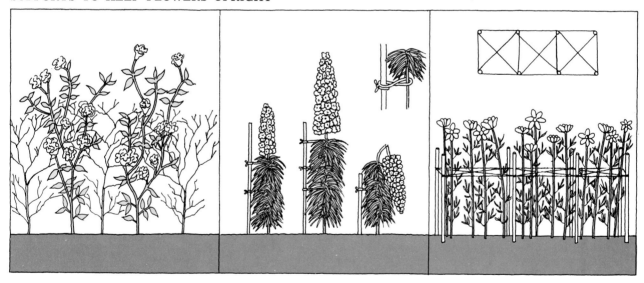

A branch of twiggy brush stuck into the soil will brace a sprawling plant or a weak-stemmed one with a tendency to flop, such as a clarkia. As the plant matures, it grows over and conceals the supporting twig.

Support a tall-growing plant like a delphinium by tying it loosely (inset) to a stake that is 4 to 8 inches shorter than the plant's ultimate height (left and center). With too short a stake, the stem may snap.

A bed full of slender-stemmed plants like cosmos is held upright inside triangles of string crisscrossed between two rows of stakes (inset). The plants are not tied, and the string is hidden by the foliage.

enough in diameter to do the job but small enough to be inconspicuous. Narrow wooden slats, about ¾ inch wide, can also be used; redwood or cedar slats are especially good for this purpose since both kinds of wood resist rotting. Stores also sell supports with horizontal wire loops at the top that hold many-stemmed plants like daisies or coreopsis with no need for tying; or you can make your own wire loops from coat hangers.

The stakes should be 4 to 8 inches shorter than the ultimate height of the plant, and they should extend into the ground 8 to 10 inches. Place them as close to the plant as possible but not so close as to risk damaging the plant's roots. Tall heavy-stemmed plants like larkspurs should have individual stakes, with each plant tied to its supporting stake at several points. In beds of annuals like cosmos, whose stems are more delicate, the plants are best supported by strings crisscrossed in triangular fashion between two rows of stakes *(drawings, page 43)*. Use soft string, preferably green garden twine, which is least conspicuous.

WATERING AND MULCHING — More than most plants, annuals tend to grow to maturity with a minimum of care. They should be weeded from time to time, preferably by hand since a hoe or other cultivating implement might damage their shallow roots, and preferably when the ground is

WATERING THE FLOWER BED

One way to assure an even, gentle "rainfall" over a flower bed is to lay out a perforated triple-tubed plastic sprinkling hose and sprinkle long enough for the water to penetrate down to the plants' feeding roots.

A tubular closed-end "soaker" made of porous canvas (inset) also waters gently. Attached to a faucet or a garden hose, it allows water to seep out and gradually soak the soil as shown in the cross section above.

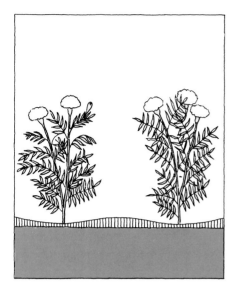

MULCH TO HOLD MOISTURE

To curtail the rapid loss of soil moisture through evaporation, spread a mulch (shaded area in drawing) around and between plants. Cover the surface of the flower bed with a 1- to 2-inch layer of mulch except directly around the stems of plants; since foliage shades the soil there, mulch these areas only to a depth of ¼ to ½ inch. The mulching material can be almost any coarse organic substance from leaf compost to ground peanut shells, wood shavings or sawdust. Such materials not only conserve moisture in the soil and keep the soil surface cool but they also tend to discourage the growth of weeds.

damp so that the weeds pull out more easily. They should also be watered occasionally, especially during dry periods. Although many annuals are native to arid regions of the earth, even these types can go without moisture for only a limited time because the root structure is so slight. If the ground around the plants is getting dry, it is time to get out the garden hose.

Annuals should be watered gently. Use the fine-spray setting of an adjustable nozzle or one of the hose attachments specially designed for watering. One of these is a length of soft plastic tubing perforated with fine holes; another is a canvas "soaker," also tubular, through which water gradually seeps into the soil *(drawings, page 44)*. Whatever method you use, remember that a thorough watering at infrequent intervals is far superior to a quick daily watering, which does little more than dampen the surface. Remember, too, that early morning is the best time of day for watering, so the leaves will have a chance to dry during the day. Evening or nighttime watering invites fungus diseases.

Gardeners in hot, dry areas have long known about an alternative to frequent watering: mulches. A mulched soil will retain moisture for weeks on end. For gardeners with limited gardening time, and those who garden only at weekend homes, mulches can make the difference between having fine flowers and not having flowers at all. A mulch can be anything that keeps the sun off the soil and blocks evaporation. Many truck gardeners spread strips of opaque plastic over the ground between plants. Most home gardeners, however, use organic mulches, which look more natural in a garden. Some of the commonly used mulches are chunky peat moss, leaf mold, ground corncobs, peanut husks, buckwheat hulls, cocoa-bean hulls, salt hay, pine needles, sawdust and ground tree bark. Choose one that is available at a local garden-supply store and spread it to a depth of about an inch over the entire bed except around the stems of plants, where it should not exceed ½ inch.

SUPPLEMENTARY FEEDING A mulch has one side benefit—and one drawback. On the credit side it cuts down on weeds by depriving weed seeds of the sun they need to germinate (the few weeds that do come through the mulch are easy to pull). But a mulch may also deprive plants of nitrogen; as mulch decomposes, the microorganisms in the soil multiply and use up the soil's nitrogen content. When this happens the leaves of the mulched plants turn a uniform pale green, and a booster shot of nitrogen is necessary. One common way to supply this is in the form of a "side dressing," the farmer's term for the fertilizer he applies to his crops after they are under way. For this purpose choose a fertilizer that is rich in nitrogen, such as 10–6–4. Sprinkle the fertilizer around the base of each plant in a circle slightly larger than the plant's leaf spread (the roots of a plant usually extend slightly beyond the spread of its foliage). Be careful, however, not to let the fertilizer touch the plant stem; the active ingredients are powerful chemicals and can burn growing plants. A teaspoonful of 10-6-4 per plant is usually sufficient. Repeat the dose every two to three weeks until the leaves regain their healthy deep green color; it is better to use several small feedings than to overwhelm the plant with one massive dose.

The same nitrogen-rich fertilizer can also be used for the supplementary feeding that experienced gardeners give their plants when the buds are showing color, just before they bloom. An extra shot of nitrogen at this stage improves the color of the flowers and prolongs their bloom. It can be applied in the form of a side dressing, as above, or by a more recently developed method called foliar feeding. With this technique, soluble powder or liquid concentrates sold for the purpose are mixed with water and sprayed directly onto the leaves, bypassing the roots. Foliar feeding, somewhat like the direct intravenous feeding of humans, is a quick source of energy. It can produce spectacular results but it can also be overdone. Applied too often, foliar fertilizer produces giant leaves but not much in the way of desirable flowers. Use these compounds in the proportions the manufacturer suggests, and never use them more often than once every three or four weeks.

MULTIPLYING THE BLOSSOMS Annuals are productive even if ignored, but they will blossom more profusely over a longer period if you keep cutting the flowers off. So long as blossoms are plucked before the seed pods form, the plant will in effect try again to produce seeds—resulting in more blooms. Annuals are also responsive to "disbudding," a kind of horticultural interference commonly practiced by people who want to grow very large flowers for show purposes. In disbudding, all the buds along one stem are pinched off except for the one at the very end. This leaves all the plant's energy available for the single end bud, and it produces a truly spectacular bloom.

Among the many good things about annuals is their comparative immunity to insects and diseases. Their short life partly accounts for this. The pests and parasites that thrive on permanent plants have little chance to settle on plants that live at best a brief six months. But this immunity is also a matter of breeding. Plant breeders have eliminated many of the weaknesses in certain annuals that made them likely candidates for disease. For example, a gardener who likes asters or snapdragons—species once notoriously vulnerable to the fungi called wilt and rust—can now buy resistant strains when they select seeds.

Annuals do have some enemies. Among insects, aphids are probably the most troublesome, but other pests that can afflict annuals from time to time are cutworms, various kinds of beetles and a tiny member of the spider family called a red spider mite. In damp weather and in low-lying gardens that get little circulation of air, various fungus diseases can also be a problem. The commonest are leaf spot, powdery mildew, rusts and wilt. On pages 48 through 51 is a chart listing detailed information on what these enemies look like, what they do and what you can do to eradicate them.

If insects and fungus diseases reach epidemic proportions only chemical pesticides can control them. But when pests strike in limited numbers, it is sometimes easier to go after them manually than chemically. A stream of water directed at the aphids on a zinnia stem will knock them to the ground (too strong a stream, however, will knock down the zinnias too). For an aphid, the return trip is long and arduous, and he may never make it. Japanese beetles, when they first appeared in this country earlier in the century, were dealt with by holding a jar of kerosene under the plant and gently tapping the beetles into it to drown; the method still works. Cutworms, smooth, fat caterpillars that inch their way along the ground at night to chew through the stems of tender plants, can be blocked from their meals by paper collars (chart, page 51). Or they can be trapped after they have fed: a cutworm habitually curls up just beneath the soil beside its meal to "sleep it off," at which point it is easy to uncover it with a stick, lift it out and destroy it. With only a little care an abundance of healthy, unblemished flowers—to enjoy in the garden, to cut for bouquets, to dry for winter flower arrangements—will reward your efforts.

BUGS AND GERMS

A QUEEN'S CARNATION

A carnation almost enabled Queen Marie Antoinette to escape from the Bastille when she was imprisoned there before being beheaded during the French Revolution in 1793. Her friend and champion, the Chevalier de Rougeville, gained access to her cell and left behind a carnation, hiding in its petals the message that he would try to get her out. When the eager Queen attempted to acknowledge his message, her own note was intercepted and the plan to rescue her was foiled.

Diseases and pests afflicting annuals, and how to control them

Although garden pests and diseases do not create as much of a problem with annuals as they do with other plants, there are some you should look out for. In wet and humid weather virus and fungus diseases can spot the plants' leaves and stunt their growth. And from time to time various pests find their succulent leaves and stems irresistible. Symptoms of the most common of these afflictions are described in the accompanying charts, together with recommended treatments.

The simplest and best controls are those that involve no chemicals. A garden that is not overcrowded with plants and is kept clean of weeds, twigs, leaves, debris and, particularly, infected plants will naturally be less susceptible to pests and disease. Proper watering practices (page 44) will also help. (Such preventive care is the only weapon against diseases such as wilt, for which no cures are known.) Simple measures can be taken against some pests: a bowl of beer set in a flower bed will attract and drown slugs, and you can knock leaf-eating beetles into a can of water coated with kerosene or oil.

When you do turn to a chemical insecticide or fungicide, choose the right one for the job and apply it when it will do the most good. Insecticides are designed for two kinds of pests: those that pierce plants to suck their juices and those that chew them. Sucking pests are generally killed by contact with the poison; chewing pests must ingest it. Insecticides can be applied after infestation, for they attack the troublemakers directly. Fungicides, however, do not. In general, they protect plants by shielding them from fungus attack, not by killing the organism that causes it, and for this reason they must be applied before the trouble starts in order to be most effective.

DISEASES	SYMPTOMS
DAMPING OFF	Stems rot near the soil surface, and seedlings fall over and die. Damping off is most prevalent when soil is cold and wet, and is caused by fungi that are present in most soil.
LEAF SPOT	Red, brown or yellow spots of varying sizes and shapes appear on leaves in humid weather; the spots sometimes fall out, leaving holes in the foliage. Spots usually appear on lower leaves first and as they work upward may merge to form large blotches, which can kill the plants.
POWDERY MILDEW	Plants become coated with a white or gray mealy substance. Leaves usually curl and turn dry; buds shrivel before they open. Especially prevalent in humid weather, this fungus afflicts plants that grow too close together and receive too much shade.
RUST	Yellow, orange or reddish brown pustules resembling warts appear, usually first on the underside of leaves, which soon wither. The pustules may burst, especially when it rains, and the disease is then carried to other plants by splashing water or wind. Snapdragons are particularly susceptible and may wilt and die. Rust flourishes in dampness, cool nights and humid days.
WILT	Wilt occurs most frequently during dry spells. Leaves become limp, turn yellow or brown and drop prematurely as the disease causes water-conducting vessels inside the stem to cease to function.

Insecticides and fungicides come in various forms. The simplest to use are the ready-mixed dusts and sprays packaged in shaker cans, or squeeze-plastic or pressurized containers. For larger jobs, wettable powders and liquid concentrates, used in spray tanks or hose attachments, are more economical.

Before you buy an insecticide or fungicide, read the label to make sure it contains the chemicals suited to the problem. The labels specify chemicals by their common names, and it is these names, rather than trade names, that are listed in the chart. The labels also indicate the pests and diseases the contents are intended to control. Always use the dosage specified —too little is better than too much—and *always observe the precautions printed on the label.* Many of these products are poisonous to humans if taken internally, and may burn the skin or injure the eyes.

And others, harmless to humans, may kill animals, fish, birds and honeybees.

For safety's sake none of these garden chemicals should be used when it is windy or while anyone is eating, drinking or smoking; do not, of course, inhale the spray. Do not use chemicals near vegetables, fruits or drinking water unless the label specifically says it is safe to do so. Mix only enough for the job and use it up; leftover chemicals should not be poured down a drain or thrown out to form puddles that animals or birds can drink from. Wash your hands and face thoroughly after using any insecticide or fungicide, and always store these products in a safe place out of the reach of children.

For help in identifying your problem and determining the proper treatment, consult your county agricultural extension service or a local garden center.

EXAMPLES OF ANNUALS AFFECTED	CHEMICAL CONTROLS	OTHER METHODS OF CONTROL
amaranth, cockscomb, coleus, petunia, portulaca, snapdragon, sweet alyssum, wallflower, zinnia. Others may also be harmed.	captan ferbam folpet zineb	When starting seeds indoors use sterile soil mix. Outdoors, be sure seedlings are thinned to recommended intervals to prevent crowding and make sure soil drains well.
California bluebell, campanula, cleome, cockscomb, coleus, hollyhock, impatiens, marigold, nasturtium, phlox	captan ferbam folpet maneb zineb	Avoid excessive wetting of foliage. Plant refuse and dead leaves are usually breeding grounds for leaf spot, so thorough garden cleanup is important. Be sure to dispose of all afflicted leaves and twigs.
ageratum, candytuft, China aster, cornflower, dahlia, phlox, sweet pea, verbena, zinnia	dinocap folpet sulfur	Avoid overcrowding and locations that are especially damp or shady.
ageratum, calendula, China aster, cleome, dianthus, hollyhock, marigold, snapdragon, sweet William	ferbam maneb zineb	Buy rust-resistant varieties (so marked on seed packets). Space plants so there is good air circulation. Avoid wetting foliage any more than necessary.
China aster, dahlia, forget-me-not, impatiens, marigold, snapdragon, sweet pea, verbena		Buy wilt-resistant seed (so marked on seed packets). Feed and water plants regularly to obtain vigorous growth. No chemicals can control wilt directly, although several such as carbaryl will halt the spread of the disease by insects.

PESTS	DESCRIPTION	SIGNS OF INFESTATION
APHIDS	Pear-shaped insects, usually wingless, of many colors—green, black, yellow, brown and pink. They are less than ⅛ inch long.	Aphids settle on the underside of leaves, along stems, at the base of buds and particularly on new shoots. They suck the plant's juices, causing leaves to curl and buds or flowers to be malformed. Aphids secrete a sweet, sticky substance called honeydew, which may form on leaves and attract ants; a fungus resembling a sooty mold may form on old honeydew. Aphids also transmit fungus and bacterial diseases to plants.
LEAF HOPPERS	Elongated suckers, 1/16 to ¼ inch in size, that fold their wings in a wedge shape. They may be colored light green, yellow, gray or white.	Leaf hoppers work on the undersides of leaves, creating a white, stippled effect on the tops of the leaves and causing their edges to curl and look as though they had been burned. When disturbed, the insects hop quickly away. Like aphids, they can be carriers of virus diseases.
WHITE FLIES	White-winged sucking insects, only 1/16 inch long fully grown. Barely visible, they lie motionless on plants. If they are disturbed, they fly away like fine white dust.	White flies suck on the undersides of leaves. Infested foliage turns mottled yellow or silvery in color and may finally drop off. Like aphids, white flies secrete a mold-forming honeydew.
BEETLES	Among the most harmful to annuals are the night-feeding Asiatic Garden Beetle, which is brown and about ⅜ inch long; the ¼-inch-long cucumber beetle, greenish yellow with black spots; and the Japanese Beetle, ½ inch long and colored a metallic bronze.	Beetles chew the foliage, stems and flowers, making sizable round or irregularly shaped holes in the leaves. The larvae feed on plant roots.
CUTWORMS	Fat, greasy-looking, hairless moth caterpillars, from 1 to 2 inches long and usually black or brown in color.	Cutworms curl up just beneath the top of the soil during the day. At night they emerge to feed on seedlings by chewing through their stems, often at ground level. Some kinds of cutworms climb up the stems of older plants to feed on the leaves and flower buds.
SPIDER MITES	Eight-legged, spiderlike creatures about as big as a fleck of paprika —only 1/75 of an inch—and sometimes paprika colored, although they may also be green or yellow.	Mites attack plants by sucking the juice from leaf cells, causing foliage to appear stippled red, yellow, gray or brown and creating silvery cobwebs on the undersides of the leaves. They thrive in hot, stagnant air; frequent victims are plants next to a sun-warmed wall.
SLUGS AND SNAILS	Both are mollusks, belonging to the same family that includes clams and oysters. Slugs are ¾ inch to 5 inches long, fat, legless and colored gray, yellow white, brown or black. Snails, usually ½ to 1½ inches long, are the same colors as slugs but have a shell.	Slugs and snails feed at night and on damp, overcast days. They attack foliage near or on the ground, chewing holes in leaves and leaving a trail of silver slime.

EXAMPLES OF ANNUALS AFFECTED	CHEMICAL CONTROLS	OTHER METHODS OF CONTROL
asclepias, browallia, calendula, campanula, China aster, cineraria, coreopsis, cornflower, cosmos, dianthus, heliotrope, impatiens, larkspur, lobelia, marigold, nasturtium, primrose, sunflower, sweet pea, wallflower	malathion pyrethrum	Knock aphids off the plant with a stream of water from a garden hose, adjusting the nozzle so that you don't knock down the plant.
amaranth, anchusa, browallia, calendula, China aster, clarkia, cornflower, dahlia, geranium, lobelia, marigold, sweet William	malathion methoxychlor	China asters and dahlias can be protected by growing them in light structures enclosed in cheesecloth.
ageratum, China aster, cineraria, coleus, gourds, heliotrope, impatiens, lantana, morning glory	diazinon malathion	Provide good air circulation by spacing plants at proper intervals.
ageratum, China aster, cineraria, coleus, cosmos, dahlia, geranium, gourds, heliotrope, hollyhock, impatiens, morning glory	carbaryl malathion methoxychlor	Pick off beetles by hand and destroy them, or knock them into a can containing water covered with a thin film of oil or kerosene. Specially designed traps are sold in garden-supply stores.
cineraria, dianthus, nicotiana	poison bait sold at garden centers	Protect plants with collars pushed into the ground around their stems. These can be made from strips of cardboard 9 or 10 inches long and 3 or 4 inches high, rolled into tubes and stapled at the ends.
abutilon, ageratum, geranium, hollyhock, larkspur, marigold, petunia, primrose, snapdragon, sunflower	dicofol malathion chlorobenzilate	
campanula, cineraria, hollyhock, primrose	metaldehyde	Leave a bowl of beer on the ground near plants to lure and drown slugs. Circle the inside edge of flower beds with narrow strips of coarse sand, cinders or ground limestone.

An abundance of beauty in small spaces

Lord Abercrombie, a distinguished British horticulturist, once summed up his advice to novice gardeners in a single sentence: "Find out what you can grow, and grow lots of it." The words are particularly applicable to the gardener who tries to grow flowers in cramped quarters, whether in a city back yard or a small suburban garden. What he can grow, and grow lots of, are annuals. No other type of plant is better suited to constricted spaces and often unfavorable growing conditions. The relatively shallow root systems of most annuals require a modest amount of scarce earth, so that dozens of annuals can be massed in miniature beds, planters or pots to provide spectacular bursts of almost any desired color. The plants' requirements for light are also easy to meet. Marigolds, petunias or zinnias shoot up quickly from seeds or store-bought plants if given several hours of sun each day. Where there is little sun, as in the tiny garden on the opposite page, shade-tolerant wax begonias, impatiens and geraniums thrive.

Annuals, compared to other plants, are also less affected by the concomitants of crowded living areas, the pollutants that often fill the air in and near large cities. Where the cumulative effect of soot and gases can prove deadly to perennial shrubs, flowers and trees, annuals absorb relatively little of such poisons in their short life spans, and plants grown from fresh seeds each year are born with no ill effects. Because of their short life, annuals are also less vulnerable to common plant diseases such as leaf spot and powdery mildew.

Gardens can be started in the very smallest of spaces. Many suburbanites with sizable back yards, but little interest in gardening, have learned the trick of planting one or two easy-to-grow beds of massed annuals to decorate their patios or pools. For the apartment dweller whose only outdoor area is a narrow balcony or terrace, a few well-placed tubs of annuals provide a splash of color high above the city streets. Where nothing else is available, a window box filled with easy-to-grow petunias, offering the broadest spectrum of color of all annuals, can provide much the same cheerful effect (*page 61*).

A 7-foot-wide Philadelphia garden, seen from above, is brightened by pink geraniums, wax begonias and impatiens.

A garden from the past

An upper-class status symbol in colonial America was a formal garden, still unsurpassed as a means of lending elegance to a small area. Its meticulously tended beds of flowers—including such then-exotic annuals as geraniums from South Africa and zinnias from Central America —were each tiny, self-contained gardens arranged in precise symmetry and divided by walks of crushed stone. The charm of such a setting, complete with grape arbor and gazebo, is re-created in the Philadelphia garden at left, using modern hybrids of 18th Century flowers.

An unusual mixture of colors is provided by three kinds of annuals (above), which are grouped in one of the beds of the garden shown at left. A stand of purplish Dark Opal basil, a fragrant herb used in salads and jelly, separates pink dwarf zinnias from yellow gazanias.

This replica of a small formal garden of the 1750s, adjoining the Philadelphia headquarters of the Pennsylvania Horticultural Society, contains 16 hedge-enclosed flower beds called parterres in four symmetrical groups. Among the flowers in the corner beds are red geraniums.

A compact garden on a hillside

What does the gardener do when he finds himself with garden space that stretches up the side of a steep hill? One solution is to create a tiny garden within a garden. The intimate terrace garden shown here was carved out of the hillside behind the owner's home, leaving the upper slope for a free-growing, informal garden accessible by steps and a winding path. Behind and to the sides, wooden retaining walls prevent earthslides and form a rustic base for raised beds of annuals selected for both their appearance and fragrance: sweet alyssum, marigolds and petunias. These, as well as the sweet peas climbing up the wall at the right, have strong and distinctive scents; they fill the garden with perfume in the early evening, when the owners like to entertain. The potted annuals around the terrace and lining the steps at the rear—red and white geraniums and yellow calendulas —complement the colors of the informally planted flowers, including yellow and white marguerites, that form a pleasant jumble of blossoms on the hillside.

A handsome San Francisco terrace garden blends the formality of annuals in containers with the casual appearance of free-growing plants on the hillside above. The flowers in the beds include white alyssum and yellow marigolds (foreground); the pots beneath the umbrella contain pink geraniums.

Portable gardens for paved areas

In many back yards, a paved patio takes up space that might otherwise be used for a small garden. But it is possible to have both cookouts and flowers too by getting the flowers up off the ground and out of the way either in raised plant beds or in containers that can be moved about wherever desired.

A number of attractive effects can be obtained by growing flowers in pots, planters and urns, or even an old wheelbarrow. The large picture at right shows what can be done by using portable containers to accent the broader expanse of blooms in a raised bed. Grouping several different kinds of annuals around an unusual centerpiece (far right, above) produces a pleasing miniature garden in a few square feet of space. The same amount of space can be used to produce colorful combinations within a single container (far right, below). When fall comes, some varieties of tender perennials treated as annuals—wax begonias and geraniums, for example—can be taken indoors to be enjoyed as house plants.

On a shady Denver patio a low tortoise-shaped planter mirrors the blooms of a large raised bed, both containing white wax begonias. In front of the French doors a planter box, on wheels so that it can be moved around, contains yellow marigolds and white geraniums.

Ivy, grown on a frame shaped like a bear, is set off by potted annuals. From upper right: pink petunias; pink Martha Washington geraniums; ageratum, lobelia and impatiens; tufted pansies; and more geraniums, white and violet.

A large ornamental tub with bright dwarf celosia, or cockscomb, in red and orange stands beside a pot of yellow marigolds, the colors of the flowers harmonizing with the rich ocher and brown tones of the container.

Flowers in the heart of the city

It is in the center of a large city, where space is so scarce apartment dwellers cherish every square inch, that annuals prove their value for cramped quarters. They transform a small terrace, like the one shown in the photograph below, into a flowery dell, or beautify an old town house with blossom-filled window boxes *(right)*.

Most annuals that bloom in suburban gardens readily adapt to city life, and some varieties have come to be particular favorites. The geranium has earned a reputation as an all-around "city flower" that thrives in pots and boxes in almost any location. Zinnias and marigolds, either giant or dwarf varieties, are particularly suited to spots where there is plenty of sunshine. Petunias and browallia, on the other hand, tolerate the shadows cast during part of the day by nearby buildings, while impatiens and wax begonias will flourish in heavier shade.

A terrace on a sixth-floor rooftop in New York City is the setting for a city-bred rock garden. The flowers include red and white petunias, yellow lantana, pink wax begonias, tall golden marigolds, red impatiens and pink geraniums.

Window boxes filled with pink petunias (right) add a festive touch to the dignified front of an old brick home on Boston's Beacon Hill. Petunias and geraniums, both sturdy plants, have long been favorites of window-box gardeners.

Bringing
outdoor beauty
indoors

3

Annuals are a double pleasure. Not only do they brighten the garden, but they also make splendid displays when cut and brought indoors. Most cut annuals will last the better part of a week and a few long-lasting varieties—notably China asters, Canterbury bells, coreopsis, marigolds and zinnias—may stay fresh and lovely for as long as two weeks. Certain annuals can even be enjoyed indefinitely —in the form of dried flowers. Best of all, none of this robs the garden of color, for the more annuals are cut, the more they blossom.

Flowers remain alive and growing even after they are cut, and their life can be extended greatly by proper cutting and care. The procedures for keeping cut flowers fresh are all designed to help them take up and hold an adequate supply of water. The largest part of a plant's bulk is water—and this water serves a dual function. Not only does it transport food to the plant cells but it also makes them turgid, that is, it fills the cells with water as a balloon is filled with air. The swelling is what holds the plant upright; deprived of water a plant droops and eventually dies.

This concern for conserving flowers' moisture governs every step of their gathering and handling. They are most suitable for picking before they reach their prime, when the buds are half to three-quarters open. In the case of flowers that bloom in clusters, like those of sweet William and candytuft, pick clusters in which only half the flowers are in bloom; the remaining buds will open later in water indoors. However, zinnias, calendulas, dahlias, marigolds and China asters, whose development ceases shortly after they are cut, should be picked just as they become fully opened and not when they are in bud.

The best time of day to cut annuals for fresh flowers is in the morning or evening; stems are apt to wilt quickly if cut in the midday sun when they are losing water. In the morning and evening they are full of water and thus better able to survive.

Whenever possible cut the flowers just above a side branch on which another flower is forming (this encourages more blooms).

A cutting garden of annuals, like this one dominated by painted tongues in rich yellows, browns and purples in front of yellow marigolds, provides not only beauty outdoors but bouquets for indoor pleasure.

Make the cut with a sharp knife or garden shears so as to crush or bruise the stem as little as possible. At this point it is a good idea to strip off some of their lower leaves. Flowers continue to transpire, or give off moisture through their leaves, as long as they are alive; they need to retain some leaves as a source of energy but can spare those near the bottom of the stem. Now the flowers should be plunged into water as quickly as possible. Most people make the mistake of using cold water—they think that cold water freshens flowers. Quite the opposite is true. The life processes within plants, as in other living things, are stimulated by warmth and slowed by cold. Since the most critical need of flowers after they are cut is acceleration of the process that takes in water, it follows that they should be placed in warm rather than cold water. When florists receive shipments from growers, they place the flowers in vases containing water at a temperature of 100° to 110° and then put the vases in a cool place until the stems have become completely filled with moisture. It is the combination of warm water around the stems and cool air around the tops that does the trick: the cut flowers take on water faster than they lose it. When I go into my garden to cut flowers, I take along a wide-mouthed vase of warm water and plunge each stem into it the instant I cut it. When the vase is full but not crowded, I let it stand in the coolest part of the house.

KEEPING FLOWERS FRESH

After the flowers are sufficiently "conditioned" by the warm water and cool air treatment—this usually takes about two hours—they are ready for arranging. Be sure to strip off any leaves that would fall below the water line in the arrangement. Left on, they will decompose and not only create an unpleasant odor but also foul the water with bacteria, clogging the flower's water-conducting apparatus and hastening its death.

The stems should also be trimmed at this point. Many tests have been made to determine whether stems should be cut straight across or on a slant, with a knife or with shears. It was found that these factors have no bearing upon the life of the flowers. Squeezing stems may compress some of the cells and restrict the easy intake of moisture, and for that reason most florists use a sharp knife or a keen two-bladed pair of shears rather than the blade-and-anvil type of clipper.

Some flowers need special treatment. Dahlias, snow-on-the-mountain, poinsettias and poppies, for example, should be sealed at their stem ends. Untreated, the stems of these flowers ooze a liquid that coagulates at the cut ends of the stems, clogging the tubes that absorb water. To halt the seepage, the stems must be seared for an instant over a gas or candle flame or a match or dipped momentarily in boiling water. If the latter method is used, keep the flower head out of the rising steam by dipping the stem on a slant; only the tip of the stem, ¼ to ½ inch, should go in the water.

There are countless other recipes for making cut flowers longer; most are useless. The practice of dropping an aspirin tablet into the water does no harm, but neither does it do any good. Nor does another common trick: placing a few copper pennies in the water. One widely held belief can lead to harm. Some people claim that sugar extends the life of flowers by providing them with energy, and in fact sugar is an ingredient of some of the commercial flower preservatives. But sugar alone does more harm than good; it stimulates the growth of stem-clogging bacteria.

Most of the commercial preservatives do actually help flowers. Along with quick-energy sugar, they also provide other useful substances: a bacteria-inhibiting material to control the spread of those organisms that clog the ends of the stems; an acidic material to lower the alkalinity of the water and to reduce the growth of microorganisms; metallic salts to maintain color in the petals; and respiratory inhibitors to cut down the flowers' metabolic rate. Under the best of circumstances these preparations can double a cut flower's life. But so many other factors are also operative in the life span of a flower—including the conditions under which it grew in the garden—that the performance of these preservatives is not entirely predictable. If you want to use them, begin to use them as soon as the flowers are cut; put the preservative into the vase or pail of water you carry into the garden. The flowers will then begin to absorb the chemicals when the chemicals will do the most good.

Nothing benefits cut flowers more than a scrupulously clean environment. Make sure the container is free of any scum left from a previous flower arrangement, and give the flowers fresh water at 100° to 110°, not cold—every day. If you have time, remove the flowers entirely and refill the container. If a preservative is used, it is not necessary to change the water; simply add fresh warm water daily to replace that used by the flowers. Cut flowers will also last longer if they are kept out of drafts and strong sunlight, both of which speed up the transpiration process.

Annuals come in so many sizes, shapes and colors that whatever the flower, there is a container to suit it: pottery bowls, ceramic vases, copper pots, china pitchers and soup tureens, teacups and brandy snifters. Make sure the container is deep enough for the water to cover at least an inch or two of the stem ends. Wide-mouthed containers are much less likely to crowd the stems. Besides, flowers tend to look better in wide-mouthed containers that allow stems to curve naturally rather than stand stiffly erect.

USING PRESERVATIVES

THE FLEETING PRIMROSE
The primrose is one of the first flowers to bloom in the spring—and one of the first to wither, a fact mourned by English poets from Chaucer to Wordsworth. Wrote Milton in his "Ode on the Death of a Fair Infant":
O fairest flower! no sooner blown but blasted,
Soft silken primrose falling timelessly.

HOLDERS FOR FLOWERS

65

There are all sorts of stem-holding devices nowadays for helping flower arrangements to stay put. The most popular is probably the weighted metal block of needle-sharp spikes, like an Indian fakir's bed of nails, onto which stem ends are impaled; it can be fastened firmly in place in a bowl with a sticky clay sold by florists. The cheapest holder is still the crumpled ball of chicken wire. But undoubtedly the most convenient holder is the one made of expanded plastic foam, which can be cut with a knife to fit snugly into the container. When thoroughly saturated it becomes soft enough for any but the most fragile stems to be poked into. (In the case of fragile stems, poke holes in the foam with a pencil, then insert the stems.) Stems placed in foam holders stay put until removed.

THE ART OF ARRANGING

As practiced by experts, the arranging of flowers is an art. It takes into account intricate relationships between color, form and line, and it draws upon two classic approaches to the use of flowers. One is the familiar floral bouquet, massing the blooms for a joyful display of color; the other is the Japanese *Ikebana,* which seeks to suggest each flower's quintessential nature by a disciplined arrangement of lines and shapes. Both are surrounded by a catechism of regulations. But special knowledge of traditional rules is never really necessary. Trust your own instinct. A few daisies or cosmos in a crystal pitcher, a bowl of pansies on a coffee table, a pottery jug full of marigolds will bring the pleasures of the garden indoors —and that is the whole purpose of cut flowers.

FLOWERS THAT LAST

Long after the garden has gone, its pleasures can remain. For centuries gardeners have preserved flowers by drying them, and have included in their gardens certain plants especially suited to this purpose. These are the "everlastings." Their flower heads are composed of tiny true flowers surrounded by bracts—the parts ordinarily referred to as flowers—that are exceptionally colorful and tough. These blossoms retain their form and color indefinitely after they dry out. Among the familiar everlastings are strawflower, statice, Swan River everlasting and common immortelle. Along with them gardeners have traditionally included ornamental grasses that also dry well. The graceful seed panicles of such grasses as cloud grass, quaking grass, animated oats, Job's tears, rabbit-tail grass and fountain grass lend an airy, delicate quality to dried bouquets.

Unlike flowers intended for fresh bouquets, whose moisture must be conserved, flowers meant for drying are picked in the heat of the day when there is the least amount of moisture in their petals. The blossoms should be cut when their color is at its maximum, just before the centers of the flowers unfold. Their leaves should be stripped off, and the stems bound together in small bunches. You will find that it is better to slip rubber bands around the stems than it is to tie them with string, since the bands will take up the slack when the stems shrivel, while string-tied bunches may loosen and fall apart *(drawing, page 68)*. Hang the flowers upside down in a dark, dry closet or attic. After a week or two of dry summer weather, the blooms will be dry enough to use, but it should be noted that if the stems are turned upright during a humid period they may take on moisture and droop. For that reason everlasting flowers are not usually arranged permanently until cool weather, when home heating assures a dry indoor atmosphere. Prepared in this way, the stems of grasses and flowers become stiffly straight.

Many kinds of annuals besides the everlastings have also been dried—with varying degrees of success—by hanging them in the air or by burying them in various drying compounds, such as sand and borax. But in the past few of them could be depended upon to hold their color as well as the everlastings and the procedures for drying them successfully were difficult to control. Now, thanks to a modern material called silica gel, any number of annuals dry satisfactorily. Among them are ageratum, snapdragon, calendula, China aster, Canterbury bells, cockscomb, cornflower, cosmos, daisies, dahlia, dianthus, larkspur, tassel flower, snow-on-the-mountain, candytuft, lupine, stock, salvia, bells-of-Ireland, pincushion flower, marigold, pansy and zinnia.

The silica gel used to dry these flowers is a compound that looks like sugar and has the capacity to absorb up to 40 per cent of its weight in water. It is widely used industrially to shield delicate instruments and dehydrated foods from dampness; cameras, for instance, are often packed with a small cloth envelope of silica-gel crystals. In the form used for drying flowers, the basic sugarlike crystals are mixed with larger crystals that have been impregnated with a nickel compound that is blue when dry but turns pink when wet. These crystals warn the user that the silica has absorbed all the water it can. Before the silica is used again, it must be dried in a warm oven, about 250°, for about 30 minutes —until the pink crystals turn blue again.

When not in use, silica gel must be stored in airtight containers to prevent the material from picking up moisture from the air. An ideal container for this purpose is the round tin in which fruitcakes are sold at Christmas, because it can also double as a container for the actual flower-drying process. Like air-dried flowers, flowers dried in silica gel must first be stripped of their foliage. If the stems are fragile, these may also be removed, and only the flower head dried. A false stem can be fitted on later if a wire is inserted through the flower head.

DRYING WITH CHEMICALS

THE USES OF BASIL

The ancient Greeks thought that basil, an aromatic annual, would dull the sight and breed worms and scorpions; 18th Century Italians, on the other hand, believed it would engender love. Persians, Malaysians and Egyptians planted or strewed it on graves to honor their dead. So conflicting were the myths surrounding the plant that the 17th Century English herbalist Nicholas Culpepper remarked: "This is the herb which all authors are together by the ears about and rail at one another (like lawyers)." Today, of course, basil is widely grown as an ornamental annual (Ocimum basilicum, page 140) and used as an herb in cooking.

Place flower heads face up, or long, spiky clusters like lark-spur horizontally, on a layer of silica gel about 1½ inches deep in the cake tin. Sprinkle more silica gently around and over the flowers until they are completely covered. Be sure the flowers are far enough apart to keep their petals from touching. Put the lid on the tin and seal it with freezer or masking tape; leave it for four to seven days, depending upon the thickness of the flower —pansies, for instance, dry quicker than zinnias do.

When the flowers are dry, brush away the silica gel and gent-ly remove them. If you lose a petal, do not despair—a drop of transparent glue applied with the end of a toothpick will refasten it. Store the blossoms for future use in screw-top glass jars, add-ing a teaspoon or two of silica gel to preserve them. Silica-dried flower heads can be used stemless, just as they are, as a sort of pot-pourri of blooms inside a decorative glass jar. But they can also be used for bouquets by equipping them with stems made of flo-rists' wire wrapped with green florists' tape.

PRESSING FLOWERS IN GEL   Silica gel also hastens the preparation of another old-fashioned fa-vorite—pressed flowers, producing them within several days instead of several weeks. The best flowers for pressing are those that are naturally flat, such as pansies and African daisies. They

AIR-DRYING FLOWERS FOR PERMANENT ARRANGEMENTS

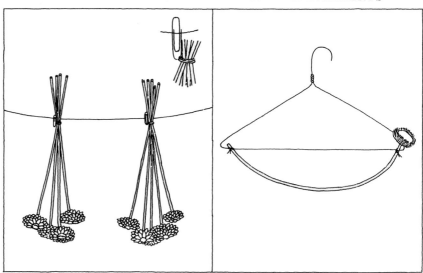

When air-drying "everlasting" flowers for year-round display, hang them blooms down if straight stems are desired. Fasten them to a line in a dry, dark place as shown in the inset. Leave eight to 10 days.

To dry everlastings so that their stems will be curved instead of straight, tie each end with a bit of string to a wire coat hanger, as illustrated. Then hang in a dry, dark place for eight to 10 days.

should be picked at their prime. It is best to remove the stems and press them separately if you intend to use them.

To press flowers you need these materials: a board of a size that will accommodate the laid-out flowers, enough white blotting paper to cover the board twice, some white facial tissue, a small amount of silica gel, a plastic bag large enough to hold the board and its flowers, and a few bricks or heavy books for weights. Start by placing a layer of blotting paper on the board; then cover it with a thin layer of silica gel. Spread two thicknesses of tissue over the silica gel. The flowers should then be laid out without touching one another and the above process repeated in reverse—that is, apply tissue paper, silica gel, then blotting paper. The board and its floral sandwich are then placed inside a large plastic bag and finally weighted with bricks or books. Last of all, seal the end of the plastic bag with masking tape, excluding as much air as possible.

At the end of a week remove the pressed blossoms and store them in tissue paper in suitable containers, such as small plastic boxes, until the day when you want to convert them into decorations for greeting cards, bookmarks or wall plaques. In this form they can recall the loveliness of the garden long after the garden itself lies dormant, awaiting a new crop of flowers.

DRYING FLOWERS IN SILICA GEL

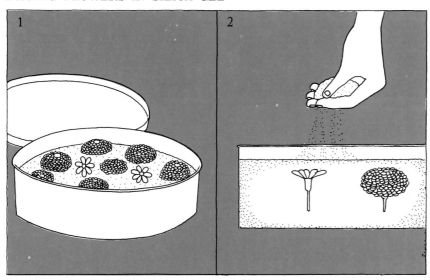

To dry flower heads in the desiccant powder silica gel, cover the bottom of a fruitcake tin with about an inch and a half of the powder. Insert the stem ends in the powder, spacing them so the petals do not touch.

Gently sift more gel through your fingers until the flowers are covered. Cover the tin, seal the lid with tape and set aside for four to seven days; the heads may now be attached to wire stems with florist's tape.

Bouquets for every room

One of the great pleasures of annuals is that they provide a steady supply of fresh cut flowers for every room in the house. Arranging the flowers is largely a matter of personal taste; anyone with an eye for form and color can create an attractive bouquet and have fun in the process.

Most experienced flower arrangers follow a few simple, almost obvious rules. First of all, they choose a container —whether it is a vase, a jug or even a soup tureen—to suit the type of flowers used and the height and form of the arrangement. Short-stemmed pansies, for example, go well in small, low containers like a small pot or sugar bowl, while long-legged sunflowers or larkspur generally look better in a taller, more substantial vase. Skillful arrangers usually steer clear of extremely fancy containers with complex lines or busy decoration because they are apt to distract attention from the flowers themselves.

Bouquets can be tailored closely to different uses. A tall, spreading arrangement can hide the black opening of an empty fireplace during the summer months. A small, cheerful bouquet brightens a kitchen without getting in the way. A bouquet on a bedroom night table not only looks pretty but also freshens the room with a delicate scent. A big circle or oval of flowers makes a fine centerpiece for a dining table or large coffee table, provided it is low enough so that people can see over it to carry on a conversation.

A wide selection of flowers is not necessary for attractive bouquets, and the most appealing are often the most restricted in their variety. A big cluster of yellow chrysanthemums, for example, can produce a stunning effect. More often a mixture of either colors or flower varieties is used to create harmony and contrast. If the flowers are all of one color the contrast and interest are provided by the different sizes, shapes and textures of the different varieties—for example, blue heliotrope, larkspur and ageratum. If a single kind of flower is used to create the harmony, the contrast can come from a range of colors, like the sweet peas in the photograph at right.

A cluster of sweet peas—pink to purple,
accented by cream and white—flares
from a clear glass vase on a porch table.

Yellow common sunflowers, bicolored cucumberleaf sunflowers and pampas grass leaves fill an empty fireplace in the summer.

Dwarf dahlias make a compact bouquet that brightens a kitchen without using up enough space to interfere with work. The rust-reds and yellows of the flowers pick up the color of the wallpaper behind.

Yellow marigolds and red and orange zinnias in a white crockery bowl echo the colors of a living room; the circular grouping, with flowers on several levels, looks well from all parts of the room.

A delicate bouquet in a small, round bowl scents a bedroom. The bold red nicotianas and the tiny-flowered heliotropes, both fragrant, are set off by pink and lavender China asters.

On a sunny terrace, an arrangement in yellow and green is keyed to fresh outdoor colors and to the shape of a long, low table.

Snapdragons, mixed with the fernlike foliage of Irish lace marigolds, rise above white nicotiana and yellow-centered dahlias.

A head start for the flower garden 4

If you are willing to take a little extra time and trouble, there is a method by which you can enjoy your annuals earlier in zones with cold climates. You can do this by starting some of the seeds indoors when it is still too cold to plant them in the ground; when these seedlings sown indoors are transplanted into the garden, they already have a head start over the plants whose seeds were sown later in the garden, and thus will blossom first. Of course you can achieve the same result by purchasing seedlings to set out in the garden; but growing them yourself is cheaper, and for many gardeners more satisfying. It does, however, require proper care and timing.

Many an impatient gardener, looking forward eagerly to spring, sows his seeds indoors too early. To his dismay the plants are ready for the garden weeks before warm weather arrives. Trying to hold back their growth, he cuts down on water and fertilizer; this slows the plants' growth, but it can also stunt them permanently and make their stems hard and woody. When such plants are finally set out in the garden, their growth nearly halts. Their youthful vigor is gone, their cell walls have toughened, and they grow very slowly. Often the outdoor-sown seeds surpass them, defeating the whole purpose of starting annuals indoors. So the first rule to remember in starting annuals indoors is that every species develops from seed to flower at its own rate; some, such as dwarf marigolds, develop flowers in five weeks while others such as petunias take as long as three months or more. (Maturing times for annuals that vary from the normal six to eight weeks are in the encyclopedia starting on page 89.)

As important as the starting time is the starting medium. Ordinary garden soil will not do; it may be full of weed seeds, disease organisms and insects that will flourish when the soil is brought into the warm house. Also, garden soil usually has insufficient organic matter and poor drainage qualities—it compacts easily and cakes on the surface, inhibiting the development of seed into seedling. What is needed for indoor gardening is "potting soil," which can be

Knee-deep in dazzling yellow and orange marigold hybrids, a harvester of a California seed company gathers the seeds in time for gardeners to start their plants indoors and be prepared for the arrival of spring.

purchased at most garden centers prepackaged and ready to use.

You can even mix your own potting soil if you want to. The most commonly used formula calls for two parts loam (a crumbly mixture of sand, silt and clay) to one part peat moss (dried moss ordinarily used as a soil additive) and one part sharp sand (the coarse sand used by builders—if you rub it between your fingers it will make a grating sound); to each bushel of this mixture add 1½ ounces of superphosphate (a fertilizer) and ¾ ounce of ground limestone. All are sold by garden-supply stores. This potting soil should be thoroughly mixed. One good way to make sure is to stir it up, then rub it through a piece of ½-inch-wire-mesh screen called "hardware cloth," available at most hardware stores.

Indoor potting soils that you mix yourself should also be sterilized to rid them of weed seeds, soil-borne diseases and insects. This is normally done with heat (at about 180°; the process actually is closer to pasteurization than sterilization). The sterilization process can be performed in the kitchen oven. The soil is placed in a covered pan and baked for 30 minutes after soil temperature, checked with a meat thermometer, reaches 180°. But since the operation usually produces an earthy, long-lasting odor that will not enhance the atmosphere of your kitchen, you may prefer to purchase presterilized, ready-mixed potting soil. Some gardeners use a chemical soil disinfectant, packaged under such trade names as Vapam, Terraclor, Larvacide and Dowfume. They should be used exactly as directed, and they should always be mixed outdoors because chemical sterilants can produce fumes that are dangerous if inhaled. (Some soil sterilants are toxic to some plants.)

You can even start seedlings indoors with no soil. What are called "soilless soils" have become popular as growing mediums for indoor seedbeds. Developed by various agricultural institutions as a substitute for loam-based potting soils, these nonsoil "soils" are generally based on a mixture of peat moss and one or the other of two forms of silica—vermiculite or perlite. The soilless soils are light in texture and weight, and thus seedlings grown in them can be transplanted much more easily. They are relatively sterile and thus need not be heated or treated with chemical sterilants. But they have no nutritional value, so nutrients must be added.

One of the best known of these soilless soils is a type of Cornell Mix, developed by Cornell University. Its base is peat moss and fine vermiculite mixed half and half, to which various nutrients are added. To make a bushel of Cornell Mix, use two 2-gallon pails full of peat moss, the same amount of Number 4 vermiculite, four level tablespoons of 20 per cent superphosphate, eight tablespoons of ground limestone, six tablespoons of ammonium nitrate or, instead of ammonium nitrate, one cup of 5–10–5 fertilizer. Run this mixture through a screen of ½-inch-mesh hardware cloth and moisten it thoroughly before using it.

The simplest container for starting seeds indoors is a clay or plastic flowerpot; I prefer a plastic one because it does not dry out as rapidly as a clay one. But you must be careful not to provide too much water if you use plastic. The size most commonly used is 4 to 6 inches in diameter. Use a single pot for each kind of seed that you are starting; you don't want different kinds coming up at different times in the same pot. If you are planting a great many of one kind of seed, a rectangular seed flat may be more practical than a flowerpot. The flat, of wood or plastic, can be of any convenient size; it is usually 3 to 4 inches deep, and 12 to 18 inches wide by 18 to 24 inches long. If you make your own seed flats from scraps of·wood, be sure to bore drainage holes in the bottom or leave ¼-inch spaces between the bottom slats.

Starter beds that use Cornell Mix or a similar soilless soil need no special preparation beyond filling the pot or seed flat with the mix. (If potting soil is used, see illustrations on page 80.) If you are using flats, mark off the surface in tiny furrows, called drills, by pressing it lightly with the edge of a ruler to a depth suitable to the size of the seeds to be sown. Most seeds should not be sown deeper than two or three times their diameter, and fine seeds need no soil covering at all. The distance between drills also depends on the size of the seeds; rows of small seeds may be 2 inches apart while rows of large seeds should be 3 inches apart.

The seeds should be sown far enough apart so that each seedling, as it grows, will have some soil, air and sunshine of its own. It is every bit as important indoors as it is outdoors to avoid the temptation to sow seeds too close together. The less the seedlings have to compete with one another from the moment of germination, the sturdier and bushier they will be. And sowing seeds thinly also inhibits the spread of "damping off," a fungus disease that attacks crowded seedlings and can kill them overnight.

The actual technique of sowing seeds thinly is simple. All it requires is a gentle tap on the edge of the seed packet crimped between finger and thumb to release the right number of seeds at the right intervals. Large seeds can be poured into the palm of the hand and deposited in the soil one by one. With very fine seeds, it is a good idea, if possible, to buy the pelleted seeds that are offered by some seedsmen. One or a few seeds are enclosed in a ball of inert material large enough to handle. Pelleted seeds, however, cost more. There are a couple of less expensive tricks that can be employed. Fine seeds can be mixed with fine sand, so as to dilute the number of seeds sown. If the seeds are too dark to be distinguished in the fur-

FROM SEED TO SEEDLING

STARTING PLANTS
FROM SEEDS INDOORS

1. *A flowerpot becomes a seedbed after it is filled as shown here. The bottom layer is pebbles or shards (pieces of a broken pot), then comes a thin layer of peat moss, then enough potting soil to reach within ½ inch of the top and, finally, ¼ inch of vermiculite or milled sphagnum moss.*

2. *Sow large seeds onto the firmed soil before adding moss or vermiculite. Tiny seeds are dusted onto the vermiculite or moss and are not covered.*

3. *To moisten the seeds without disturbing them, stand the pot in water, which will rise to dampen the surface. Then lift the pot out and let it drain.*

4. *To hasten germination, slip a clear plastic food-storage bag over the pot, tucking the open end underneath (arrow). Leave ample air space at the top. Give the seedbed subdued light and a steady temperature of 65° to 75° until the seeds sprout. Then remove the bag and put the pot in a sunny window; keep the soil moist.*

5. *When the first true leaves appear just above the "seed leaves," moisten the soil and prick out the seedlings with a pencil or plant marker. Lift soil with the roots; steady the plant by a leaf to avoid injuring the delicate stem.*

6. *Each seedling is set into potting soil in a 2- to 3-inch pot, and the soil is gently firmed. Keep the pots in trays at a sunny window. Put a little water in the trays each morning, no more than can be absorbed by midafternoon.*

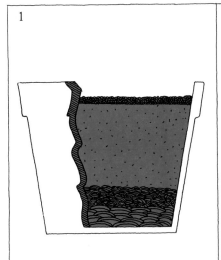
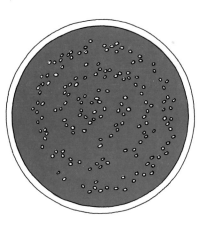
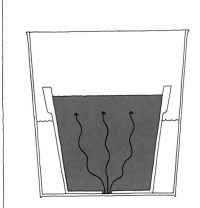

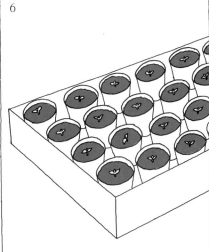

row, the surface of the seedbed can be dusted with light-colored sand to make them more visible. Of course, if too many seedlings germinate in a small area, you can always thin them out.

After the seeds are sown, the requirements for germination are few but critical—water, a humid atmosphere, warmth and shade. If a pot is used, the moisture can best be supplied by standing it in a pan of water immediately after sowing and leaving it there until the surface of the soil becomes damp—not waterlogged, just damp. Then lift the pot out of the water and drain it. To preserve humidity for the seeds cover them with clear plastic household bags; they come in a variety of sizes. Simply slide the pot or flat inside the bag and tuck the open end underneath, leaving some air space around the container. Props will be required to keep the bag from sagging; pencils, plant labels or even unbent paper clips can be used. The rounded top and sides of the bag will help carry off the condensation, and the atmosphere inside will stay moist. After the initial watering you probably will not have to water again until the plants have started growing.

Warmth is essential to the germination process. The optimum temperature for a seedbed for most plants is between 65° and 75°; some professional plant growers keep this temperature constant by placing their seed flats on waterproof electric heating pads. There is no need for such measures in the home unless the thermostat is set so the temperature falls below 65°. In that case the pot or flat should be placed closer to a radiator or other heat source, but not on top of it. Do not use an ordinary home heating pad unless you can protect it thoroughly from moisture.

Partial shade, the final requirement for germination of most seeds, is a simple matter of keeping the pot or flat out of bright light. One common shading device is a tent made of a sheet or two of newspaper to reduce the amount of light the seedbed receives.

USING ARTIFICIAL LIGHT

Once the seeds have sprouted, the seed pot or flat should have the plastic cover removed. Moreover, the requirement for partial shade ends. Now bright illumination is what you want. The paper tent should be taken down and the seedlings should be placed on a sunny window sill or under a fluorescent light. Sunlight is free. But even the sunniest window sill receives its illumination from only one side, and the plants must be turned every day or two in order to maintain an even growth rate and to keep them from leaning toward the light source. Furthermore, the number of plants is limited by the number of brightly lighted window sills in the house.

For these reasons many home gardeners as well as commercial florists have turned to fluorescent lamps. There are lamps made especially for growing plants and seedlings but they are not essential; you can use the widely sold types labeled "cool white," "white" or "daylight."

While it is possible to build elaborate artificially lighted indoor gardens, it is easier to purchase one of the commercially available fluorescent-lighted plant stands. These units, complete with waterproof flowerpot trays, are constructed so that the light fixture can be raised or lowered according to the height of the plants.

FROM SEEDBED TO POT   As soon as the seedlings show their first pair of identifiable true leaves (not the seed leaves that appear initially), they are ready for transplanting. This should be done as soon as possible. Although some plant varieties are able to survive transplanting at almost any stage of their development, others suffer no matter when it is done—but suffer least as tiny seedlings. If transplanting is delayed until several sets of leaves have appeared, the shock is greater and the plant, made tall and spindly by its confinement in the seedbed, is less able to withstand it.

Although some gardeners, for reasons of space, transplant seedlings into flats, it is better for the plants if they are moved to individual containers so their roots do not become intertwined. The best pot size for this purpose is one that has a 2- or 3-inch top diameter, and the type of pot used—clay, plastic, peat—is largely a

HASTENING GROWTH WITH ARTIFICIAL LIGHT

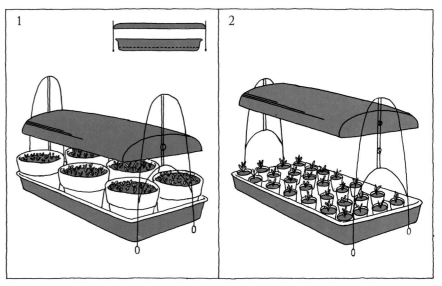

1

2

To grow seedlings faster, keep their seedbed pots under a two-tube fluorescent unit set 6 to 8 inches above the soil. Stand the pots on gravel in a shallow tray containing a little water (side view).

After transplanting the seedlings to individual 2- to 3-inch pots—as soon as the first true leaves have developed—raise the light unit 10 to 12 inches above the soil. Keep the light on for 14 to 18 hours a day.

matter of individual preference. Each has its advantages. Seedlings grown in clay or plastic pots are taken out of the pots when transplanted into the garden, and their roots come in immediate contact with the garden soil. Also, clay and plastic pots are reusable. Peat pots, on the other hand, are easier to set out in the garden, for pot and plant go into the ground together. Crush the fragile peat pot slightly as you set it in the ground; the roots then grow through the disintegrating pot and into the garden soil. Also, crumble away the top edge of the peat pot if it shows above the soil, since it sometimes acts as a wick, depriving the seedling of vital soil moisture.

A refinement of the peat pot is the peat pellet, a flat disk of compressed peat moss impregnated with fertilizer and held together by plastic mesh. When moistened the disk expands to pot size and is used as a pot is used. Because its composition is looser than that of the standard peat pot, the pellet permits the roots to pass through more easily into the garden soil. Still another medium for seedlings is a "planting block," which is made of soft wood pulp impregnated with fertilizer and can also be set directly in the garden.

If you choose a pot or flat for the intermediate stage between germination and transplanting outdoors, fill the container with potting soil to within ½ inch of the top. Make a hole big enough to accommodate the seedling's root system without crowding; for this you can use a pencil or a pointed stick, rotating it to make a cone-shaped hole. Remove the seedlings from the seedbed individually by lifting each one with a plant label or tongue depressor, taking with each root a small bit of soil to keep the root from drying out. If several seedlings are growing so close together they may have intertwined roots, remove them in the following manner: Rap the pot or flat sharply against the edge of a table or workbench; this compacts the soil enough so you can slide your fingers under a clump of seedlings. Lift a clump and drop it gently on the work surface; the soil will fall away from the roots and the seedlings will separate. Lift each seedling gently, supporting it by a leaf rather than the stem, and set it in the hole you have poked in the soil of its new container. Make sure it is placed no deeper than it was in the seedbed—many a seedling has died of rot or shock because it could not adjust to a new soil height around its stem. Press the soil gently around the plant, not touching the stem; water it; shade it for a day or two; and then set it in full sunlight.

Sowing seeds and helping them germinate is not the only method of preparing flowers indoors for the outdoor garden. You can also grow new plants from pieces of old plants.

A number of the plants grown as annuals are not true annuals; they may be woody shrubs or perennial herbs in their native

THE VERSATILE SUNFLOWER
Explorers in the New World found that the Indians made many uses of a flower unknown to Europe, the sunflower. The Incas worshiped it as an emblem of the sun; the Plains Indians of North America placed its seeds on the graves of their dead to provide food for the journey to heaven. The Hurons used its leaves for animal fodder, its petals for a yellow dye and its fibrous stalks for weaving textiles. Today the sunflower remains a highly useful plant. Its seeds —a single flower bears more than 2,000 of them—not only provide a tasty snack for humans and a major ingredient in bird feed, but the oil extracted from them is used in margarine, salad dressings, paint, soap, plastics, and even in processing iron and steel.

HOW TO ROOT CUTTINGS

Containers into which seedlings from a seedbed can be transplanted include flat peat pellets that swell into pot shapes when wet (top, left); ordinary flowerpots (top, right); cellulose planting blocks impregnated with nutrients (bottom, left); compressed peat pots (bottom, right).

land. In colder climates they can be carried over through the winter in a home or greenhouse and set into the garden in the spring. Typical plants of this group are geranium, patient Lucy, flowering maple and coleus. While these particular types may also be grown from seeds, gardeners who wish to perpetuate a particularly fine plant can do so by "vegetative propagation," i.e., taking cuttings. Not all plants can be propagated by cuttings, but many of the popular house and garden plants can.

There are several types of cuttings, but the tip, or terminal, cutting is the one most often used. It consists of a piece of the stem taken from the end of a branch and is usually 2 to 6 inches long. Leaves should be removed from the lower inch of the stem cutting so it can be inserted into the rooting medium to take root. Any flowers or flower buds should be pinched off so they will not drain energy from the cutting. Treated this way the cutting will retain enough energy to tide it over until new roots form at the base.

A 6-inch flowerpot of clay or plastic is easy to handle and holds enough cuttings to suit most needs. The rooting medium can be any of these mixtures: one-half coarse sand and one-half vermiculite; one-half coarse sand and one-half peat moss; coarse sand alone; or vermiculite or perlite alone. All these rooting media are porous enough to admit plenty of water and air. They should be moist when the cuttings are inserted and should be kept moist during the rooting period, but should not be allowed to become soggy with water as this may cause the cuttings to rot. No drainage material is needed in the bottom of the pot.

Before inserting the cutting to be rooted, it is helpful to dip the bottom inch of the premoistened stem into a rooting powder, tapping the cutting to remove excess powder. These root-promoting chemicals speed the rooting process and increase the number of roots. Many different rooting powders are available at garden supply centers. Be sure to get the right one; some are suitable for easy-to-root plants while others are for the more difficult.

Insert cuttings ½ to 1 inch deep and far enough apart so that they do not crowd each other. The rooting media should be pressed firmly around the stems, and the pot should be well watered. To maintain humidity, cover the pot with a plastic bag in the same way you covered the pots during seed germination. As with the seeds, it is generally unnecessary to moisten the plants again until they form roots and are ready for transplanting to separate pots. If no plastic coverings are provided, it is a good idea before transplanting cuttings to set inside each large pot a tiny, empty clay pot with its drainage hole plugged by a cork; water poured into this small pot will seep through its porous sides and keep the surrounding rooting medium in the large pot moist. A bit of shade

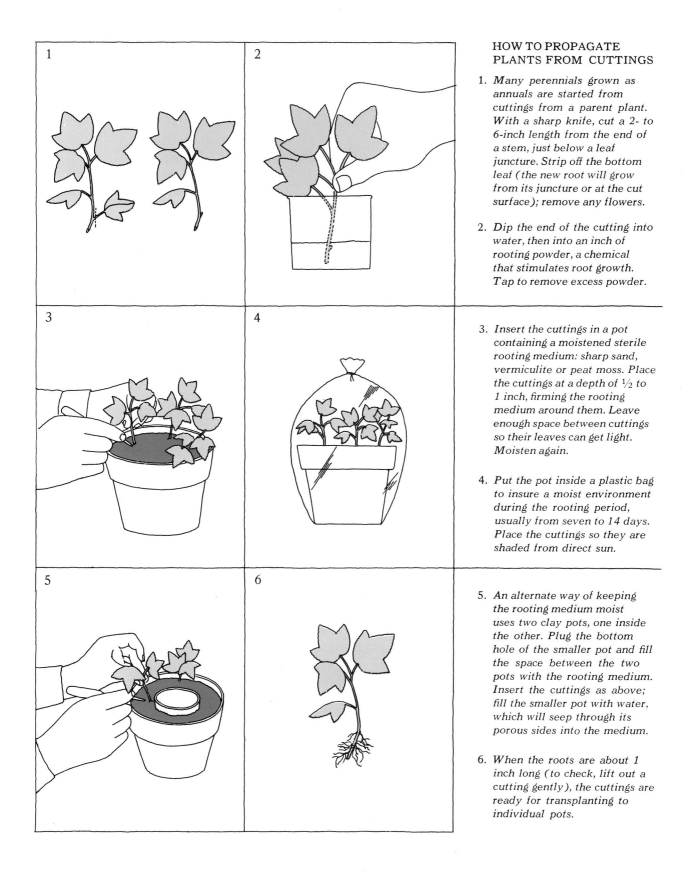

HOW TO PROPAGATE PLANTS FROM CUTTINGS

1. *Many perennials grown as annuals are started from cuttings from a parent plant. With a sharp knife, cut a 2- to 6-inch length from the end of a stem, just below a leaf juncture. Strip off the bottom leaf (the new root will grow from its juncture or at the cut surface); remove any flowers.*

2. *Dip the end of the cutting into water, then into an inch of rooting powder, a chemical that stimulates root growth. Tap to remove excess powder.*

3. *Insert the cuttings in a pot containing a moistened sterile rooting medium: sharp sand, vermiculite or peat moss. Place the cuttings at a depth of ½ to 1 inch, firming the rooting medium around them. Leave enough space between cuttings so their leaves can get light. Moisten again.*

4. *Put the pot inside a plastic bag to insure a moist environment during the rooting period, usually from seven to 14 days. Place the cuttings so they are shaded from direct sun.*

5. *An alternate way of keeping the rooting medium moist uses two clay pots, one inside the other. Plug the bottom hole of the smaller pot and fill the space between the two pots with the rooting medium. Insert the cuttings as above; fill the smaller pot with water, which will seep through its porous sides into the medium.*

6. *When the roots are about 1 inch long (to check, lift out a cutting gently), the cuttings are ready for transplanting to individual pots.*

for a few days may be necessary to help the cuttings become acclimated so they will not wilt. Shortly the cuttings can be exposed to light. They should then be kept in a well-lighted location, but out of direct sunlight, during the rooting period.

Most plants form new roots within seven to 14 days. They should be planted in separate pots when the new roots are about 1 inch long. If roots are allowed to become much longer, they become fragile and break off when the cutting is moved to its own pot. This is also true of cuttings that have been placed in plain water for rooting; they often are quite fragile, as well as long, stringy and sparse.

COLD FRAMES AND HOTBEDS

At this point you will probably develop a space problem. The 50 young marigolds that occupied only 6 or 8 square inches as tiny seedlings, or the 20 geraniums that were little cuttings, suddenly take up much more room as young plants in separate pots. Now you face the problem of giving over every available window sill to your plants, and still not having enough room. The solution is a hotbed or cold frame.

These are identical outdoor structures, except that the hotbed is artificially heated and the cold frame is heated only by the sun. The advantage of a hotbed over a cold frame is that it can be used earlier in the season; when warm weather comes, the heat can be turned off and the hotbed becomes a cold frame.

Nearly all hotbeds and cold frames are rectangular. The standard size is 3 by 6 feet, but they can be larger or smaller. The back of the structure, facing north, should be 18 to 30 inches high; and the front, facing south, should be 12 to 24 inches high. The sides should slope about 1 inch per foot of width. This frame is topped with glass or plastic, allowing the sun's rays to hit all plants equally; the cover also carries off rain.

You can build permanent frames of masonry or decay-resistant wood (redwood or cypress). Some stores carry aluminum frames, which are convenient because they can be dismantled and stored. In a very cold climate it is wise to pack a mound of earth around frames for extra protection against the weather. An inexpensive and simple cold frame can be made at home by building a wooden frame to support an old storm window or a piece of heavy-gauge plastic tacked on a separate wooden frame.

The heating element in a hotbed is an electric cable, laid under six inches of sand in a regular pattern. Cable units, complete with thermostats, can be purchased from most large garden supply houses. Installed in a standard 3-by-6-foot frame and plugged into any outlet, the unit uses about ½ to 1½ kilowatt hours per day —comparable to the electricity used by a 100-watt light bulb in 10 hours—depending on the outdoor temperature.

In both hotbeds and cold frames, set the pots or flats inside, close the top and wait for warmer weather.

Meanwhile your plants will get more light than in your home. They will grow into more robust specimens, and since they grow at cooler temperatures, they will suffer less when they are moved into the open garden. The temperature inside the hotbed or cold frame should range between 70° and 75° during the day, and should drop no lower than 45° at night. To help you measure the temperature, hang a thermometer inside the hotbed or cold frame where you can read it through the glass, but be sure it is shaded from the sun. While a thermostat will control the addition of heat to the hotbed, on sunny days it will be necessary to prop open the cover slightly to allow excess heat to dissipate—otherwise your tender seedlings may parboil. And on very cold nights you may have to cover a cold frame with a tarpaulin to hold in the day's heat. In addition, you will need to water the plants whenever the surface of the soil in pots or flats seems dry. Watering should be done early in the day so foliage and soil surface are dry before nightfall.

As the weather gets warmer you can open the sash wider and for longer periods during the day until warm weather finally arrives. At that point your house-grown, hotbed-nurtured plants are at last ready for the open garden *(Chapter 2)*.

USING COLD FRAMES AND HOTBEDS

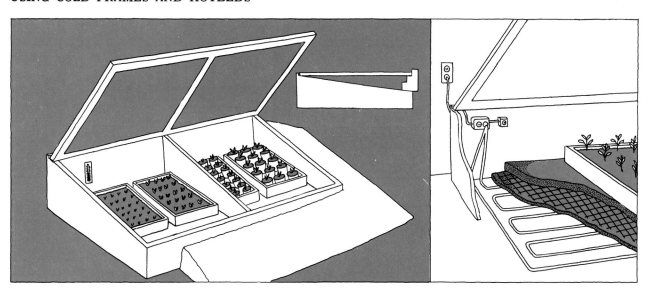

To accustom indoor-grown seedlings to the outdoors, move them to a cold frame. Prevent overheating on warm days by propping the top open (side view). In cold climates, bank earth or mulch around the sides of the frame.

For weather too cold for a cold frame use a hotbed—a frame with an electric heating cable looped inside. Lay the cable over 2 inches of sand and cover with hardware cloth and 4 inches more of sand, as shown in the cutaway above.

An illustrated encyclopedia of annuals 5

Among the most important—and for many people most fascinating —aspects of gardening is deciding which annuals to grow. There are hundreds of species and thousands of varieties, each seeming to promise more delight than another. Should you select one of the reliable old standards like marigolds or petunias or zinnias, or would something exotic like Cupid's dart be more fun? Which plants come in the color and height that you want for a particular spot in your garden? What is the blossom size of a particular plant? The leaf shape? How long will it bloom? Is it fragrant? Will it prosper under your garden's conditions of soil, moisture and exposure to sun? If so, when and how do you plant it?

The following encyclopedic chapter answers such questions about the annual flowers available to home gardeners in the United States and Canada; also included are biennials and perennials that blossom the first year and can therefore be grown as annuals. Each plant is listed alphabetically under its botanical name. You will note that this Latin name has more than one part, for example, *Browallia speciosa major.* The first part—in this case *Browallia* —refers to the plant's genus: a group of plants marked by common characteristics in leaves, flowers and seeds. Considerable variation can occur within a genus, particularly in height, color and hardiness. The second part of the name refers to the species, a subdivision of plants potentially capable of interbreeding, in this example *speciosa.* The third part of the name, when used, identifies a particular variety of the species, in this case *major,* meaning larger, a reference to the size of the flowers.

For the convenience of those who know most flowers by their common English names, those names have been included and cross-referenced. But common names can be confusing; they vary from region to region, and sometimes one name refers to several distinct species. The name "daisy," for example, applies to at least 18 different plants. For this reason the description of a flower appears under the internationally recognized Latin name of its genus.

The color, abundance and extraordinary variety of annuals—from the tiny edging lobelia at bottom right to the big gloriosa daisy at upper left—are suggested in a medley drawn by Allianora Rosse.

PINK SAND VERBENA
Abronia umbellata

FLOWERING MAPLE
Abutilon hybridum

SUMMER ADONIS
Adonis aestivalis

A

ABRONIA

A. umbellata (pink sand verbena).

Pink sand verbenas are trailing plants that stand about 6 inches high and have dense, round-topped flower clusters about 2 inches across made up of delicately colored ½-inch blossoms. (The name is misleading: pink sand verbenas are not true verbenas (see *Verbena*) but have verbenalike flowers, and their color is more a rosy lavender than pink.) Perennials in the mild areas of their native West Coast, they are widely used as annuals where they are unable to survive the harsher winters.

USES. Pink sand verbenas are versatile plants. Because they are low-growing, they make effective edgings for walkways and borders. Because they trail and have a pleasing fragrance, they are excellent for window boxes and hanging baskets and as potted plants on balconies (wind does not damage them). And though their stems are short, they provide long-lasting cut flowers. They are splendid for seaside gardens since they need abundant sunshine, cool temperatures and light, sandy, rather dry soil.

HOW TO GROW. Sow seeds indoors in the spring about six weeks before the last frost is due. In dry areas of Zones 9-10, seeds may be sown outdoors in the fall. Seedlings of pink sand verbenas are difficult to transplant successfully except when very small, so move them first into individual 2- to 3-inch peat pots as soon as the first true leaves appear. This step will be spread over two to three weeks, for the seeds will not all germinate at the same time. Then transplant them into the garden, pots and all, when all danger of frost has passed. Set them 6 to 9 inches apart.

ABUTILON

A. hybridum (flowering maple).

Flowering maples, of uncertain origin, derive their name from their leaves, which are shaped like those of a maple tree. (They are not true maples, which are members of the *Acer* genus.) In Zones 9-10 they grow as garden shrubs, becoming as tall as 4 feet and blossoming year after year; elsewhere they reach a height of 12 to 18 inches. The gracefully drooping branches have bell-shaped blossoms, 1½ to 2½ inches across, and come in a wide choice of colors, including apricot, salmon, white, rose, yellow or purple.

USES. In most of the U.S., where flowering maples grow only a foot or so in height and are not winter hardy, they are popular as border plants. They are even more delightful in window boxes and hanging baskets because of the way their flower-laden stems cascade over the edges. They flourish in moist, fertile soil, in full sun or light shade.

HOW TO GROW. Sow seeds indoors eight to 10 weeks before the last frost is due, then pot the plants individually when the first maplelike leaves appear. Wait until the plants are 4 to 6 inches tall and night temperatures are not likely to drop below 50° before putting them outdoors. Space them 12 inches apart. Outdoor plants may be repotted and brought into the house for winter flowering. Cuttings can also be rooted *(page 85)*.

ACHYRANTHES See *Alternanthera*
ACROCLINIUM See *Helipterum*

ADONIS

A. aestivalis (summer adonis, pheasant's eye). *A. autumnalis,* sometimes called *A. annua* (autumn adonis, pheasant's eye, red Morocco, flos adonis).

These European annuals grow to be feathery-leaved 15-inch plants topped by a great number of bright red, buttercuplike flowers. The blossoms of summer adonis are about 1½ inches across; those of autumn adonis are half that size, with black centers.

USES. Both summer adonis and autumn adonis form large mounds of color that are effective in borders. They do not, however, provide long-lasting cut flowers. Both species grow best in light but moist, rich soil. They will grow in full sun or partial shade but cannot stand extreme heat, thriving best in cool coastal or mountainous regions where night temperatures in summer drop below 65°.

HOW TO GROW. Adonis does not transplant successfully, so sow seeds directly into the garden borders in late fall, just before the ground freezes, or as early in the spring as the soil can be cultivated. Space seeds so plants will stand 12 inches apart. The seeds need about two weeks to germinate. Despite the common names, summer adonis and autumn adonis, both species blossom in July and August.

AFRICAN DAISY See *Arctotis* and *Dimorphotheca*
AFRICAN MARIGOLD See *Tagetes*
AGATHAEA See *Felicia*

AGERATUM

A. houstonianum, also called *A. mexicanum* (ageratum, flossflower).

Ageratums, descendants of wild plants from Mexico, bear abundant clusters of fuzzy ¼- to ½-inch blossoms that are misty blue or, less commonly, pink or white. Most varieties grow in compact mounds, 3 to 6 inches tall and 8 to 10 inches across; a few varieties reach 2 feet in height.

USES. Ageratums prosper in average soil if placed in full sun and will tolerate some light shade. Low varieties are well suited for borders and window boxes; taller ones provide splendid background plantings and cut flowers.

HOW TO GROW. Ageratums are usually grown from seeds, which germinate in five to 10 days, but they may also be propagated from cuttings *(page 85)*. Young plants are tender and develop slowly, so start them indoors six to eight weeks before the last frost is due. Set plants 6 to 9 inches apart in the garden. In mild West Coast areas, seeds may be planted in late summer for fall flowers.

AGROSTEMMA

A. githago (corn cockle).

No plant more dramatically demonstrates how a garden variety can differ from the original wild version than the corn cockle. It is a small, purplish, undistinguished weed in European grain fields, but the garden variety of the corn cockle, named Milas, is a hardy, lovely annual with soft 2- to 3-inch lilac-pink blossoms atop 2- to 3-foot willowy stems. It is named for the town in Turkey where its ancestor was discovered growing wild.

USES. The corn cockle makes an excellent cut flower. It needs sun but will prosper in any soil and can stand a good bit of wind and moisture.

HOW TO GROW. Sow seeds outdoors any time in the fall or as soon as the soil can be spaded and raked in the spring. Space plants 12 inches apart.

AGROSTIS

A. nebulosa (cloud grass).

A Spanish member of the genus that includes some of the finest lawn grasses, cloud grass has long clusters of small white flower spikes atop stems about a foot high.

USES. Grouped together, the plants create a soft, hazy effect (hence the name cloud grass), useful when you want to conceal the spindly lower portions of background plants. The stems of cloud grass make unusual and interesting additions to cut-flower arrangements. They can also be dried

AGERATUM
Ageratum houstonianum

CORN COCKLE
Agrostemma githago

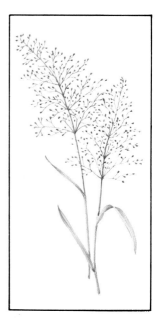

CLOUD GRASS
Agrostis nebulosa

For climate zones and frost dates, see maps, pages 164-165.

MASK FLOWER
Alonsoa warscewiczii

ALTERNANTHERA
Alternanthera amoena

HOLLYHOCK
Althaea rosea

for year-round use if they are picked just before the blossoms open and hung upside down to dry in a shady place. Cloud grass needs sun but will grow in almost any soil.

HOW TO GROW. Sow seeds outdoors any time in the fall, or as early in the spring as the soil can be cultivated. Space plants 6 inches apart. The plants may remain where sown or may be transplanted.

ALGERIAN STATICE See *Limonium*
ALKANET See *Anchusa*

ALONSOA
A. warscewiczii (mask flower).

This native of the Andean Mountains has stems 1½ to 2 feet tall covered along their lengths with a profusion of small scarlet flowers.

USES. Mask flowers thrive in light, fertile soil and full sun but do not tolerate hot weather well. They do best in cool coastal or mountainous regions where night temperatures in summer can be expected to drop below 65°. A dwarf variety about 9 inches tall is valuable as a long-flowering edging plant. Both dwarf and full-sized varieties make unusual house plants.

HOW TO GROW. Mask flowers require four months to grow from seed to flower. Sow seeds indoors two to three months before the last frost is due. Or sow them in the garden after all frost danger is past. Plants should stand 10 to 12 inches apart.

ALPINE POPPY See *Papaver*
ALPINE STRAWBERRY See *Fragaria*

ALTERNANTHERA
Sometimes sold as *Telanthera* or *Achyranthes*. *A. amoena*. *A. bettzichiana*. *A. versicolor*. (All called alternanthera.)

These tender herbs from the jungles of Brazil are grown for their leaves, brilliantly colored in shades of yellow or red, or green blotched with yellow, red or orange. The plants range in height from 6 to 12 inches: *A. amoena* is very small, *A. bettzichiana* is medium height and *A. versicolor* is the tallest of the three. The flowers are inconspicuous.

USES. Alternantheras are among the plants most commonly used as "carpet bedding" to work out designs and edgings for flower beds. They need sun but grow well in almost any soil.

HOW TO GROW. Because alternantheras must be propagated by cuttings or division during the winter, most home gardeners buy small plants. Set them directly in the garden in the spring when all danger of frost has passed. Space them 4 to 5 inches apart. When used in a floral design (like the "clocks" sometimes seen in public gardens), plants may be clipped with shears to keep them a uniform height. A few plants may easily be carried over the winter in pots indoors. Cuttings from these can be rooted in the spring for the following garden season *(page 85)*.

ALTHAEA
A. rosea (hollyhock).

There was a time when all hollyhocks were biennials, bearing flowers only during the summer after the year they were planted. Today, seed catalogues list annual varieties that make robust plants 4 to 6 feet tall and flower the first season—and with luck bloom the second year as well. Their tall stalks bear great numbers of single, semidouble and double flowers, 4 inches or more across, some with frilled edges, in red, rose, pink and yellow, as well as white.

USES. Hollyhocks, natives of the Orient, are dramatic

enough to make attention-getting accent plants but look best in rows against a wall, fence or garage. They need sun and average soil.

HOW TO GROW. Sow seeds indoors six to eight weeks before the last frost is due. When the first true leaves appear, transplant the seedlings into individual 3-inch pots and grow them in a cold frame until you can be sure the temperature will not drop below 50° at night. Then set them into the garden about 12 to 24 inches apart. The annual varieties grow quickly in a relatively dry time of the year, hence are rarely bothered by the rust disease that often disfigures the biennials. If orange-brown spots do appear on the leaves, dust the plants at weekly intervals with a fungicide. Spider mites can be a problem; for ways to control them, see chart, pages 50-51.

ALYSSUM See *Lobularia*
AMARANTH See *Amaranthus*
AMARANTH, GLOBE See *Gomphrena*

AMARANTHUS

A. caudatus (amaranth, love-lies-bleeding, tassel flower). *A. hypochondriacus,* also called *A. hybridus hypochondriacus* (amaranth, prince's feather). *A. salicifolius* (amaranth, flaming fountain, fountain plant). *A. tricolor,* also called *A. gangeticus melancholicus tricolor* (amaranth, Joseph's coat, molten fire, summer poinsettia).

Amaranths are brilliant, heavy-looking plants from the tropics of the Far East. They become 3 to 5 feet tall in rich soil and only slightly smaller—and even more brilliantly colored—in poor soil. Love-lies-bleeding has large green or red leaves and great drooping, tassellike red flower heads that cascade from the tops of the plants. The leaves of prince's feather may be purple, red or green; the tips of its stems are crowned with large erect spikes of tiny bright red flowers. Flaming fountain bears mounds of long, narrow leaves that turn from a bronze green to a striking orange red. The most colorful amaranth of all is Joseph's coat; its leaves vary from reddish green at the base to a neon red at the top and some varieties seem fluorescent.

USES. Amaranths are extremely long lasting—one tassel may last for eight weeks before fading. They are tall enough to serve as a temporary substitute for shrubbery, but their blazing colors can overwhelm a garden if not used with discretion. They are easy to grow in any average to dry soil so long as they have full sun.

HOW TO GROW. Sow seeds indoors about six weeks before the last frost is due, or in the garden, 18 to 36 inches apart, when you can be sure the night temperature will not drop below 50°. Amaranths transplant easily.

AMMOBIUM

A. alatum (winged everlasting).

Winged everlastings, natives of Australia, get their name from the raised ridges, or "wings," on their stiff stems. They grow 3 feet tall and have soft, silvery leaves and 1- to 2-inch white flowers with large yellowish centers.

USES. These flowers thrive in full sun and sandy soil (*Ammobium* is Latin for "living in sand"). Later, winged everlastings can be used in dry winter bouquets. For this purpose they should be clipped just before the flowers are fully open and hung upside down in a dry, shady place.

HOW TO GROW. Sow seeds indoors about six weeks before the last frost is due and set seedlings outdoors, 9 inches apart, when night temperatures do not fall below 50°. Seeds may also be sown outdoors as soon as the soil can be spaded and raked in the spring. Winged everlastings are easy to transplant at any stage of their development.

LEFT: LOVE-LIES-BLEEDING   RIGHT: JOSEPH'S COAT
Amaranthus caudatus   *A. tricolor*

WINGED EVERLASTING
Ammobium alatum

For climate zones and frost dates, see maps, pages 164-165.

TOP: PIMPERNEL
Anagallis arvensis

BOTTOM: FLAXLEAF PIMPERNEL
A. linifolia

TOP: SUMMER FORGET-ME-NOT
Anchusa capensis

BOTTOM: WHITE SUMMER FORGET-ME-NOT
A. capensis alba

ANAGALLIS

A. arvensis (pimpernel, shepherd's clock, poor man's weather glass). *A. linifolia* (flaxleaf pimpernel).

The scarlet pimpernel, a native of Europe, bears bright orange-red blossoms ¼ inch across on trailing stems that lie almost prone on the ground; blue and white varieties are also available. The flaxleaf pimpernel, native to North Africa, is a compact plant, 6 to 18 inches tall, bearing large clusters of ¾-inch flowers. It is available in a spectrum of colors from scarlet to blue, but many gardeners consider the deep blue varieties the finest of all blue annuals. Both species close at night and on cloudy days and open in sunshine —hence their other common names, shepherd's clock and poor man's weather glass.

USES. Pimpernels are effective in the dry pockets of rock gardens, in window boxes and in hanging baskets and are also used for edgings. They thrive in full sunlight and light, sandy loam.

HOW TO GROW. Start pimpernels indoors six weeks before the last frost is due, or sow seeds directly in the garden when frost danger has passed, spacing them so plants will stand 6 inches apart.

ANCHUSA

A. capensis (summer forget-me-not, alkanet, bugloss, Cape forget-me-not).

Most blue annuals are not really blue at all—their colors veer toward lavender or purple. Summer forget-me-nots, natives of South Africa, are an exception: The best variety, Blue Bird, has five-petaled flowers that are a true sky blue. Like the other varieties, its blossoms have white centers resembling forget-me-nots but are larger, about ¼ to ½ inch across; they grow in clusters on hairy 15- to 18-inch stems. An all-white variety, *A. capensis alba,* is also available. Summer forget-me-nots are not true forget-me-nots, which are members of the genus *Myosotis.*

USES. Summer forget-me-nots are most effective massed in beds and borders in such a way as to dramatize their unusual color. They thrive in moist, fertile soil in sunshine or light shade.

HOW TO GROW. Start seeds indoors six to eight weeks before the last frost is due. Or sow seeds directly in the garden when all frost danger has passed; plants should stand 10 to 12 inches apart. After their first flush of bloom, cut plants back to within 6 to 8 inches of the ground; they will rejuvenate quickly and be more beautiful than ever.

ANGEL'S TRUMPET See *Datura*
ANIMATED OAT See *Avena*

ANTIRRHINUM

A. majus (snapdragon).

Snapdragons, native to the Mediterranean region, are a particular favorite of children, who like to pinch the tiny individual blossoms and make the "dragon mouth" open and close. Modern varieties provide large, blossom-laden flower heads, faintly fragrant, in a wide assortment of bright colors. The vertical flower spikes, opening gradually from the bottom to the top, are available in three heights: small varieties range from 6 to 9 inches; intermediates, 18 to 24 inches; and large types, as tall as 3 or 4 feet. A single snapdragon plant may produce seven or eight blossom spikes in the course of a summer. A strain with open-faced cup-shaped blossoms, typified by the variety called Bright Butterflies, comes in both single and double versions.

USES. The tall varieties are striking as cut flowers but when growing must be supported by stakes. The small plants excel in beds and at the front of borders. The most useful of all are the intermediates; they need no staking, yet are stately in the garden and have stems long enough for use as cut flowers. Gardeners used to be less than enthusiastic about snapdragons as cut flowers because blossoms tended to "shatter"—drop off shortly after being fertilized by bees. But plant breeders have developed shatterproof strains in lavishly petaled double blossoms as well as the conventional singles. Snapdragons flourish in well-fertilized soil and full sun.

HOW TO GROW. Sow seeds indoors six to eight weeks before the last frost is due, moving seedlings outdoors as early as a planting bed can be spaded and raked. In Zones 8-10, seedlings started in a sheltered seedbed may be moved outdoors any time in the fall for winter and spring flowering. Seeds may also be sown outdoors, but the seed is so fine and the seedlings are so delicate that controlled growing conditions give better results. Plants should stand from 6 to 12 inches apart, depending on the ultimate size of the variety selected. Seedlings bought from a garden center, where they have been grown under the carefully controlled conditions only a florist's greenhouse can provide, will flower earlier than plants started at home from seeds. Whether starting from seeds or seedlings, choose varieties that are specifically marked rust resistant. When the plants are 2 to 4 inches tall, pinch off the stem tips if shorter but more abundant flowers spikes are desired. Then, as the flowers mature, use them freely for bouquets; the cutting will force plants to produce additional stems that will bloom later in the season.

APHANOSTEPHUS
A. skirrhobasis (lazy daisy).

The small daisylike flowers of lazy daisy, about an inch across, are white with yellow centers, but the reverse side of the petals is tinted with shades of pink or purple. They bloom singly on 15- to 18-inch stems, raised high above hairy gray-green leaves. As wild flowers they grow on the sandy prairies of the Southwest and northern Mexico.

USES. Lazy daisies are useful for planting in areas with light, dry soil and rather strong winds. They also provide long-lasting cut flowers. They need full sunshine.

HOW TO GROW. Sow seeds indoors about two months before the last frost is expected, or sow them directly in the garden when the danger of frost has passed. Plants should stand 8 to 12 inches apart.

APPLE, BALSAM See *Momordica*

ARCTOTIS
A. grandis, also called *A. stoechadifolia grandis* (arctotis, African daisy).

Its woolly gray leaves would make arctotis, native to South Africa, attractive even without flowers, but it has those too. The most common variety has pearl-white blossoms with gold-rimmed steel-blue centers and a reverse side of lavender. In addition, hybrid strains are available in shades of yellow, pink, brown, terra cotta, wine and mauve, often with contrasting colors at the base of the petals. Blossoms are about 3 inches in diameter. Most varieties grow less than 1 foot tall but some reach 2 feet.

USES. Arctotis has a long stem that makes it desirable for flower arrangements, though the flowers close at night. It will withstand drought, and does best in full sun and light, sandy loam in areas where summer nights are cool.

HOW TO GROW. Sow seeds indoors in early spring, about six to eight weeks before the last frost is due, or outdoors when you can be sure night temperatures will not drop below 50°. Space plants 12 inches apart.

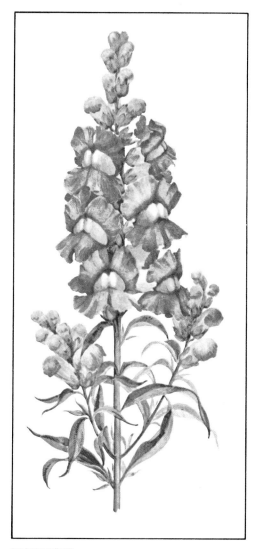

SNAPDRAGON
Antirrhinum majus

LAZY DAISY
Aphanostephus skirrhobasis

ARCTOTIS
Arctotis grandis

For climate zones and frost dates, see maps, pages 164-165.

PRICKLY POPPY
Argemone grandiflora

BLOOD FLOWER
Asclepias curassavica

ANNUAL WOODRUFF
Asperula orientalis

ARGEMONE

A. grandiflora. A. mexicana. (Both called argemone and prickly poppy.)

The flowers of *A. grandiflora* are satiny white and about 4 inches across; those of *A. mexicana,* yellow and 2 to 3 inches across. Of Mexican origin, both species grow about 2 feet tall. The leaves have scalloped edges tipped with tiny spines, hence the common name prickly poppy.

USES. Prickly poppies make dramatic border plants. They need sun, a hot location and sandy loam.

HOW TO GROW. Prickly poppies do not transplant easily. If they are started indoors, sow the seeds about six weeks before the last frost is due, putting them directly in individual 3-inch peat pots rather than in the usual seedbed; this minimizes shock when seedlings are moved to the garden, pots and all, after all frost danger has passed. Or sow seeds outdoors where they are to grow when all the frost has left the soil. Plants should stand about 9 inches apart.

ASCLEPIAS

A. curassavica (blood flower, bloodflower milkweed).

The blood flower is well named. Its blossoms, less than an inch across, are deep purplish red and orange, appearing in clusters from the base of leaves and at the top of 2- to 4-foot stalks. It is a perennial in tropical America, as well as in Zones 8-10 of the United States, but is treated as an annual in Zones 3-7. The flowers bloom in late summer.

USES. Blood flowers stand out in summer gardens, especially as a background planting, and the seed pods make interesting material for dried arrangements. The plants require a sunny spot in moist, fertile soil.

HOW TO GROW. Sow seeds indoors six to eight weeks before the last frost is due. Set seedlings in the garden, 15 to 18 inches apart, when frost danger is past. To induce branching, pinch off the tips of stems when the plants are 4 to 6 inches tall.

ASPERULA

A. orientalis, usually sold as *A. azurea setosa* (annual woodruff).

This little annual, originating in the Caucasus, bears clusters of tiny, very fragrant, pale blue flowers on 9- to 12-inch-tall plants. The flower stems trail along the ground, clothed with whorls of slender, bristly leaves.

USES. The annual woodruff is one of the few plants that are at their best in a moist, shady place, and is often planted along the banks of a stream. It makes a fine edging plant and may be used as a short-stemmed cut flower.

HOW TO GROW. For best effect, plant annual woodruffs in masses. Scatter seeds outdoors as thinly as possible as soon as the ground can be cultivated in the spring. Rake seeds lightly into the soil. Little thinning is necessary, but the plants grow best if they stand 4 to 6 inches apart. The plants bloom 10 to 12 weeks after sowing. Annual woodruff may scatter its own seeds in favorable locations so that the plants renew themselves each springtime.

ASTER

A. tanacetifolius, often sold as *Machaeranthera tanacetifolia* (Tahoka daisy).

When gardeners think of annual asters, they usually have in mind the China aster, belonging to the genus *Callistephus.* But the genus *Aster* offers an excellent annual, the Tahoka daisy. It bears long-lasting pale blue 2-inch flowers with yellow-orange centers that grow 1 to 2 feet tall amid wispy, threadlike foliage. The wild Tahoka daisy variety is native to a wide area of North America stretching from Mexico and California to Montana and South Dakota.

USES. The Tahoka daisy is valued in summer borders because it blooms continuously from midsummer until frost with virtually no attention. It thrives in full sun or light shade, in average soil, and withstands heat well.

HOW TO GROW. Sow seeds of Tahoka daisies indoors six to eight weeks before the last frost is due, outdoors any time in the fall, or outdoors very early in the spring as soon as the earth is warm and dry enough to be cultivated. Space plants 6 inches apart.

ASTER, CHINA See *Callistephus*

ATRIPLEX
A. hortensis (orach, sea purslane, French spinach).

This fast-growing annual from Asia is notable for its ornamental dark red foliage. The leaves are arrowhead-shaped and are covered with a crystalline substance when the plants are young. The plants bear tiny purplish flowers and reach a height of 4 to 6 feet.

USES. Orach is often used as a temporary hedge or screen because of its rapid growth. The red foliage makes a decorative addition to an indoor arrangement. It prefers a sunny, open area but will thrive in almost any soil and is not damaged by wind.

HOW TO GROW. Sow seeds outdoors when frost danger is past, spacing them so plants will stand 12 inches apart. Or sow the seeds indoors four to six weeks earlier. Seeds can be purchased by mail from English seedsmen.

AUTUMN ADONIS See *Adonis*

AVENA
A. sterilis (animated oat).

The strange grass known as animated oat comes from the north coast of Africa. The awns of its seeds—those slender tannish bristles sometimes called the beard—twist and turn in reaction to the amount of moisture in the air. Mature plants are 18 to 24 inches tall.

USES. The long seed clusters of animated oat are effective both in the garden and in dried arrangements. The plant will grow in any sunny location and average soil.

HOW TO GROW. Sow seeds outdoors in midfall or as early in the spring as the soil can be spaded and raked. Space plants 1 foot apart. For winter bouquets, stand the cut stems upright in a container to dry; the weight of the seed head will curve the stems gracefully. Other stems can be hung to dry upside down.

AZTEC MARIGOLD See *Tagetes*

B
BABIES'-BREATH See *Gypsophila*
BABY BLUE-EYES See *Nemophila*
BACHELOR'S BUTTON See *Centaurea*
BALLOON VINE See *Cardiospermum*
BALM, MOLUCCA See *Molucella*
BALSAM APPLE See *Momordica*
BALSAM, BUSH See *Impatiens*
BALSAM, GARDEN See *Impatiens*
BALSAM PEAR See *Momordica*
BARKHAUSIA See *Crepis*
BARTONIA See *Mentzelia*
BASIL See *Ocimum*
BASKET FLOWER See *Centaurea*
BEAN, CASTOR See *Ricinus*
BEAN, HYACINTH See *Dolichos*
BEAN, SCARLET RUNNER See *Phaseolus*
BEAN, WHITE DUTCH RUNNER See *Phaseolus*

TAHOKA DAISY
Aster tanacetifolius

ORACH
Atriplex hortensis

ANIMATED OAT
Avena sterilis

For climate zones and frost dates, see maps, pages 164-165.

WAX BEGONIA
Begonia semperflorens

ENGLISH DAISY
Bellis perennis

SWAN RIVER DAISY
Brachycome iberidifolia

BEARD TONGUE See *Penstemon*
BEEFSTEAK PLANT See *Perilla*

BEGONIA

B. semperflorens (wax begonia).

Wax begonias, natives of Brazil, are tender flowering herbaceous perennials but are widely used as annuals because they flower prolifically the first year. They bear 1- to 2-inch clusters of delicate pink, white or red flowers, and come in single- and double-petaled varieties; some are so voluminously and broadly petaled that they resemble miniature Christmas-tree balls. The blooms grow close together, often hiding the glossy red or green foliage. Wax begonias grow 6 to 9 inches tall, occasionally taller.

USES. Wax begonias are among the most popular of all garden plants. They are superb for window boxes, beds and borders, and also are widely grown as house plants. They flourish in shady areas as well as in full sunshine, provided they have rich, moist soil.

HOW TO GROW. Begonia seeds must be sown four to six months before the last frost is due, so most people prefer to buy plants in the spring to put directly into the garden. But wax begonias can be started from seed at home, provided you are willing to devote the necessary time to tending the seedlings. Then, when you can be sure the night temperature will not drop below 50°, set the plants into the garden 6 to 8 inches apart. They will soon begin to flower and will bloom continuously until cut down by frost; in Zones 9-10 they will flower most of the year. Wax begonias may be dug up before the first frost and potted as house plants; they will grow and blossom indefinitely. Cuttings (*page 85*) started from house plants in the spring root readily to provide specimens for the summer garden.

BELLFLOWER See *Campanula*

BELLIS

B. perennis (English daisy, true daisy).

The name "daisy" is applied to many plants, but the original "day's eye" of literature is the English daisy, of European as well as British origin, a bushy plant about 6 inches high topped with quantities of single or double white, pink or red flowers, 1 to 2 inches across, with centers of golden yellow.

USES. English daisies serve well in the front of a border and in rock gardens. They thrive in full sun or light shade, in almost any soil as long as it is moist. In climates like that of San Francisco, where winters are temperate and summers cool, the seeds they cast germinate easily, maintaining a continuous growth of blooming plants during much of the year.

HOW TO GROW. The English daisy is grown as an annual in Zones 8-10; plants started from seeds sown outdoors in the fall grow through the mild winter and flower in very early spring. In Zones 3-7, where the ground freezes in winter, the species acts as a biennial; seeds sown one spring will blossom the following spring. In all cases, space plants 8 to 9 inches apart.

BELLS, CANTERBURY See *Campanula*
BELLS, IRISH See *Molucella*
BELLS-OF-IRELAND See *Molucella*
BELVEDERE See *Kochia*
BLACK-EYED SUSAN VINE See *Thunbergia*
BLANKETFLOWER See *Gaillardia*
BLAZING STAR See *Mentzelia*
BLOOD FLOWER See *Asclepias*

BLOODLEAF See *Iresine*
BLUE BELLS, CALIFORNIA See *Phacelia*
BLUEBONNET, TEXAS See *Lupinus*
BLUEBOTTLE See *Centaurea*
BLUE CUPIDONE See *Catananche*
BLUE DAISY See *Felicia*
BLUE LACE FLOWER See *Trachymene*
BLUE MARGUERITE See *Felicia*
BLUE SUCCORY See *Catananche*
BLUE THIMBLE FLOWER See *Gilia*

BRACHYCOME

B. iberidifolia (Swan River daisy).

Multitudes of fragrant, daisylike blossoms of blue, rose, violet or white about 1½ inches across cover this annual from Australia. It rarely grows more than a foot tall.

USES. Masses of Swan River daisies are effective in borders, window boxes and terrace planters; they also may be used as short-stemmed cut flowers. They require rich soil and full sun.

HOW TO GROW. Sow seeds outdoors in late spring after all frost danger has passed. Or start seeds indoors four to six weeks before the last frost is due and set the plants outside when the earth is warm and dry enough to be cultivated. Space plants 6 inches apart. Place brushy twigs between the plants to hold the slender stems upright.

BRASSICA

B. oleracea capitata (ornamental or flowering cabbage). *B. oleracea acephala* (ornamental or flowering kale).

Foliage rather than flowers makes these low-growing plants notable. (The two species look alike and are usually sold interchangeably or as a mixture.) The leaves, which open out from a center point, are either off-white or deeply tinged with pink, rose, red or purple, especially toward the centers. The plants are really tender biennials, blooming the second year, but they are killed by freezing so flowers are rarely seen north of Zone 7. Even in Zones 8-10, where they survive the winter months to blossom, the flowers are such an undistinguished mustard color they are seldom considered justification for growing the plant.

USES. Ornamental cabbage and ornamental kale make unusual bedding plants and are prized by flower arrangers because their colored leaves are effective in fall arrangements dominated by shades of gold and russet. They grow in average soil but need full sun. Like all members of the mustard family, they are most colorful in cool weather.

HOW TO GROW. Start seeds indoors four to six weeks before the last frost, then set the plants in the garden, 12 to 18 inches apart, when night temperatures are not expected to drop below freezing. Or sow seeds outdoors in early spring as soon as the planting bed can be prepared. Another sowing in midsummer will produce plants with the small leaves desirable for fall arrangements.

BRIZA

B. maxima (large quaking grass). *B. minor*, also called *B. gracilis* and *B. minima* (lesser quaking grass).

The ornamental feature of quaking grass is its colorful seeds, which group themselves into the shape of arrowheads that droop from slender stems and tremble in the slightest breeze. The seed heads of large quaking grass are about an inch long, hanging on stems 18 to 24 inches tall. Lesser quaking grass has seed heads only about ⅛ inch in size on 9- to 12-inch stems. The colors of the seeds include silvery red, reddish brown and purplish green.

USES. Quaking grass makes a decorative dried arrangement. For this purpose, stems should be cut before the

For climate zones and frost dates, see maps, pages 164-165.

ORNAMENTAL CABBAGE
Brassica oleracea capitata

LEFT: RIGHT:
LARGE QUAKING GRASS LESSER QUAKING GRASS
Briza maxima   *B. minor*

99

BROWALLIA
Browallia speciosa major

seeds ripen to prevent the seeds from falling off, then hung upside down to dry in a shady place. It will grow in average or dry soil if planted in full sun.

HOW TO GROW. Sow seeds outdoors in early spring, as soon as the ground can be spaded and raked. Space them 9 inches apart.

BROWALLIA
B. speciosa major. B. viscosa compacta. (Both called browallia.)

Browallias show their kinship to petunias by the trumpetlike shape and velvety texture of their blossoms. Varieties of *B. speciosa major* have blue or white flowers 1 to 2 inches across. In *B. viscosa compacta,* the variety Sapphire has dark blue, white-throated blossoms about an inch across. All grow to a height and spread of 12 to 15 inches.

USES. In window boxes and hanging baskets, the slender stems trail gracefully over edges. Browallias are easy to grow; they flourish in sun and a moderately rich soil but will grow well in partial shade.

HOW TO GROW. Most gardeners buy young plants, but browallias can be started from seeds indoors six to eight weeks before the last frost is due. When you can be sure the night temperature will not drop below 50°, transplant the seedlings into the garden, setting them 8 to 10 inches apart. They start to bloom about 12 weeks after the seeds are sown. Six to eight weeks before the first frost of autumn, dig up a few plants for indoor growing as house plants. Cut them back severely and put them in pots on a sunny window sill. They will flower freely all winter.

BUGLOSS See *Anchusa*
BURNING BUSH See *Kochia*
BUSH BALSAM See *Impatiens*
BUSH MORNING GLORY See *Convolvulus*
BUSY LIZZIE See *Impatiens*
BUTTER DAISY See *Verbesina*
BUTTERFLY FLOWER See *Schizanthus*

C
CABBAGE, ORNAMENTAL See *Brassica*
CACALIA See *Emilia*

CALANDRINIA
C. grandiflora (rock purslane). *C. menziesii,* also called *C. speciosa* (rock purslane, red maids). *C. umbellata* (rock purslane).

Rock purslanes are colorful plants in sunshine but, like their relative *Portulaca,* close their blossoms in cloudy weather and darkness. *C. grandiflora,* from Chile, grows 18 to 24 inches tall and has cuplike rose-colored blossoms about 2 inches across, red stems and long, thin, pointed leaves. *C. menziesii,* a California wild flower called red maids, grows 3 to 12 inches tall and bears its smaller deep purple-crimson blossoms on short stems growing off a main stem. The most popular species is *C. umbellata,* a native of Peru. It grows only 4 to 6 inches tall and has clusters of magenta flowers. Though a perennial that will live through winter in Zones 8-10, it is usually treated as an annual; it will flower about 15 weeks after seed is sown.

USES. Rock purslanes thrive in dry to average soil in the hottest of gardens so long as they have sun. *C. umbellata,* which is the smallest of the rock purslanes and tends to trail, is excellent for rock gardens and window boxes and is sometimes used in edgings.

HOW TO GROW. Sow the tiny seeds indoors four to six weeks before the last frost is due. When all danger of frost has passed, set out the plants 6 inches apart in the garden.

ROCK PURSLANE
Calandrinia umbellata

Seeds can also be sown directly into the garden very early in the spring, as soon as the earth can be spaded and raked.

CALENDULA

C. officinalis (calendula, pot marigold).

Few annuals are easier to grow or produce more abundant blossoms than these colorful natives of the Mediterranean region. Their 2- to 4-inch flowers come in both daisylike and chrysanthemumlike varieties, and range in shade from white through cream and lemon, to bright yellow, apricot and orange. The plants rarely grow more than 18 inches tall.

USES. Calendulas make bright flower-bed plantings and splendid cut flowers. They thrive in full sun, fertile soil and cool growing weather. They also will produce satisfactory flowers, though on shorter stems, under any growing conditions except deep shade and extreme heat.

HOW TO GROW. Plant seeds outdoors, 1¼ inches deep, as soon as the ground can be spaded and raked in the spring. Space them so plants will stand 12 to 15 inches apart (calendulas are easy to transplant). A second sowing in early summer gives a luxuriant autumn crop of flowers in areas where night temperatures in summer generally drop below 65°. In Zones 8-10, the second sowing should be delayed until late summer or early fall; it will provide color throughout the winter and spring.

CALIFORNIA BLUE BELLS See *Phacelia*
CALIFORNIA POPPY See *Eschscholzia*
CALLIOPSIS See *Coreopsis*

CALLISTEPHUS

C. chinensis (annual aster, China aster).

Of all the lovely flowers to come out of the Orient, China asters are among the most widely known and cherished, although they are not among the easiest to grow. The flowers, 1½ to 5 inches across, can take a wide variety of forms—some like daisies, some like chrysanthemums, some like tight little pompons, some just shaggy. Their colors are white, creamy yellow, pink, red, blue, lavender or purple, often with yellow centers. Varieties range in height from 8 inches to 3 feet.

USES. China asters are among the most popular of plants for flower beds, often providing spectacular effects. Their long, wiry stems make them graceful in flower arrangements. They flourish in rich, well-drained soil in a sunny or lightly shaded location. If the soil is acid, it may be necessary to add lime.

HOW TO GROW. Sow indoors, barely covering the fine seeds, five to six weeks before the last frost is expected. When the first true leaves appear, transplant the seedlings to 3-inch pots and place them in a cold frame to adjust to outdoor conditions. Set them into the garden, 12 inches apart, when all danger of frost is past. China asters have very shallow roots, so cover the soil with a 1-inch mulch of grass clippings or peat moss to maintain moisture and keep the soil cool. They may also be grown from seed sown directly in the garden when all danger of frost has passed. Asters come in early, midseason and late-flowering varieties, so you can enjoy them through summer and fall. Plant them at two-week intervals because the blooming season of any one plant is relatively short—only about four weeks. And unlike most annuals, China asters tend to stop blooming when they are cut. Do not plant China asters for two successive years in the same location because they are vulnerable to fungus diseases that tend to build up in the soil. Look for stunted yellow foliage on stems that fail to blossom; it may be "yellows," a virus disease that is spread

CALENDULA
Calendula officinalis

CHINA ASTER
Callistephus chinensis

For climate zones and frost dates, see maps, pages 164-165.

MOONFLOWER
Calonyction aculeatum

CANTERBURY BELLS
TOP: *Campanula medium*
BOTTOM: *C. medium calycanthema*

by leaf hoppers. To reduce the incidence of this disease, use only wilt-resistant varieties of China asters and spray them weekly with malathion in wettable powder form.

CALONYCTION
C. aculeatum, also called *Ipomoea bona-nox, I. noctiflora, I. mexicana grandiflora* (moonflower).

Moonflowers are twining climbers with large heart-shaped leaves and white trumpetlike blossoms, as large as 6 inches across, that open at sunset; the flowers usually close before noon the next day but remain open longer in cloudy weather. The genus name *Calonyction* means "beautiful night," and moonflowers add to their visual beauty with a heavy fragrance on summer evenings. Though they are perennials in their native tropics and in Florida, they are grown as annuals in Zones 3-8.

USES. Because they climb rapidly—10 feet or more in a single season—moonflowers make excellent screens. They will grow in average garden soil in full sun.

HOW TO GROW. Moonflowers are difficult to transplant and need to be started in individual 3-inch peat pots eight weeks before the last frost is due. To speed germination, soak the seeds in water overnight before sowing them. When night temperatures will not drop below 50°, plant the seedlings outdoors, pots and all, 9 to 12 inches apart, with an 8- to 10-foot trellis or string for them to climb on.

CAMPANULA
C. medium (Canterbury bells, bellflower).

Biennial forms of Canterbury bells, natives of southern Europe, have been garden favorites for generations; but they often have failed to survive the cold winters of Zones 3-5, even with special protection. The annual Canterbury bells grow in noteworthy 2½-foot-tall pyramids, which are covered in late summer with spikes of large bell-shaped pink, rose, lavender, blue or white blossoms, each 2 inches or more long. A "cup-and-saucer" variety, *C. medium calycanthema*, bears flowers with double bells, one inside the other. Although this variety is a biennial, it will blossom the first year if started indoors.

USES. Canterbury bells are handsome plants for use in a flower border and make unusual, long-lasting cut flowers. They require sun and rich, moist soil.

HOW TO GROW. Sow seeds in the garden as soon as the soil can be spaded and raked in the spring, or start them indoors six to eight weeks before the last frost for earlier flowering. Transplant seedlings started indoors into 3-inch pots when they are large enough to handle, then move them into a cold frame two weeks before the last frost is due to enable them to become acclimated to outdoor conditions gradually. Set them in the garden, 12 inches apart, when all frost danger has passed. Annual Canterbury bells require about six months to grow from seeds to flowers.

CANARY-BIRD FLOWER See *Tropaeolum*
CANDYTUFT See *Iberis*
CANTERBURY BELLS See *Campanula*
CAPE FORGET-ME-NOT See *Anchusa*
CAPE MARIGOLD See *Dimorphotheca*
CARDINAL CLIMBER See *Quamoclit*

CARDIOSPERMUM
C. halicacabum (balloon vine, heartseed, love-in-a-puff).

If ever a plant derived its names from its appearance, it is the balloon vine, native to the tropics. Its round black seeds form in balloon-shaped seed pods about an inch in diameter, and on each seed is a heart-shaped white spot —which led herbalists of the Middle Ages to believe that the plant would help to relieve heart ailments. The four-petaled flowers of the balloon vine are small and white. The vines climb by tendrils to a height of 10 feet or more in a summer. The vine is a perennial in Zones 9-10.

USES. The balloon vine provides a quick-growing decorative screen when planted beside a fence, trellis or wall. It thrives in sun and average soil.

HOW TO GROW. Sow seeds indoors in individual 3-inch pots six weeks before the last frost is due; transplant the seedlings to the garden when all frost danger has passed. Seeds may also be sown directly in the garden in the spring when leaves begin to unfold on trees. Space plants 12 inches apart and provide them with an 8- to 10-foot trellis, string or other support on which the vines can climb.

CARNATION, ANNUAL See *Dianthus*
CASTOR BEAN See *Ricinus*
CASTOR OIL PLANT See *Ricinus*

CATANANCHE

C. caerulea (Cupid's dart, blue cupidone, blue succory).

Cupid's dart, a perennial in its native southern Europe, is included here because it blossoms the first year from seed. Its blue flowers, which are generally about 2 inches across and resemble stiff double daisies with fringed petals, bloom atop stems about 2 feet high. A blue-and-white form (*C. caerulea bicolor*) and a pure white one (*C. caerulea alba*) are also available.

USES. The flowers of Cupid's dart make a colorful addition to a garden border, but their greatest asset is the fact that they can be dried for winter flower arrangements without losing their shape or color. To dry them, cut them at their peak and hang them upside down in a cool place. Cupid's dart thrives in a dry, well-drained, sunny location.

HOW TO GROW. Sow seeds indoors six to eight weeks before the last frost is due, or outdoors when the ground can be cultivated. Space plants 9 inches apart.

CATCHFLY See *Silene*
CATHARANTHUS ROSEUS See *Vinca*
CATHEDRAL BELLS See *Cobaea*

CELOSIA

C. argentea (cockscomb, woolflower).

Cockscomb, native to the Asian tropics, is notable for its striking flower heads that range from 2 to 10 inches in width. One variety, *C. argentea cristata,* does indeed have tops that look vaguely like the rose combs of roosters, while the blossoms of another variety, *C. argentea plumosa* (sometimes called feather or plume cockscomb), spray out like varicolored ostrich plumes. All varieties come in brilliant shades of yellow, orange, red and purple, and grow from 8 inches to 3 feet high. The flower heads are extremely long lasting; one flower head may decorate a plant for eight weeks or more before fading.

USES. Cockscombs make colorful and interesting cut flowers, and are especially suited for use in dried arrangements. To dry, cut the flowers when they are at their peak and hang them upside down in an airy, shady place. The flowers are so brilliantly colored, however, that they must be used discreetly in most gardens. They require sun and thrive when the weather is hot. They will grow in any garden soil and tolerate dry conditions.

HOW TO GROW. Start seeds indoors a month before the last frost is due. Transplant seedlings into the garden when all frost danger has passed. Or sow seeds directly outdoors in the spring when the soil can be easily spaded and raked. Space plants 9 to 12 inches apart.

BALLOON VINE
Cardiospermum halicacabum

CUPID'S DART
Catananche caerulea

LEFT: FEATHER COCKSCOMB
Celosia argentea plumosa

RIGHT: COCKSCOMB
C. argentea cristata

For climate zones and frost dates, see maps, pages 164-165.

PINCUSHION FLOWER
Cenia barbata

CORNFLOWER
Centaurea cyanus

CENIA

C. barbata, usually sold as *Cotula barbata* (pincushion flower).

The tiny golden flowers of this South African plant look like daisies at the end of a she-loves-me-she-loves-me-not game, when only the centers remain. The little round blossoms, about ⅓ inch across, are borne atop slender branched 3- to 6-inch stalks that rise out of clumps of silky, hairy, light green leaves. The whole effect accounts for the common name of pincushion.

USES. This appealing little annual is well suited for use as an edging plant. It grows in any ordinary soil in dry, sunny places.

HOW TO GROW. Sow seed outdoors as soon as you can be sure night temperatures will not drop below 50°. Plants should stand 4 inches apart.

CENTAUREA

C. cyanus (cornflower, bachelor's button, bluebottle, ragged sailor, French pink). *C. americana* (basket flower). *C. cineraria,* also known as *C. rutifolia* and *C. candidissima* (dusty miller). *C. gymnocarpa* (dusty miller, velvet centaurea). *C. moschata,* also known as *C. imperialis, C. odorata, C. suaveolens* and *C. amberboi* (sweet sultan).

Within this large genus of plants is one of the world's most widely grown annuals—the cornflower. Its cheerful, ragged blossoms, about 2 inches across, are at home in temperate-zone gardens around the world. Besides the old favorite blue cornflower, there are newer varieties in pink, red, maroon, lavender and white. They bloom so prolifically with so little care that they often are the first plants that children grow on their own. Cornflower blossoms are borne on plants from 1 to 3 feet tall, contrasting with the gray-green foliage. The name "cornflower" comes from the fact that the plant grows wild in the grainfields of southern Europe. Two close cousins of the cornflower are the basket flower and sweet sultan. The basket flower gets its name from the fact that the flower buds appear to be encased in little baskets; the opened blossoms look like cornflowers but are much larger—4 to 5 inches across, on plants that become 5 or 6 feet tall. Basket flower blossoms may be pink, white or lavender. Sweet sultan, from the Near East, bears fuzzy 3- to 4-inch blossoms, delicately scented, in shades of yellow, pink or lavender as well as white; it grows 1½ to 3 feet tall. Two other species of *Centaurea, C. rutifolia* and *C. gymnocarpa,* are valued primarily for their unusual foliage. Both called dusty miller, they bear white, fernlike leaves and grow about a foot tall.

USES. The flowering kinds of *Centaurea* are effective when massed for color in beds and borders, in foregrounds or backgrounds, depending on the height specified on the seed packet. The unusual foliage of dusty millers makes them striking edging plants. The plants will prosper in any well-drained soil but need a sunny location. Dusty millers also do well in window boxes since they require a relatively dry soil. In the frost-free areas of Zones 9-10, dusty millers are treated as perennials and are favored as a ground cover for hot, dry sites.

HOW TO GROW. Sow cornflower seeds outdoors any time in the fall, so they will start to grow before the first frost is expected; fall seeding in any zone will produce plants that will start to bloom early in the spring. Or sow seeds in the garden in the spring as soon as the soil can be spaded and raked. Seeds may also be sown indoors about a month before the last frost is expected; transplant the seedlings into the garden when the ground can be spaded and raked. Plants should stand about 12 inches apart. Sow sweet sultan and basket flowers outdoors as soon as the soil can be cultivated, spacing them so plants will stand 6 to 10 inches apart. Dusty millers are slow growing but can be started indoors six to eight weeks before the last expected frost and moved outdoors, 8 to 9 inches apart, when all danger of frost is past.

CERINTHE
C. aspera (honeywort).

An annual, honeywort is a wild flower native to southern Europe. At the ends of 1- to 2-foot stems are pendant clusters of yellow tubular flowers with chocolate-colored bases, each about 1¼ inches long. Honeyworts are believed to get their name from the fact that they are often visited by bees, which obtain honey from the flowers. The stems are clothed in smooth gray-green clasping leaves.

USES. This plant is unusual enough in form and color to stand out in a garden but the flowers do not last long after cutting. Honeyworts blossom for about six weeks in midsummer and are at their best when grown in full sun. Almost any soil will suit them and they are able to withstand windy places and driving rain.

HOW TO GROW. Sow seeds outdoors as soon as the ground can be spaded and raked. Or start them indoors about two months before the last spring frost is expected and move them into the garden when danger of frost is past. Plants should stand 6 inches apart.

CHARIEIS
C. heterophylla (charieis).

This dainty daisylike annual from South Africa has bright blue flowers about 1 inch across borne profusely on sprawling plants only 6 to 12 inches high. American seedsmen do not list this plant but English seed catalogues still offer it under its old name, *Kaulfussia amelloides,* although the name has been known to be incorrect for generations.

USES. Charieis is well suited for rock gardens or for edging. A sunny site and light, sandy loam are desirable. Because of their short, sturdy stature, the plants stand up well to wind and rain. The flowers of charieis are delicately fragrant and long lasting when cut but they stay open only during daylight hours.

HOW TO GROW. Seeds may be sown indoors four to six weeks before the last frost is due or they may be sown outdoors in the spring when the soil can be spaded and raked. Space plants 6 inches apart. In the frost-free areas of Zones 9-10, seeds may also be sown outdoors in early fall for bloom in late winter and early spring.

CHEIRANTHUS
C. cheiri (English wallflower). C. allionii, more correctly Erysimum asperum (Siberian wallflower).

Springtime gardens in England would be incomplete without their masses of fragrant wallflowers, of European origin, bearing spikes of inch-wide blossoms in shades of yellow, orange, red, purple or brown. There are dwarf varieties 6 to 9 inches tall and others that grow as high as 18 inches. Wallflowers are usually grown as biennials but early strains will flower in about five months from seeds; look for seeds marked "early flowering" or "annual variety."

USES. Dwarf varieties are attractive when planted in rock gardens or in the chinks of stone walls and they will thrive in such well-drained sites. Taller annual varieties may be massed for late-summer color in a flower bed. Wallflowers will grow in full sunshine or light shade and do best in coastal and mountainous areas where the·summer weather is cool (night temperatures below 65°) and damp. They require a neutral soil, so lime may have to be added if there is excessive acidity.

HONEYWORT
Cerinthe aspera

CHARIEIS
Charieis heterophylla

LEFT: ENGLISH WALLFLOWER
Cheiranthus cheiri

RIGHT: SIBERIAN WALLFLOWER
C. allionii (Erysimum asperum)

For climate zones and frost dates, see maps, pages 164-165.

ANNUAL CHRYSANTHEMUM
CLOCKWISE FROM TOP:
*Chrysanthemum carinatum, C. segetum, C. parthenium,
C. coronarium*

PLUMED THISTLE
Cirsium japonicum

HOW TO GROW. To grow wallflowers as annuals, sow seeds indoors six to eight weeks before the last frost is due. When transplanting seedlings to individual pots, pinch off the bottom tip of the main root—the taproot—of each seedling to encourage development of a bushy root system. When frost danger is past, put the seedlings in a cold frame for a week or two to acclimate them gradually to outdoor conditions before planting them, 6 to 12 inches apart, in the garden. Seeds may also be sown outdoors in midspring, but the plants will produce only foliage the first year and blossom early the following spring.

CHERRY PIE See *Heliotropium*
CHINA ASTER See *Callistephus*
CHINA PINK See *Dianthus*
CHINESE FORGET-ME-NOT See *Cynoglossum*
CHINESE HOUSES See *Collinsia*

CHRYSANTHEMUM

Hybrids of *C. carinatum, C. coronarium* and *C. segetum* (all called annual chrysanthemums). *C. parthenium,* also known as *Matricaria capensis* and *Pyrethrum parthenium* (feverfew).

Annual chrysanthemums, native to southern Europe and Morocco, differ in appearance from the huge perennial varieties in evidence during the football season. Their leaves are generally smaller and more succulent, and their flower heads, about 2 to 3 inches across and single or semidouble, look like those of daisies. Colors include yellow, purple, scarlet, orange, salmon and white, usually with a ring of contrasting color near the center of each flower. Most varieties grow about 2 feet tall. One perennial chrysanthemum, feverfew, blooms the first year from seed and is not reliably hardy in areas of severe frost, so it is often grown as an annual. There are two types of feverfews, one that grows about 2 feet tall and bears double white flowers, and another that grows only 6 to 9 inches tall and has double white or yellow flowers. Some hardy perennial chrysanthemums, described as "early flowering," will also bloom the first year if started from seed sown indoors six to eight weeks before the last frost is due.

USES. Annual chrysanthemums grow rapidly from seed and provide masses of color in flower beds if planted in rich soil and full sun. They provide fine cut flowers that are long lasting in the manner of all chrysanthemums. The taller feverfews are excellent for bouquets; the smaller type is used as an edging plant. They will grow in full sun or light shade.

HOW TO GROW. Annual chrysanthemums are among the easiest plants to grow. As soon as the earth can be cultivated in the spring, scatter seeds thinly over prepared soil in the garden and rake them in lightly. Thin or transplant seedlings so plants stand about 18 inches apart; annual chrysanthemums transplant easily at any time. Feverfews can also be sown outdoors as soon as the soil can be cultivated in the spring, or started indoors six to eight weeks before the last expected frost for even earlier flowering.

CIGAR PLANT See *Cuphea*
CINERARIA See *Senecio*

CIRSIUM

C. japonicum (plumed thistle).

Thistles are usually thought of as pestiferous weeds with fluffy-headed lavender flowers, but a strain of *C. japonicum* with deep rose-red flowers, 1 to 2 inches across, makes a fine addition to any garden. The rather coarse plant grows about 2½ feet tall and has dark green, deeply lobed, spiny leaves. The plumed thistle is a biennial but like an annual will flower the first year from seed.

USES. These plants are useful as background planting toward the rear of a flower border. Full sun or light shade suits them and they do best in light, well-drained soil. Seed catalogues note that seeds of the plumed thistle cannot be mailed to California, presumably because the plant scatters its seed so freely that it might become a weed.

HOW TO GROW. Sow seeds outdoors any time in the fall to have flowers late the following spring, or sow outdoors any time in the spring to have flowers in late summer. Plants should be spaced 2 feet apart.

CLADANTHUS

C. arabicus (cladanthus), also known as *C. proliferus* and *Anthemis arabica.*

The yellow daisylike cladanthus, a wild flower in Spain and Morocco, is unfamiliar to many American gardeners. When it first blooms, the end of each stem carries a solitary golden-yellow flower, approximately 2 inches across. But about the time this flower opens, a number of other stems, each with a flower bud, form just beneath it. Eventually the entire plant is covered with blooms. The lacy foliage has a strong but not unpleasant aroma. Plants may become 2 to 3 feet high and equally broad.

USES. Cladanthus provides an abundance of bright and cheerful flowers in an annual border. It needs a sunny, well-drained location and grows well in most soils.

HOW TO GROW. Sow seeds thinly outdoors as soon as the ground can be spaded and raked in the spring. Seeds germinate in about a month and the plants begin to bloom 12 to 14 weeks later. The plants should stand 12 inches apart.

CLARKIA

C. elegans and *C. pulchella* (both called clarkia, Rocky Mountain garland).

Clarkias are among the most beautiful of western wild flowers and deserve a place in any garden that can meet their rather special needs. Mostly of western U.S. origin, they were named for Captain William Clark of the Lewis and Clark expedition. Their delicate blossoms, each about an inch across, are borne all along the 2- to 3-foot stems. Seed catalogues offer only double-flowered varieties, available in shades of salmon, pink, mauve, rose, carmine, purple, red or white, but occasionally single-flowered varieties, like the wild flower, appear among the seedlings. Some plants classified and sold as *Godetia* are now classified by some botanists as *Clarkia* (see *Godetia*).

USES. Clarkias thrive in the cool summers and dry, sandy loam found in mountainous areas of the West. They grow well in full sun or partial shade, and bloom most profusely where the soil is rather low in nitrogen. They make longlasting, decorative cut flowers.

HOW TO GROW. Sow seeds outdoors early in the spring as soon as the ground can be spaded and raked. Space plants 9 inches apart. Do not start seeds indoors; they do better in the cooler outdoors. In Zones 8-10, sow seeds outdoors any time in the fall for blossoms the following spring.

CLARY See *Salvia*

CLEOME

C. hasslerana, also known as *C. spinosa* (cleome, spider flower). *C. lutea* (yellow cleome, yellow spider flower)

Cleomes grow swiftly to a dramatic height of 3 to 5 feet and produce big, airy flower clusters, 6 to 8 inches across. *C. spinosa,* a native of tropical America, comes in pink, lavender or white; *C. lutea,* a wild flower in the western

CLADANTHUS
Cladanthus arabicus

CLARKIA
LEFT: *Clarkia elegans*
RIGHT: *C. pulchella*

CLEOME
Cleome hasslerana

part of the U.S., bears bright golden-yellow flowers. Each blossom is graced with a delicate tracery of long stamens. As blossoms fade, decorative seed pods sprout from the flower heads like spider legs. Cleomes are best admired at a little distance; some gardeners find their strongly scented blossoms too pungent to enjoy.

USES. Cleomes are effective as a background planting, especially beside a wall or along a fence. They are also useful in terrace pots. They grow in almost any soil and prefer a rather hot, dry location but will tolerate some shade.

HOW TO GROW. Sow seeds outdoors when all frost danger has passed, or start them indoors four to six weeks before the last frost is due. Or purchase seedlings and set them outdoors when you can be sure night temperatures will not drop below 50°. Plants should stand 2 feet apart.

CLOCK VINE See *Thunbergia*
CLOUDGRASS see *Agrostis*

COBAEA

C. scandens (cup-and-saucer vine, cathedral bells).

The cup-and-saucer vine, a vigorous climber from Mexico, is well named. The showy cups of blossoms, about 2 inches long and 1½ inches across, look as though they were sitting in large green saucers of foliage. Colors of the cups range from white through greenish purple to violet. The vine, clinging by tendrils, grows rapidly in hot weather, often reaching a height of 15 to 25 feet in one summer. In frost-free areas of Zones 9-10, the vine becomes woody —it does not die to the ground—and grows for years.

USES. To cover a wall, trellis or fence in a hurry, the cup-and-saucer vine is ideal, though temporary. It requires a light, rich soil and full sun.

HOW TO GROW. Plant the large, flat seeds on edge, two to a 3-inch pot, indoors six to eight weeks before the last frost. Barely cover the top edges of the seeds. Germination may take three weeks; when both seeds in the pot sprout, remove the weaker seedling. Set the young plants outdoors when all danger of frost has passed, placing them 18 to 24 inches apart. Provide a trellis, wall or string for the vine to climb on. In frost-free areas of Zones 9-10, cup-and-saucer vines may be planted directly outdoors in early spring. Set the seeds on edge in the ground.

COCKSCOMB See *Celosia*

COIX

C. lacryma-jobi (Job's tears).

The broad-leaved ornamental grass known as Job's tears is grown for the decorative effects of its hard-shelled seeds, which come in white, pearl gray, brown or black, and are about the size of cherry pits. They are borne in clusters on 2- to 6-foot stems in late summer. The plant is native to the East Indies, and in parts of Asia a soft-shelled variety, *C. lacryma-jobi mayuen*, is cultivated as a cereal grain.

USES. Stems with seeds in place make interesting additions to dried winter arrangements. Dry the stems in a cool, airy place, upright in a vase if curved stems are desired, hung upside down if straight stems are wanted. Cut the stems before the seeds become dry enough to fall off. Individual seeds are often used to make necklaces and bead curtains.

HOW TO GROW. Before planting the seeds, soak them in water for a day to soften the seed coat and stimulate faster germination. Plant them in dry to average soil in a sunny spot after all frost danger has passed, or start them indoors in early spring, four to five weeks before the last frost is due. Plants should stand 12 inches apart.

CUP-AND-SAUCER VINE
Cobaea scandens

JOB'S TEARS
Coix lacryma-jobi

COLEUS
Coleus blumei

COLEUS

C. blumei (coleus).

Coleus, tender perennial herbs from the islands of the South Pacific, grow so rapidly from seeds to decorative plants that they can also be used effectively in the annual garden. They range in height from 6 inches to 2 feet and are admired for their bizarre foliage, which may be chartreuse, yellow, pink, white, red or green, often with multihued leaf patterns.

USES. Coleus are spectacular plants for beds, borders or window boxes. They thrive in sun or partial shade and have no special soil requirements.

HOW TO GROW. Sow seeds indoors in early spring, 10 weeks before the last expected frost; seeds sprout in about 10 days and, though the seeds are tiny, the plants grow rapidly. As the plants grow, pinch off the tips of the branches to create a compact mound of foliage. Seedlings may also be bought at a garden center. Set the plants in the garden after all frost danger has passed, spacing them 8 to 10 inches apart. Young coleus seedlings show little leaf color other than green, but brilliance develops as they grow. The slower-growing seedlings usually produce the most intense colors. Plants that have especially attractive coloring may be multiplied by stem cuttings *(page 85)*, which can be carried through the winter as house plants and from which still more cuttings can be started.

COLLINSIA

C. heterophylla, also known as *C. bicolor* (collinsia, Chinese houses, pagoda collinsia, innocence).

Most collinsias are wild flowers in California, where they are found in shady areas on mountain slopes. As garden flowers they seem to be more valued abroad than in·the U.S. Collinsia blossoms, borne in many-flowered spikes, are about an inch across, composed of two deeply cleft lips, the upper one white and the lower pink or lavender. Whorls of dark green pointed leaves are spaced along the flower stalks. Plants grow 1 to 2 feet tall.

USES. Collinsias make lovely, free-flowering border plants. They will thrive in light shade and in nearly any soil, so long as night temperatures in summer generally fall below 65°; they do not tolerate heat well. They do tolerate dryness and are often used in rock gardens. As cut flowers they are long lasting.

HOW TO GROW. Sow seeds outdoors any time in the fall, or as early in the spring as the seedbed can be spaded and raked; space so the plants will stand 12 inches apart.

CONSOLIDA

Hybrids of *C. ambigua* (widely known as *Delphinium ajacis*), *C. regalis regalis* (*D. consolida paniculata*) and *C. orientalis* (annual delphinium, larkspur).

Since larkspurs are so different in appearance from perennial delphiniums, botanists have decided that they constitute a genus of their own, *Consolida*. But the older name *Delphinium* will no doubt continue to be applied to these plants in seed catalogues for some time to come. By either name, larkspurs, which are natives of southern Europe, will continue to be cherished for their tall, beautiful spikes of feathery, petaled flowers, in shades of blue, salmon, rose, lilac, purple or white, set amid lacy bright-green foliage. Two strains are available: the branching type, which produces a number of flower stalks on each plant, and the hyacinth-flowered type, which has only one massive stem per plant. Each type grows 3 to 5 feet tall. In addition, among the hyacinth-flowered varieties, there is a dwarf strain that grows only about 12 inches tall but bears large and lovely flowers. There are also a number of true pe-

COLLINSIA
Collinsia heterophylla

LARKSPUR
Consolida ambigua

For climate zones and frost dates, see maps, pages 164-165.

DWARF MORNING GLORY
Convolvulus tricolor

COREOPSIS
TOP: *Coreopsis drummondii*
BOTTOM: *C. tinctoria*

rennial delphiniums, all hybrids but often sold under the names *D. elatum, D. belladonna* and *D. bellamosum,* that blossom the first year from seeds sown early in the spring. One of the most famous strains consists of the Pacific hybrids; in Zones 9-10 these are planted early in the fall.

USES. The tall, stately, heavily flowered spikes of larkspur provide a mass of color as a background planting along a wall or fence. Used in flower arrangements, the spikes are long lasting and exceptionally graceful. Larkspurs need fertile, well-drained soil. They are tolerant of light shade, especially in areas that have hot summers.

HOW TO GROW. Larkspurs are hardy annuals; their seeds may be sown outdoors in the fall as well as early spring. In Zones 7-10, sow larkspur seed in the fall early enough to allow the plants to begin growth before cold weather arrives. North of Zone 7, delay seeding until just before the first frost is expected so that the seeds will not germinate until very early in the spring. Even with the delayed seeding, the plants will blossom from midspring until early summer. A sowing made as early as the ground can be spaded and raked in the spring, followed by another three weeks later, will provide flowers through midsummer and early fall. Since larkspurs are not easy to transplant, sow the seeds where the plants are to remain. Fall or early sown seeds will become twice as tall as late-sown seeds. Space plants 8 to 15 inches apart, depending on anticipated height —the taller the plants, the greater the distance between them should be. The tall varieties may require staking to keep them from bending under the weight of the blossoms.

CONVOLVULUS
C. tricolor (dwarf morning glory, bush morning glory).

Climbing morning glories (*see Ipomoea*) have always been popular, even though their blossoms close early each day. Dwarf morning glories, native of southern Europe, have flowers that stay wide open all day. These lovely plants do not climb; instead they make solid mounds of blue, lilac, red, pink or white flowers, usually about 1 foot tall and of greater spread. The name *tricolor* refers to the fact that each flower has a band of white between its yellow throat and the flaring blue, lilac, red, pink or white trumpet of the blossom, which is 2 inches across.

USES. Dwarf morning glories are among the best plants for edging or in window boxes and hanging baskets since they bloom constantly in dry, sunny locations. They will prosper in almost any kind of soil.

HOW TO GROW. Give the plants a head start by sowing seeds indoors in early spring, five to six weeks before the last frost is due. To speed germination, nick the hard seed coat with a file, then sow two seeds each in 3-inch pots and discard the weaker of the two seedlings when they sprout. Set the plants 12 inches apart in the garden. Seeds may also be sown directly outdoors when you can be sure night temperatures will not drop below 50°.

COREOPSIS
C. drummondii and *C. tinctoria,* also known as *C. elegans* and *C. marmorata.* Sometimes available: *C. douglasii,* also called *Leptosyne douglasii,* and *C. stillmanii,* also called *Leptosyne stillmanii.* (All known as coreopsis, calliopsis, tickseed.)

The annual forms of coreopsis are often known as calliopsis. By either name, the gay, 1½- to 2-inch, daisylike blossoms are bright with toothed petals, often in double layers. They come in shades of orange, maroon, crimson, gold and mahogany, with small, brownish yellow centers, and seem to dance on wire-thin stems at the slightest breeze. Some varieties grow less than 1 foot tall, others exceed 3 feet. Two species, *C. douglasii* and *C. stillmanii,* are not always available but are native to California. Their bright 1- to 1½-inch golden flowers blossom atop 12- to 18-inch stems.

USES. Coreopsis blossom profusely over a long flowering season, making a brilliant showing in borders. They are also grown for their value as long-lasting cut flowers. They need a sunny location but will do well in almost any soil.

HOW TO GROW. Coreopsis are among the easiest flowering plants to grow. Sow seeds very early in the spring, as soon as the seed bed can be cultivated. Sow where plants are to grow, since seedlings are difficult to transplant successfully. Space plants 6 to 8 inches apart. Stake the plants to help the thin stems hold the heavy flower heads erect.

CORN COCKLE See *Agrostemma*
CORNFLOWER See *Centaurea*
CORN POPPY See *Papaver*

COSMOS
C. bipinnatus (cosmos). *C. sulphureus* (yellow cosmos).

Few plants grow as rapidly as cosmos, and fewer still have such graceful flowers. These natives of Mexico become 4 to 6 feet tall, sometimes taller, and bear airy, daisylike blossoms 2 to 4 inches across. The wide, serrated petals circling yellow centers may be pink, red or white. The foliage is delicate and feathery. The species known as yellow cosmos, which seldom grows more than 3 feet tall, used to begin flowering so late in the season that fall frosts often nipped the first blossoms. But now there are early flowering yellow, orange and red varieties, including the double-flowered, golden-yellow Goldcrest, the superb orange-scarlet Sunset and the fiery red Diablo.

USES. Cosmos grow so tall that they are among the most valuable of plants to use at the back of garden beds and borders. In addition, they produce graceful and long-lasting cut flowers. They will grow in any soil in full sun, and will tolerate partial shade as well. They flower earlier and more freely if the soil is fairly dry and not especially fertile.

HOW TO GROW. Sow the seeds outdoors after all danger of frost is past. Or sow the seeds indoors five or six weeks before the expected time of the last frost. Plants should stand 12 inches apart in the garden. Seedlings transplant easily. The plants may require staking to remain upright if the site is windy.

COTULA See *Cenia*
CREEPING ZINNIA See *Sanvitalia*

CREPIS
C. rubra, also called *Barkhausia rubra* (hawk's beard).

The flowers of hawk's beard resemble pink dandelions in size (about 1 inch across) and shape (narrow, ragged petals radiating from the center). Flowers grow on slender stalks about 1 foot tall, from clumps of slender leaves at the base of the plant, which is native to Italy and Greece.

USES. Hawk's beard is effective as an edging and in rock gardens. It is not good for cutting since the blossoms close in the afternoon. It thrives in poor soil if given full sun.

HOW TO GROW. Sow seeds outdoors any time in the fall or as soon as the ground can be cultivated in early spring. Space plants 4 inches apart.

CROTALARIA
C. retusa (crotalaria, rattle box, golden-yellow sweet pea).

In midsummer, crotalarias bear showy 18- to 24-inch spikes of yellow-and-purple flowers, with each blossom shaped like the familiar little sunbonnet of sweet peas.

UPPER LEFT: COSMOS   LOWER RIGHT: YELLOW COSMOS
Cosmos bipinnatus   *C. sulphureus*

HAWK'S BEARD
Crepis rubra

CROTALARIA
Crotalaria retusa

For climate zones and frost dates, see maps, pages 164-165.

CIGAR PLANT
Cuphea miniata

CHINESE FORGET-ME-NOT
Cynoglossum amabile

Hence the popular name, golden-yellow sweet pea, although crotalaria is only remotely related to the true sweet pea (see *Lathyrus*) and has little fragrance. The flowers are striking; often a dozen blossoms will open on a spike at a time. Plump seed pods with loose seeds inside suggest the other common name of this native of Asia, rattle box.

USES. Crotalarias are effective plants in borders and make lovely cut flowers. They need rich soil and full sun and are unsatisfactory where summers are cool and damp.

HOW TO GROW. Crotalarias require a long growing season. In Zones 3-7, sow seeds indoors six to eight weeks before the last frost is due. The seeds have hard coats; soak them in tepid water for 24 hours before planting to speed germination. When the night temperature will not fall below 50°, set plants out in the garden 12 inches apart. In Zones 8-10, seeds may be sown directly in the garden any time in the winter or early spring for summer flowering.

CUCUMBER, MOCK See *Echinocystis*
CUCUMBER, WILD See *Echinocystis*
CUCUMBERLEAF See *Helianthus*
CUCUMIS See *Gourds*
CUCURBITA See *Gourds*
CUP-AND-SAUCER VINE See *Cobaea*
CUPFLOWER See *Nierembergia*

CUPHEA
C. ignea, also called *C. platycentra. C. miniata*. (Both known as cigar plant.)

Cigar plants, natives of Mexico, are common as everblooming house plants, but they are also useful outdoor plants. The most familiar variety has fiery-red tubular flowers, about ¾ inch long, each with a black-and-white tip resembling a cigar ash. The flowers are borne abundantly on compact plants that rarely exceed 1 foot in height. Other varieties come in shades of lavender, lilac, pink or rosy purple. A variety of *C. miniata* called Firefly grows about 20 inches tall and has glowing cerise flowers. Cigar plants may be grown as perennials in frost-free areas of Zones 9-10.

USES. Cigar plants make colorful edgings for garden walks and borders, and are an unusual and striking choice for window boxes and hanging baskets. They are also useful in a rock garden, since they will grow in average soil, in either sun or light shade. Cuttings rooted in the fall make fine house plants for winter flowering *(page 85)*.

HOW TO GROW. Cigar plants do not begin to flower until four or five months after seeds are sown, so start seeds indoors soon after Christmas. Move the plants into a cold frame two to three weeks before the last expected frost to acclimate them to outdoor conditions. When frost danger has passed, set the plants 9 inches apart in the garden.

CUPIDONE, BLUE See *Catananche*
CUPID'S DART See *Catananche*
CUTHBERTSON See *Lathyrus*

CYNOGLOSSUM
C. amabile (Chinese forget-me-not, hound's tongue).

Chinese forget-me-nots can be used to give garden borders lovely brushstrokes of blue. The small blossoms, ¼ inch across, resemble those of true forget-me-nots (see *Myosotis*) and are borne along graceful, branching sprays 1½ to 2 feet tall. There are also less common varieties in white and pink, as well as biennials that blossom the first year from seed. The name "hound's tongue" refers to the leaves of this East Asian native, which are soft textured and shaped like a dog's tongue. The seeds of all varieties are stick-tights that adhere to clothing and animals.

USES. The long spraylike branches of Chinese forget-me-nots make them useful in the middle of an annual bed or border when blue color is desired. They are attractive but not long lasting as cut flowers. They thrive in almost any soil, in full sun or partial shade, and tolerate both wet and dry locations. They tend to scatter their seed and care must be taken that they do not become a nuisance.

HOW TO GROW. Sow seeds outdoors as soon as the ground can be cultivated. Space plants 12 inches apart. They will germinate in about two weeks and begin blooming in late spring. Since they flower so quickly, there is little advantage in starting seeds indoors.

CYPRESS, SUMMER See *Kochia*
CYPRESS VINE See *Quamoclit*

D

DAHLBERG DAISY See *Thymophylla*

DAHLIA
Several hybrids grouped under the name *Dahlia*.

Named for the Swedish botanist Dr. Andreas Dahl, dahlias cultivated as annuals range from 1 to 2 feet in height, although some wild species grow as tall as 20 feet. They are tender perennials from Mexico, but early flowering dwarf types are grown from seed each year and treated as annuals. They blossom prodigiously, producing brilliant 2- to 3-inch flowers in every color except blue.

USES. Massed in a flower bed, dwarf dahlias add striking color to any garden. They are long lasting as cut flowers. They require fertile, well-drained soil and full sun at least half of each day.

HOW TO GROW. Sow seeds indoors six to eight weeks before the last frost is due, then set seedlings outdoors about 15 inches apart when danger of frost is past. Started dwarf dahlia plants are also available at garden centers. Water the plants often enough during dry weather to keep the ground slightly moist. Dwarf dahlias are short and sturdy and do not require the staking needed by taller types.

DAISY, AFRICAN See *Arctotis* and *Dimorphotheca*
DAISY, CROWN See *Chrysanthemum*
DAISY, ENGLISH See *Bellis*
DAISY, GLORIOSA See *Rudbeckia*
DAISY, KINGFISHER See *Felicia*
DAISY, LIVINGSTON See *Mesembryanthemum*
DAISY, PAINTED See *Chrysanthemum*
DAISY, SUNSHINE See *Gamolepis*
DAISY, SWAN RIVER See *Brachycome*
DAISY, TAHOKA See *Aster*
DAISY, TRUE See *Bellis*

DATURA
D. metel (trumpet flower, angel's trumpet).

Native to the tropics, the trumpet flower grows 3 to 5 feet tall. Its spectacular lilylike blossoms, about 10 inches long and 4 inches across the face, come in white, yellow, purple, red or pink. The flowers may be single or double.

USES. The flowers and seeds of trumpet flowers contain a poisonous alkaloid called hyoscyamine. Children must be cautioned not to eat them. The plant will prosper in a hot, sunny location in soil that is rich and rather dry. In the frost-free climates of Zones 9-10, trumpet flowers may be grown throughout the year in terrace pots as well as in the garden.

HOW TO GROW. Start seeds indoors two or three months before the last frost is due. Set the plants in the garden 18 inches apart when all danger of frost has passed.

DAHLIA
Dahlia hybrid

TRUMPET FLOWER
Datura metel

For climate zones and frost dates, see maps, pages 164-165.

UPPER LEFT: CHINA PINK
Dianthus chinensis

RIGHT CENTER: ANNUAL CARNATION
D. caryophyllus

BOTTOM: ANNUAL SWEET WILLIAM
D. barbatus

TWINSPUR
Diascia barberae

DELPHINIUM See *Consolida*
DEVIL-IN-A-BUSH See *Nigella*
DEVIL'S CLAW See *Proboscidea*

DIANTHUS

D. chinensis (China pink). *D. caryophyllus* (annual carnation). *D. barbatus* (annual sweet William).

Botanists agree that there are many species of *Dianthus* (about 300), but they disagree as to their exact number because of the ease with which various species hybridize. Even such categories as "annual" or "perennial" fail to apply firmly to *Dianthus*, since types that blossom readily the first season may continue to thrive for several years in well-drained soil. Three species have a place in the annual garden. China pinks, which are native to East Asia, grow 6 to 12 inches in height and produce an enormous quantity of 1- to 2-inch single, semidouble or frilled flowers on erect stems. They come in shades of pink, rose, scarlet, crimson and white, with some bicolored. The foliage is gray-green in color. China Doll, an All-American Selection, is an excellent strain of China pink, as is the variety *D. chinensis heddewigii*. Annual carnations, natives of southern Europe, have flowers that rival those of the greenhouse-grown carnations sold by florists. Not only are they comparable in color—yellow, white, red, pink and mixtures—but in size of blossom (1 to 3 inches across), height (1 to 2 feet) and spicy fragrance. The foliage is blue-gray in color. Annual sweet Williams, of which outstanding strains are Red Monarch, Bravo and Wee Willie, resemble the more common biennial sweet William. They have closely packed, flat-topped, nonfragrant flower clusters, 2 to 4 inches across, in shades of red, pink, rose-purple, white or a combination of these colors. The foliage is dark green. Strains vary in height from 6 to 12 inches. Annual sweet Williams are native to both southern and eastern Europe.

USES. The smaller *Dianthus* varieties are among the most popular plants for garden edgings. All varieties provide dramatic color effects when massed in beds and borders, and all make attractive, long-lasting cut flowers. They need full sun and well-drained alkaline soil to do their best.

HOW TO GROW. If the soil is on the acid side (page 11), add lime to neutralize it. Sow seeds of China pinks indoors six to eight weeks before the last frost is due, then about a month later move the seedlings to a protected cold frame; they need cool temperatures to thrive at this stage. When danger of frost is past, set them in the garden 6 to 10 inches apart. Seeds may also be sown outdoors early in the spring as soon as the soil is warm and dry enough to be cultivated. Start annual carnation seeds indoors six to eight weeks before the last frost; seeds germinate in about 10 days but it takes five months for the plants to come into flower. For large specimen flowers, remove all but the top bud from each stem of the annual carnation. Especially fine plants may be obtained by rooting cuttings of side shoots (page 85). In Zones 8-10, annual carnations act as biennials or perennials, living for two years or more in the garden; in colder climates (Zones 3-7) young plants started from cuttings can often be saved in a cold frame over the winter. Annual sweet William plants will flower by midsummer if seeds are sown outdoors as soon as the soil can be spaded and raked in the spring; space plants 8 to 10 inches apart. For earlier flowering, sow seeds indoors six to eight weeks before the last frost is due. Even earlier blossoms, starting in midspring, are possible if seeds are sown outdoors any time in the fall. This enables them to germinate and achieve some growth before winter. Young fall-sown plants benefit from a light winter mulch of salt-marsh hay in areas where the ground freezes.

DIASCIA

D. barberae (twinspur).

Twinspur is a lovely 10- to 12-inch-tall annual from South Africa. Its slender stalks, rising above a mound of gleaming, deep green leaves, bear clusters of saucerlike pink flowers about ¾ inch across. Each blossom has a yellow throat dotted with green, and on its reverse side are two curving hornlike spurs, which account for the common name. Some strains have deep pink or orange flowers.

USES. The flowers of twinspur are exquisite in a garden border, but they are not suited for cutting. This abundantly flowering annual will grow in average soil, provided the location is sunny.

HOW TO GROW. Sow seeds indoors six to eight weeks before the last expected frost. When the young plants are 2 inches tall, pinch off the stem tips, and when the new shoots that arise from this pinching are 2 inches long, remove their tips in turn. This will develop bushy plants. Set them into the garden 6 inches apart when danger of frost is past. Seeds can also be sown directly into the garden in early spring, as soon as the soil can be spaded and raked. Plants will flower about 14 weeks after sowing. When the first crop of flowers has faded, clip all the flower stalks back to the mound of foliage at the base of the plant; it will soon blossom again. This process can be repeated throughout the summer.

DIDISCUS See *Trachymene*

DIGITALIS

D. purpurea, annual type (annual foxglove).

Since time immemorial, foxgloves have made vegetative growth the first year and sent forth blossoms the second, in the manner of all biennials. This pattern has been changed by plant breeders who produced a strain called Foxy. Derived from *D. purpurea,* a native of western Europe, Foxy blossoms from seed the first year as well as the second. The Foxy foxglove grows 2 to 3 feet tall and has sturdy, compact spikes of 2- to 3-inch-long bell-shaped flowers with mottled throats. Colors include white, cream, yellow, pink, lavender, magenta and purple.

USES. Foxgloves provide color even in cool, shady spots where few plants will flower, but the soil must be well drained. They are also among the showiest of tall plants to use at the rear of a sunny border or as individual accents.

HOW TO GROW. Foxy foxglove seeds started outdoors any time in the fall will produce flowers in spring and early summer; space plants 12 to 18 inches apart. You also can sow seeds indoors six to eight weeks before the last frost, or buy started plants, since a growing season of about five months is needed to produce flowers. Set seedlings into the garden as soon as the ground can be cultivated in the spring. Foxy often reproduces from its own scattered seeds.

DILL-LEAF URSINIA See *Ursinia*

DIMORPHOTHECA

Several hybrids grouped under the name *Dimorphotheca* (Cape marigold, star-of-the-veldt, African daisy).

Cape marigolds are natives of South Africa that grow about a foot tall and produce a profuse number of 3½- to 4-inch daisylike blossoms, whose colors range from white through brilliant shades of yellow, salmon or rose. The reverse side of the petals is colored in shades of blue or lavender. Some of the multicolored hybrid strains are sold as *D. aurantiaca,* the correct botanical name for an orange-flowered species. They are not true marigolds, which belong to the genus *Tagetes.*

ANNUAL FOXGLOVE
Digitalis purpurea

CAPE MARIGOLD
Dimorphotheca hybrid

For climate zones and frost dates, see maps, pages 164-165.

HYACINTH BEAN
Dolichos lablab

WILD CUCUMBER
Echinocystis lobata

VIPER'S BUGLOSS
Echium plantagineum

USES. Cape marigolds provide masses of unexpected color in the garden as long as they have plenty of sunlight and well-drained soil. They do particularly well in hot, dry areas. They are rarely used as cut flowers, since they close at night and on cloudy days.

HOW TO GROW. Seedlings begin to blossom when they are about nine weeks old and are rarely without flowers until cut down by frost. Seeds may be sown indoors four to five weeks before the last frost is due, but the young plants should not be set into the garden until night temperatures average about 50°. Alternatively, sow seeds outdoors where they are to grow when the danger of frost is past. Plants should stand 10 inches apart. In dry, frost-free climates of Zones 9-10, sow Cape marigolds in late summer, and they will bloom throughout the winter and spring.

DOLICHOS
D. lablab (hyacinth bean).

Hyacinth beans are rapidly climbing vines from the tropics with large, decorative leaves and long spikes of purple or white pealike flowers. They will climb 15 to 30 feet in a single summer. The name is misleading; hyacinth beans are not true beans, which belong to the genus *Phaseolus,* nor are they related to hyacinths.

USES. Hyacinth beans grow so rapidly, even in average soil, that they are useful as a quick covering wherever vines are needed, as on a fence or trellis. But since they are tropical plants, they do well in the cold climates of Zones 3-4 only if planted in a warm, sunny, sheltered place. The plant is a perennial in frost-free climates of Zones 9-10.

HOW TO GROW. Since hyacinth beans are difficult to transplant, sow the seed directly in the garden where they are to grow when you can be sure night temperatures will not drop below 50°. Space plants a foot or more apart. Provide cord or wire supports for the tendrils to cling to. In Zones 3-5, earlier flowering can be achieved by starting seeds indoors, six to eight weeks before the last frost is due. Sow seeds in individual 3-inch peat pots and move them, pots and all, to the garden when all danger of frost is past.

DROOPING CATCHFLY See *Silene*
DRUMMOND PHLOX See *Phlox*
DUSTY MILLER See *Centaurea* and *Senecio*
DUTCH RUNNER BEAN, WHITE See *Phaseolus*
DWARF MORNING GLORY See *Convolvulus*

E

ECHINOCYSTIS
E. lobata (wild cucumber, mock cucumber).

This vine, native to North and South America, grows rapidly to a height of 20 feet or more. Its small, fuzzy, greenish white flowers are followed by spiny, egg-shaped seed pods 2 inches long. The lobed leaves are 3 to 5 inches long.

USES. The vine provides a quick cover for any unsightly object, as well as for a trellis or fence. It will grow in any soil as long as it has sunlight, but it requires a support for the tendrils to cling to.

HOW TO GROW. Wild cucumbers are easily grown from seed, which may be sown outdoors any time in the fall or in the early spring as soon as the soil can be spaded and raked. Space plants 12 inches apart. Or start vines indoors four to five weeks before the last expected frost and move plants to the garden when danger of frost has passed.

ECHIUM
Hybrids of *E. plantagineum,* classified by some botanists as *E. lycopsis* (viper's bugloss).

The name "viper's bugloss" is rather unappealing, which

may explain why few gardeners grow this showy native of the Mediterranean. The name *Echium* comes from the Greek word for viper and refers to the seeds of this plant, which look like tiny snake heads. The name "bugloss" is also derived from Greek and means "ox tongue," a reference to the broad, rough, tongue-shaped leaves. Although the wild species, *E. plantagineum,* grows 3 feet tall, garden varieties are usually only 12 to 18 inches in height. They bear great quantities of bell-shaped flowers in shades of blue, lavender, purple, rose or white. These flowers, about ½ inch across, appear along branching stems covered with bristly gray hairs. The variety Blue Bedder has masses of violet-blue blossoms that turn pink as they age.

USES. Viper's bugloss is a long-flowering annual, especially suited to dry, sunny locations with poor soil. It is excellent for a seashore garden. In rich soil, the plants tend to have much foliage and few flowers.

HOW TO GROW. Start seeds of viper's bugloss indoors six to eight weeks before the last frost is due and move them to the garden when frost danger is past. Or sow them in the garden as soon as the soil can be spaded and raked in the spring. Space plants 15 to 18 inches apart. They will become compact, bushy plants and begin flowering about three months after sowing. In frost-free areas of Zones 9-10, seeds may be sown outdoors in the fall as well as in the spring. Plants from fall-sown seeds will blossom at least a month earlier than those started in the spring.

EDGING LOBELIA See *Lobelia*

EMILIA

E. flammea, also known as *E. sagittata* and *Cacalia coccinea* (tassel flower, Flora's paintbrush).

Tassel flowers, which are wild flowers in tropical America and India, are grown for their small but brilliantly colored tassellike flower heads of red, golden orange or yellow. Flowers are borne on wiry 18- to 24-inch stems above a low cluster of gray-green foliage.

USES. Tassel flowers add a dash of color to an annual border and are long lasting as cut flowers. They will thrive in dry to average soil if given a sunny location.

HOW TO GROW. Sow the seeds outdoors when all danger of frost has passed. Or start seeds indoors four to six weeks before the last frost is due and move seedlings into the garden when frost danger is past. Plants should stand 6 to 8 inches apart; they do not mind a little crowding.

ENGLISH DAISY See *Bellis*
ENGLISH WALLFLOWER See *Cheiranthus*
ERYSIMUM See *Cheiranthus*

ESCHSCHOLZIA
Also spelled *Eschscholtzia.*
E. californica (California poppy).

Silky 2- to 3-inch cups of gold, bronze, scarlet, terra cotta, rose or white are borne abundantly by California poppies, the state flower of California. Some varieties have semidouble or double flowers, often with crinkled petals edged in a darker shade. The blossoms appear above mounds of finely cut, silvery green foliage, about a foot high and usually broader than they are tall. California poppies were found on the Pacific coast by a Russian expedition in 1815 and were named after a member of the expedition, Dr. Johann Friedrich Eschscholtz.

USES. The flowers of California poppies are spectacular in the garden, but even if there were no flowers, the lacy foliage would merit display. They also thrive in window boxes and planters. Plants do best in full sun in well-

TASSEL FLOWER
Emilia flammea

CALIFORNIA POPPY
Eschscholzia californica

TOP: ANNUAL POINSETTIA
Euphorbia heterophylla

BOTTOM: SNOW-ON-THE-MOUNTAIN
E. marginata

BLUE DAISY
Felicia amelloides

drained and rather sandy soil; they are easy to grow and often thrive where other plants will not do well.

HOW TO GROW. Sow the seeds any time in the fall or very early in the spring, as soon as the soil can be spaded and raked. Sow seeds where you want the plants to grow, since California poppies are not easy to transplant. Space plants 6 inches apart. In Zones 8-10, California poppies often act as perennials and come up year after year, tending to reproduce from their own scattered seed.

EUPHORBIA
E. heterophylla (annual poinsettia, Mexican fire plant, fire-on-the-mountain, spurge). *E. marginata* (snow-on-the-mountain).

Our native annual poinsettia is closely related to the poinsettia that is so popular as a Christmas pot plant. It grows 2 to 3 feet tall, and by midsummer the top leaves turn from dark green to brilliant red, sometimes with white markings, resembling a gigantic "flower." Snow-on-the-mountain, a wild flower in the Central States, grows 1½ to 2 feet tall in much the same manner as the annual poinsettia, except that the upper leaves have wide margins of clear white, and an occasional leaf may be all white. In both cases, the true flowers are insignificant.

USES. Both species of *Euphorbia* make showy border plants. They thrive in light, sandy loam with abundant sunshine and also do well in poor, dry soil. Branches may be used as "cut flowers" if the stem ends are seared over a flame or dipped in boiling water and then arranged in vases of warm water. This procedure prevents wilting by keeping the sap from coagulating and clogging the stems. In both species, this latexlike liquid is poisonous and should be kept away from the eyes, mouth or skin abrasions; it will raise blisters on the skin of some persons.

HOW TO GROW. Both species are easy to grow. Sow seeds of annual poinsettias outdoors after frost danger has passed or, if early leaf color is desired, start plants indoors five or six weeks before the last frost is due and move them to the garden when frost danger is past. Space plants about 12 inches apart. Sow seeds of snow-on-the-mountain outdoors very early in the spring, as soon as the ground is workable. The plant often reproduces from its own scattered seed.

EVENING PRIMROSE See *Oenothera*
EVENING STOCK See *Mathiola*
EVERLASTING, ROSE See *Helipterum*
EVERLASTING, SWAN RIVER See *Helipterum*
EVERLASTING, WINGED See *Ammobium*
EVERLASTING FLOWER See *Helichrysum*

F
FAIRY PRIMROSE See *Primula*
FANCY GERANIUM See *Pelargonium*
FAREWELL-TO-SPRING See *Godetia*
FEATHER COCKSCOMB See *Celosia*
FEATHERTOP See *Pennisetum*

FELICIA
F. amelloides, sometimes classified as *F. capensis, Agathaea coelestis, Aster rotundifolia* (blue daisy, blue marguerite). *F. bergeriana* (kingfisher daisy).

Both of these South African plants have low, dark green, hairy mounds of foliage from which grow an abundance of blue daisylike flowers. The bushy blue daisies bear 1- to 1½-inch blossoms, sky blue with yellow centers, atop 1- to 2-foot stems. Kingfisher daisies grow only 6 inches tall and are covered with ½- to ¾-inch sky-blue flowers.

USES. Both species will thrive in the dry pockets of rock

gardens. They also may be used to edge walks and flower beds and, since they withstand wind well, are often used in balcony planters. They are long lasting as cut flowers, but they may close at night and during cloudy weather.

HOW TO GROW. Start seeds indoors at least six weeks before the last frost is due. Set the plants outdoors when the danger of frost has passed, 6 to 12 inches apart, in a sheltered, sunny spot. They will thrive in any dry to average soil. In frost-free areas of Zones 9-10, blue daisies are grown as perennials; kingfisher daisies are true annuals.

FENNEL FLOWER See *Nigella*
FEVERFEW See *Chrysanthemum*
FIG MARIGOLD See *Mesembryanthemum*
FIRE BUSH See *Kochia*
FIRE-ON-THE-MOUNTAIN See *Euphorbia*
FIRE PLANT, MEXICAN See *Euphorbia*
FISH GERANIUM See *Pelargonium*
FLAME FLOWER See *Tropaeolum*
FLAMING FOUNTAIN See *Amaranthus*
FLAX See *Linum*
FLAXLEAF PIMPERNEL See *Anagallis*
FLORA'S PAINTBRUSH See *Emilia*
FLOS ADONIS See *Adonis*
FLOSSFLOWER See *Ageratum*
FLOWERING FLAX See *Linum*
FLOWERING MAPLE See *Abutilon*
FLOWERING TOBACCO See *Nicotiana*
FLOWER-OF-AN-HOUR See *Hibiscus*
FORGET-ME-NOT, CHINESE See *Cynoglossum*
FORGET-ME-NOT, SUMMER See *Anchusa*
FORGET-ME-NOT, WOODLAND See *Myosotis*
FOUNTAIN GRASS See *Pennisetum*
FOUNTAIN PLANT See *Amaranthus*
FOUR O'CLOCK See *Mirabilis*
FOXGLOVE, ANNUAL See *Digitalis*

FRAGARIA

F. vesca semperflorens (Alpine strawberry).

Alpine strawberries, which are native to Europe, form mounds of dark green, glossy foliage 6 to 8 inches high, and bear ¼- to ½-inch white flowers followed by a continuous crop of small, sweet-flavored red or yellow strawberries that may be eaten or allowed to remain on the plants for ornament. (If you are eating them, first crush them in sugar and let them stand for about two hours.) Some recommended varieties are Baron Solemacher, Harzland, Alexandria and Alpine Yellow.

USES. Alpine strawberries are perennials, but they make a sturdy ground cover from seed during the first year and are also used effectively as green edging plants. Since they do not produce runners, as most strawberries do, they are ideal for strawberry-jar planters—those large, strawberry-shaped ceramic containers with cuplike openings on their sides through which various plants, including strawberries, may be grown.

HOW TO GROW. Sow seeds indoors six to eight weeks before the last frost is due (germination is likely to be slow and erratic). Set the plants outdoors, 6 to 8 inches apart, in fertile soil, as early as the ground can be cultivated. They will thrive in full sun or light shade. Seeds may also be sown outdoors as soon as the ground can be spaded and raked in the spring, but the plants will be smaller than those started indoors.

FRENCH MARIGOLD See *Tagetes*
FRENCH PINK See *Centaurea*
FRENCH SPINACH See *Atriplex*

ALPINE STRAWBERRY
Fragaria vesca semperflorens

GAILLARDIA
Gaillardia pulchella

SUNSHINE DAISY
Gamolepis tagetes

GAZANIA
Gazania longiscapa

G

GAILLARDIA

Hybrids of *G. amblyodon* and *G. pulchella* (gaillardia, blanketflower, Indian blanket).

Gaillardias are descendants of wild plants of the American West that have become popular garden plants both in North America and abroad. Most annual types grow about 18 inches tall, some with single and semidouble daisylike blossoms, others with shaggy ball-shaped flower heads as large as 3 inches in diameter. Colors range from creamy white to yellow, orange and red; many types are bicolored.

USES. Gaillardias will flourish in full sun in any garden soil and will withstand heat waves and drought better than most flowering plants. Since they do tolerate dry soil, they are useful for window boxes and planters. They also provide lasting long-stemmed cut flowers.

HOW TO GROW. Sow seeds indoors four to six weeks before the last expected frost, then move seedlings to the garden when all danger of frost is past. Or sow seeds directly in the garden as soon as the ground can be spaded and raked in the spring. Space plants 8 inches apart. They will blossom a few weeks after being planted outdoors.

GAMOLEPIS

G. tagetes, also called *G. annua* (sunshine daisy).

The sunshine daisy is a native of South Africa that reaches 4 to 10 inches in height and bears a multitude of ½- to ¾-inch daisylike flowers ranging in color from bright yellow to orange.

USES. Sunshine daisies are suitable for rock gardens and borders, as well as for window boxes and planters, and may be used in small flower arrangements. They will thrive in sun and in average to very dry soil.

HOW TO GROW. Sow seeds outdoors as soon as the ground can be spaded and raked in the spring. Place them where you want the plants to grow—sunshine daisies are difficult to transplant except when very small. Plants should stand about 4 inches apart. Seeds may also be started indoors six to eight weeks before the last frost is due and moved to the garden when all danger of frost has passed.

GARDEN ALTERNANTHERA See *Alternanthera*
GARDEN BALSAM See *Impatiens*
GARDEN VERBENA See *Verbena*
GARLAND, ROCKY MOUNTAIN See *Clarkia*

GAZANIA

G. longiscapa (gazania, treasure flower).

Gazanias, natives of South Africa, are widely grown in the American Southwest as perennials, but some hybrids blossom so quickly from seeds that they may be treated as annuals in Zones 3-7. Their stalks rise 6 to 12 inches directly from the ground and bear single daisylike blossoms, up to 4 inches across, in bright yellow, gold, cream, yellow orange, pink or bronze red, each with a dark rim around the center. Their 6- to 9-inch-long, thick leaves are usually dark green on top, felty white underneath.

USES. Gazanias grow well in windy places and in balcony planters. Their blossoms close in cloudy weather and at night, hence are unsatisfactory as cut flowers. They may, however, be lifted from the garden in the fall and potted for use as ever-blooming house plants. In the garden they need full sun and will prosper in light, sandy loam even if it is very dry. They grow best when summer temperatures are in the 80s and 90s.

HOW TO GROW. Start plants indoors four to six weeks before the last frost is due. Set plants in the garden, 8 to 12 inches apart, when all danger of frost has passed.

GENTIAN SAGE See *Salvia*
GERANIUM See *Pelargonium*

GILIA
G. capitata (blue thimble flower). *G. hybrida,* usually sold as *Leptosiphon hybrida* (stardust).

Blue thimble flowers, native to the Pacific Coast, are dainty, feathery foliaged annuals that grow 1 to 2 feet tall and are covered continuously with sky-blue globe-shaped flower heads about 1 inch across. Stardust grows 6 to 9 inches tall and has myriads of tiny starlike flowers of golden yellow, bright rose, cream, orange or red.

USES. Blue thimble flowers are long lasting and graceful as cut flowers. Stardust will withstand wind and thrives in balcony planters and window boxes; it is low enough to serve as an edging plant. Both are colorful additions to borders. They thrive in full sun in dry to average soil.

HOW TO GROW. Both species of *Gilia* are easy to grow. Sow seeds outdoors after all frost danger has passed. Space plants 12 inches apart. The taller varieties may require some support to hold them upright. Branchy twigs inserted between half-grown plants serve well and are soon hidden by subsequent growth.

BLUE THIMBLE FLOWER
Gilia capitata

GLOBE AMARANTH See *Gomphrena*
GLOBE CANDYTUFT See *Iberis*
GLORIOSA DAISY See *Rudbeckia*

GODETIA
G. amoena (farewell-to-spring). *G. grandiflora,* sometimes sold as *Oenothera whitneyi* (satinflower).

Godetias, native to the western U.S., have satin-petaled, cuplike blossoms, 3 to 5 inches across, clustered along stems varying in height from 10 inches to 2½ feet. The common name farewell-to-spring is generally applied to the taller varieties, the name satinflower to those that are shorter. Flowers are white, pink, red or lilac; the foliage is gray green. Godetias are sometimes classified as *Clarkia.*

USES. Godetias are showy additions for any part of a garden, and the tall varieties make lovely cut flowers. They grow well in light sandy loam that is not too rich, in sun or light shade. Rich soil tends to produce plants with much foliage and few flowers.

HOW TO GROW. Godetias do best in cool weather, so sow seeds outside in the spring as soon as a seedbed can be spaded and raked. Place them where you want the plants to grow; they are not easy to transplant. Space plants 6 to 12 inches apart. In Zones 9-10, sow seeds in early fall; plants will blossom abundantly in early spring. Stick twiggy brush around the taller varieties for support when they are half grown *(see page 43).*

TOP: FAREWELL-TO-SPRING   BOTTOM: SATINFLOWER
Godetia amoena   *G. grandiflora*

GOLDEN CROWNBEARD See *Verbesina*
GOLDEN CUP See *Hunnemannia*
GOLDEN FLEECE See *Thymophylla*
GOLDEN-FLOWER-OF-THE-INCAS See *Tithonia*

GOMPHRENA
G. globosa (globe amaranth, gomphrena).

Globe amaranths are native to tropical regions throughout the world. They grow in neat mounds 6 to 18 inches tall that are covered with ¾-inch round flower heads resembling those of giant-sized clover. Purple and white varieties are most commonly seen, but pink and yellow types are also available from most seedsmen. The name "bachelor's button," sometimes used for globe amaranths, more properly applies to *Centaurea cyanus,* listed under the entry for *Centaurea.*

GLOBE AMARANTH
Gomphrena globosa

For climate zones and frost dates, see maps, pages 164-165.

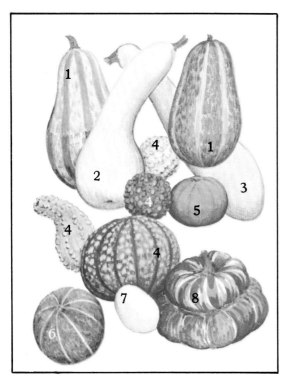

GOURDS
1 STRIPED PEAR, *Cucurbita pepo.* 2 DIPPER, *Lagenaria siceraria.* 3 DISHCLOTH GOURD, *Luffa.* 4 WARTY HARDHEADS, *C. pepo.* 5 CHITO, *Cucumis melo.* 6 MINIATURE BOTTLE, *Cucurbita pepo ovifera.* 7 NEST EGG, *C. p. ovifera.* 8 TURK'S TURBAN, *C. maxima.*

ANNUAL BABIES'-BREATH
Gypsophila elegans

USES. Globe amaranths do well in window boxes, planters and high, windy places. Dwarf varieties are suitable for edgings, taller varieties for cut flowers. They can be used in dried arrangements if they are picked just as the flowers open fully and are hung upside down to dry in a cool shady place; when dried they retain their color as well as shape. They need sun and well-drained soil, and they tolerate hot weather well.

HOW TO GROW. Start seeds indoors six to eight weeks before the last spring frost is due and move seedlings to the garden when frost danger has passed. Or sow seeds directly in the garden when night temperatures can be expected to stay above 50°. The seeds may take 12 to 14 days to germinate. Plants should stand 8 to 12 inches apart.

GOODNIGHT-AT-NOON See *Hibiscus*

GOURDS

Lagenaria vulgaris (large gourds). *Cucurbita pepo ovifera* (small gourds). Also, several species of the genera *Benincasa, Luffa, Cucumis* and *Trichosanthes.*

Ornamental gourds are tropical vines that produce brightly colored, hard-shelled, often grotesquely shaped inedible fruit. The plants grow as high as 10 to 12 feet, with fruit ranging from 2 inches to 5 feet in length.

USES. Gourd plants quickly cover fences and porch railings, trellises, pergolas, arches and poles with heavy foliage. In sun, they grow in almost any soil. Fruits should be allowed to ripen on the vine but then may be gathered before the first frost for use as table decorations. Gourds may be made shinier by the application of a thin coat of floor wax or varnish.

HOW TO GROW. Sow seeds outdoors when all frost danger has passed. Place seeds where you want the plants to grow—they do not transplant well. Space plants 10 to 12 inches apart. Gourds' vines will trail along the ground if no support such as a fence or trellis is supplied, but the fruit will be less perfect since it will lie on the ground causing that side to be less colorful or even misshapen.

GRASS, CLOUD See *Agrostis*
GRASS, FOUNTAIN See *Pennisetum*
GRASS, HARE'S-TAIL See *Lagurus*
GRASS, QUAKING See *Briza*
GRASS, RABBIT-TAIL See *Lagurus*
GRASS, RUBY See *Tricholaena*
GRASS, SQUIRRELTAIL See *Hordeum*
GRECIAN STOCK See *Mathiola*
GROUNDSEL, PURPLE See *Senecio*

GYPSOPHILA

G. elegans (annual babies'-breath).

A native of Asia Minor, babies'-breath bears delicate ¼-inch starlike blossoms in profusion on many-branched sprays that add an airy quality to summer gardens and bouquets. The plants grow 12 to 18 inches tall, and come in pink, rose and carmine, as well as the familiar white.

USES. Annual babies'-breath flowers for six weeks at most, and thus is better suited to a cutting garden than to a flower border. Its delicate flower heads are valued by flower arrangers. The plants are lime lovers—the botanical name *Gypsophila* comes from the Greek *gypsos,* or gypsum, and *philos,* or friendship—so lime should be added to acid soil (*page 12*). The plants should have sun and a soil low in nutrients; in rich soil they grow too luxuriantly and are easily beaten down by summer thunderstorms.

HOW TO GROW. Sow seeds outdoors when frost danger is past. Space plants 8 to 12 inches apart. Flowers will appear in about eight weeks, but a new seeding should be made every two to four weeks to ensure flowers throughout the summer. They grow so rapidly that it is usually impractical to start seeds indoors, although a few seeds sown in 3-inch pots two to three weeks before the last expected frost may be set directly into the ground as clumps rather than as individual seedlings.

H

HAIRY-CALYX SUNDROPS See *Oenothera*
HARE'S-TAIL GRASS See *Lagurus*
HAWK'S BEARD See *Crepis*
HEARTSEED See *Cardiospermum*

HELIANTHUS

H. annuus (common sunflower). *H. debilis* (cucumberleaf sunflower).

It might be difficult to convince a Kansas or Nebraska farmer that the freely blossoming golden wild flowers known as sunflowers are truly flowers at all. Even though the sunflower is the official state flower of Kansas, most farmers consider it a weed. But varieties have been developed—mostly from the cucumberleaf sunflower—that bear blossoms about 3 inches across in colors from pure white through many shades of yellow and orange to chestnut and even rosy lavender and maroon; some are bicolored. These garden varieties vary in height from 1½ to 4 feet and come in both single- and double-flowered forms. In addition to these garden varieties, there is the giant common sunflower, which grows as tall as 10 feet or more, with single yellow blossoms 8 to 14 inches across.

USES. The common sunflower and tall varieties of the cucumberleaf sunflower can be used effectively as temporary hedges and screens. The cucumberleaf sunflower also provides bright cut flowers, but the only other major garden function of the common sunflower is to produce seeds. It does this prolifically, and gardens containing sunflowers —cucumberleaf as well as common—are often visited by flocks of goldfinches when the seeds ripen. All varieties thrive in poor soil with very little moisture and, though their name implies otherwise, they tolerate light shade well.

HOW TO GROW. Plant seeds outdoors ½ inch deep and about 2 feet apart when all danger of frost has passed. Sunflowers grow so rapidly that little advantage is gained from sowing seeds indoors.

HELICHRYSUM

H. bracteatum (everlasting flower, strawflower, immortelle).

Strawflowers, natives of Australia, are the most brilliant of all flowers suitable for drying for year-round display. The plants grow about 2 feet tall, and one variety, *H. bracteatum monstrosum*, bears double daisylike flowers as large as 2½ inches in diameter. Strawflowers are red, salmon, purple, yellow, rose or white in color. The parts of strawflowers that look like petals are actually stiff, colorful modified leaves, called bracts. The true flowers are in the very center of each blossom.

USES. Strawflowers can be used fresh as cut flowers during the summer, as well as dried for winter bouquets. They flourish in sun in almost any soil, provided that it is not too wet. To dry, cut the flowers just before the center petals open, strip off the foliage and hang the flowers upside down in a dry, shady place.

HOW TO GROW. Start seeds indoors four to six weeks before the last spring frost, or sow them directly in the garden after all frost danger is past. Space plants to stand about 9 inches apart.

COMMON SUNFLOWER
Helianthus annuus

STRAWFLOWER
Helichrysum bracteatum

For climate zones and frost dates, see maps, pages 164-165.

COMMON HELIOTROPE
Heliotropium peruvianum

SWAN RIVER EVERLASTING
Helipterum manglesii

FLOWER-OF-AN-HOUR
Hibiscus trionum

HELIOTROPIUM

H. peruvianum, also called *H. arborescens* (common heliotrope, cherry pie). *H. corymbosum* (big heliotrope).

Although heliotropes grow year round as perennial shrubs in their native Peru, they serve as annual flowers in North American gardens. Plants are 1 to 2 feet tall, depending upon the strain, and bear flower clusters as large as 1 foot in diameter, in dark violet and white in addition to the renowned heliotrope blue. Their fragrance, once experienced, is never forgotten, whether it is the sweet vanilla scent of the common heliotrope or the heavy narcissuslike scent of the big heliotropes.

USES. Heliotropes make colorful as well as fragrant plants for borders, window boxes and terrace pots. They bring the same assets to fresh-cut bouquets. Garden-grown heliotropes require a rich soil in full sun, but when grown in pots they do best in places where they get a bit of shade during the hot part of the day.

HOW TO GROW. Start seeds indoors in midwinter, or buy seedlings in the spring. Space plants 1 foot apart.

HELIPTERUM

Often sold as *Acroclinium* or *Rhodanthe. H. roseum,* also called *Acroclinium roseum* (rose everlasting, rose sunray, helipterum). *H. manglesii,* also called *Rhodanthe manglesii* (Swan River everlasting).

The 2- to 3-inch blossoms of helipterums look much like double-flowered daisies. Originally wild flowers in Australia, they are now available in white and chamois and shades of pink, and grow atop slender 2-foot stems with oval, pointed leaves.

USES. Helipterums can be used as cut flowers, but are most outstanding when dried for winter bouquets. To dry them, cut the flowers before they are fully open and hang them, blossoms down, in a dry, shady place. Helipterums flourish in average to dry soil, in full sun.

HOW TO GROW. Helipterums are difficult to transplant, so sow seeds outdoors after the danger of frost has passed. Space 6 to 12 inches apart. Seeds germinate in 15 days, and plants begin to blossom six weeks later.

HIBISCUS

H. manihot (sunset hibiscus). *H. trionum,* also called *H. africanus* (flower-of-an-hour, goodnight-at-noon).

Since they blossom from seeds the first year, these two tender members of the hibiscus family can be grown as annuals in any area. The most familiar and impressive is the sunset hibiscus from Eastern Asia, whose reddish stems may become 8 to 9 feet tall and in late summer bear enormous sulfur-yellow or white, maroon-centered flowers 7 to 9 inches across. A much lower-growing species is *H. trionum* from the tropics of the Old World, which rarely reaches more than 18 to 24 inches in height. Its common names, flower-of-an-hour and goodnight-at-noon, point up the fleeting quality of its 1- to 1½-inch, maroon-throated, primrose-yellow flowers. The plants compensate for the brief life of their individual blossoms by flowering profusely from midsummer until late fall. Today's varieties are not quite so ephemeral as the original species; the blossoms of the new strains do not fade before noon but have been bred to last throughout most of the day.

USES. Neither variety of hibiscus can be used in cut-flower arrangements, since the blossoms die so quickly. But sunset hibiscus make excellent hedges or screens and the smaller *H. trionum* can be used effectively in an annual border. The plants grow best in rich, moist soil and full sunshine.

HOW TO GROW. Start *H. manihot* seeds indoors six to eight weeks before the last frost is due. Grow them in 3-inch peat pots; then set the plants and pots 1½ to 2 feet apart in the garden when all frost danger is past. Since *H. trionum* are difficult to transplant, wait until there is no further danger of frost and sow the seeds about 1 foot apart where you want them to grow. Both species often sow their own seeds in the garden to produce new plants year after year.

HOLLYHOCK See *Althaea*
HONEYWORT See *Cerinthe*
HOP VINE, COMMON See *Humulus*
HOP VINE, JAPANESE See *Humulus*

HORDEUM

H. jubatum (squirreltail grass).

A member of the grass family, *H. jubatum* is known as squirreltail grass because of its fluffy seedheads. Depending on soil fertility and moisture, squirreltail grass grows 9 inches to 3 feet tall. It is native to cold and dry sections of Europe, Asia and North America but grows well throughout the U.S. In parts of the West, it is known as foxtail or tickle grass. Hordeum is perennial in its growing habit but is grown in most gardens as an annual.

USES. Ornamental in gardens, squirreltail grass is useful in floral arrangements, particularly when dried. It should be cut when seedheads are fluffy and hung up to dry in a shady place. It thrives in full sun and any soil, including dry locations.

HOW TO GROW. Sow the seeds as soon as the ground can be spaded and raked in the spring. The plants should stand 1 foot apart.

HORSESHOE GERANIUM See *Pelargonium*
HOUND'S TONGUE See *Cynoglossum*
HUMBLE PLANT See *Mimosa*

HUMULUS

H. scandens, also sold as *H. japonicus* (Japanese hop vine).

The Japanese hop vine is a coarse, fast-growing annual that climbs to 20 to 35 feet in a single season by twining around almost any available support. It is grown for its foliage; its bright green, rough-textured, hand-shaped leaves grow 6 to 8 inches across and have 5 to 7 deeply indented lobes. The small, greenish flowers are without ornamental value. It is said to derive its name from *humus,* or ground, a reference to the trailing nature of the vine if it does not have something to climb on. The variegated form, *H. scandens variegatus,* has green leaves splashed with white. Both are related to *H. lupulus,* the common hop vine, a perennial, nonornamental vine that bears male and female flowers on separate plants and provides the hops used in brewing beer.

USES. Japanese hop vines make dense screens and can be used as temporary coverings for unsightly walls, fences and garage and service areas. The vines grow quickly in ordinary soil, but are even more vigorous if planted in enriched soil in a sunny location where they will receive ample moisture.

HOW TO GROW. Sow the seeds in the garden after all frost danger is past. Plant them so that plants will stand about 18 inches apart at the base of the support on which the vine is to climb—fence, trellis or stout strings. Seeds can also be started indoors four to six weeks before the last frost is due.

SQUIRRELTAIL GRASS
Hordeum jubatum

TOP: JAPANESE HOP VINE
Humulus scandens (japonicus)

BOTTOM: COMMON HOP VINE
H. lupulus

For climate zones and frost dates, see maps, pages 164-165.

HUNNEMANNIA

H. fumariaefolia (Mexican tulip poppy, golden cup).

A perennial in its native Mexico, the tulip poppy is grown in the frost zones of this country as an annual. Its blue-green, finely cut foliage and 2½- to 3-inch satiny yellow flowers are reminiscent of its close relative, the California poppy, but the plants are taller, usually growing 2 to 3 feet in height.

USES. Since the Mexican tulip poppy blossoms continuously from early summer until fall frost, it is an excellent selection for flower beds and borders. If the flowers are picked just before the buds open, and the stem ends are singed with a match or dipped briefly into boiling water, the blossoms will last nearly a week in a cut-flower arrangement. The plants should have plenty of sunlight and do particularly well in dry soil.

HOW TO GROW. Mexican tulip poppies can be started indoors, although transplanting is difficult. Sow the seeds directly into individual 3-inch peat pots containing sandy loam, 3 or 4 seeds to a pot, about four to six weeks before the last frost is due. Thin to one seedling and transplant pot and all without disturbing the roots, setting them about 8 to 10 inches apart. Seeds can be sown directly in the ground when the night temperature is unlikely to drop below 50°.

HYACINTH BEAN See *Dolichos*
HYACINTH-FLOWERED CANDYTUFT See *Iberis*
HYBRID MARIGOLD See *Tagetes*

I

IBERIS

I. amara coronaria (hyacinth-flowered candytuft, rocket candytuft). *I. umbellata* (globe candytuft, annual candytuft).

Candytufts come mainly from Europe, and their botanical name alludes to the ancient name for Spain, Iberia, where some species grow as wild flowers. The hyacinth-flowered candytuft, reaching a height of 1 to 2 feet, bears its fragrant ¾- to 1-inch white blossoms in dense hyacinth-like clusters. The globe candytuft is distinctly different. It bears tiny flowers in flat-topped clusters, grows only 7 to 12 inches tall, and has no fragrance. However, it comes in a dazzling array of colors, including pink, carmine, lilac, purple and rose, as well as white.

USES. Candytufts are among the brightest and most easily grown of annuals. The smaller globe candytuft is excellent for borders, edgings and rock gardens. The hyacinth-flowered candytuft is a dramatic border plant. Both species provide long-lasting cut flowers for indoor bouquets. The candytufts do well in average soil, in a sunny location. In areas where summer temperatures are high, they benefit if given a little light shade.

HOW TO GROW. Candytufts are not easily transplanted. Sow the seeds in early spring, as soon as the planting bed can be spaded and raked, where the plants are to flower; space the seedlings 6 to 9 inches apart. Flowers will appear eight to 10 weeks after sowing. Where summers are hot, plant at two- to three-week intervals to extend the flowering season. In Zones 3-7, candytufts may also be sown late in the fall, just before the first frost is expected, if spring bloom is desired. In frost-free areas of Zones 8-10, fall-sown seeds will grow through the winter and bloom very early in the spring.

ICELAND POPPY See *Papaver*
ICE PLANT See *Mesembryanthemum*
IMMORTELLE See *Helichrysum* and *Xeranthemum*

MEXICAN TULIP POPPY
Hunnemannia fumariaefolia

GLOBE CANDYTUFT
Iberis umbellata

IMPATIENS

I. balsamina (garden balsam, touch-me-not). *I. wallerana* (patient Lucy, busy Lizzie, patience).

The name *Impatiens* refers to the curious fact that this plant seems anxious to spread its seeds—the pods burst open at the slightest touch, a property that never fails to fascinate children. Garden balsams—*I. balsamina*—are old-fashioned flowers originally from Asia, and among the easiest to grow. The blossoms of most varieties are double or semidouble, up to 2½ inches across, and may be white, salmon, pink, purple, or deep red, as well as combinations of colors. Some varieties grow only 8 to 10 inches high; others become 3 feet tall. The short types, known as bush balsams, display their flowers at the tops of the plants. Flowers of the taller-growing varieties cling closely to the main stems and have been likened to open roses or camellias. *I. wallerana,* or patient Lucy, was a favorite plant on grandmother's window sill because it was never without flowers. Old-time varieties used to produce leggy, long-jointed 2-foot plants with a steady but rather sparse supply of flowers. Today's varieties are bushy and compact, 6 to 15 inches tall and 10 to 24 inches across, bearing a profusion of 1- to 2-inch fiery red, scarlet, orange, purple and bicolored flowers, as well as more subdued golden ones.

USES. The short varieties of garden balsams are ideal for bed and edging purposes. The taller varieties can be used in flower borders. All varieties do well in rich and moist, light, sandy loam, in the sun or shade. Patient Lucy is especially effective for beds in shady places, as well as for window boxes, planters, and hanging baskets.

HOW TO GROW. Garden balsam seeds may be started indoors four to six weeks before the last frost is due, or sown directly in the garden after all danger of frost is past. Space the plants 18 inches apart so that they can develop properly and display their flowers, which have a tendency to be hidden beneath the foliage. Balsams of all varieties can be transplanted easily, even when in blossom, if lifted with a ball of soil. Patient Lucy is more delicate, being very sensitive to cold weather. Sow its seeds indoors six to eight weeks before the last frost is due and transplant seedlings to the garden when there is no longer any threat of frost. It can also be propagated by cuttings (*page 85*).

INDIAN BLANKET See *Gaillardia*
INNOCENCE See *Collinsia*

IPOMOEA

I. purpurea and *I. tricolor* (morning glory). (For dwarf morning glory, see *Convolvulus.*)

Seed catalogues may list morning glories under their common name or the botanical name *Ipomoea*, although some botanists now classify them as *Pharbitis*. Native to the tropics, more than 200 species of morning glories come from the Americas alone. Their requirements are few, and their daily crop of freshly opened blue, purple, pink, scarlet, white or multicolored single or double trumpet-shaped flowers—some of which may be as much as 8 inches across —makes them one of the most widely grown of all annual vines. Flowers are normally open only from dawn to mid-morning, but the newer varieties tend to hold their flowers open most of the day, especially in cloudy weather. The vine's abundant leaves are heart-shaped, 4 to 5 inches long.

USES. Morning glory vines grow very fast, reaching 10 feet or more two months after seeds sprout, and they will climb on just about any support. Profusely flowering against a background of pale green foliage, they quickly form lovely hedges or screens. The vines are sometimes used as a temporary ground cover, and they may also be allowed

TOP: PATIENT LUCY
Impatiens wallerana
BOTTOM: GARDEN BALSAM
I. balsamina

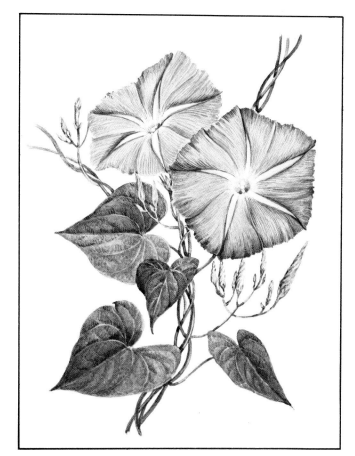

MORNING GLORY
Ipomoea purpurea

For climate zones and frost dates, see maps, pages 164-165.

to cascade from a hanging basket or raised container. They should be planted in full sun but the soil should not be too fertile or moist; otherwise the vines tend to produce a profusion of leaves instead of flowers.

HOW TO GROW. After all danger of frost is past, sow the seeds ½ inch deep, 8 to 12 inches apart, and provide a support of twine, wire or a fence or trellis for the vine to climb on. Or start seeds indoors in individual 3-inch peat pots four to six weeks before the last frost is due and set the pots into the garden when you can be sure seedlings will not be nipped by a late frost. Only pot-grown seedlings are likely to survive transplanting, and they must be transplanted pots and all—the plants generally die if their roots are pulled free of soil. Before you plant each seed, nick it with a file to help it absorb water and germinate more quickly. Alternatively, the seeds may be soaked overnight in tepid water to soften their coats.

IPOMOEA, STAR See *Quamoclit*

IRESINE
I. herbstii and *I. lindenii* (both called bloodleaf).

The common name bloodleaf is descriptive of the intense coloration of the leaves of these plants, which are widely grown for their decorative foliage. The botanical name *Iresine* comes from the Greek word *eiros,* meaning wool, a reference to the woolly appearance of the seeds and flowers. In its native settings in tropical America, bloodleaf may become 6 feet tall and shrublike, but in gardens it rarely exceeds 18 inches in height and may be kept smaller by pinching off new growth as it appears. Bloodleaf has inconspicuous white flowers, but it almost never blossoms in northern gardens because the tender plants do not become sufficiently mature to flower in a single growing season. *I. herbstii* has 1- to 2-inch-long heart-shaped leaves, usually dark red and yellow or green and yellow, while *I. lindenii* has narrow red ones. Two varieties of *I. herbstii* are of special merit: *I. herbstii aureoreticulata* has spectacular red-veined green leaves blotched with gold markings, and *I. herbstii wallisii* has blackish purple foliage and grows only 6 to 12 inches high.

USES. Because of its rich leaf colors, bloodleaf is very effective in group plantings, either in garden beds or in window boxes and planters. It needs plenty of sunlight and will thrive in average or wet soil.

HOW TO GROW. Bloodleaf must be propagated from cuttings taken during winter and early spring. Florists sell young plants in the spring, but home gardeners may grow their own by transplanting a few garden plants into pots in late summer and growing them indoors through the winter on sunny window sills. The cuttings will root readily (*page 85*) and make good-sized plants in about two months. The rooted cuttings are extremely sensitive to cold, however, and should not be set out in the garden until night temperatures are warm, preferably in the 60s.

IRISH BELLS See *Molucella*
IVY GERANIUM See *Pelargonium*

J
JAPANESE HOP VINE See *Humulus*
JOB'S TEARS See *Coix*
JOSEPH'S COAT See *Amaranthus*

K
KALE, ORNAMENTAL See *Brassica*
KAULFUSSIA See *Charieis*
KINGFISHER DAISY See *Felicia*

BLOODLEAF
Iresine herbstii

BURNING BUSH
Kochia scoparia trichophila

KOCHIA

K. scoparia trichophila (burning bush, fire bush, summer cypress, belvedere).

Burning bushes, indigenous to southern France eastward across Asia to Japan, are not grown for flowers but for their compact, globe-shaped and unusually dense mass of feathery foliage. During the summer months they are a delicate green but they become bright red in autumn. The plants grow slowly early in the season; with the advent of warm weather they develop rapidly into bushy specimens 2 to 3 feet in height.

USES. Burning bushes are often used to make low hedges and screens though they last but one season. You can shear the mature plants, just as you would any hedge, to achieve a desired height or shape. They are good for windy locations, so are sometimes grown in containers on balconies. They require plenty of sun in dry to average soil for optimum coloration and will tolerate very hot weather.

HOW TO GROW. Seeds may be started indoors four to six weeks before the last frost is due, but most gardeners sow the seeds directly into the garden after all frost danger has passed. Space the seedlings at least 18 inches apart. In warm climates the plants can become nuisance weeds since they reproduce readily by distributing their seeds.

KOREAN CHRYSANTHEMUM See *Chrysanthemum*
KUDZU VINE See *Pueraria*

L

LACE FLOWER, BLUE See *Trachymene*
LADY WASHINGTON GERANIUM See *Pelargonium*

LAGURUS

L. ovatus (rabbit-tail grass, hare's-tail grass).

It is easy to see how rabbit-tail grass got its name—at the end of each slender stem is a woolly tuft of seeds some 2 inches in size. The plant is native to the Mediterranean and now grows widely in California. Mature, it reaches 12 to 24 inches in height and displays narrow, hairy leaves.

USES. Rabbit-tail grass makes an unusual edging plant for a garden walk and is an interesting addition to fresh or dried arrangements. To preserve the stems for winter bouquets, cut them in dry weather and hang them upside down in a dark dry place. The seed heads may be dipped in dye for colorful effects. Rabbit-tail grass thrives in light, well-drained soil and tolerates heat well.

HOW TO GROW. Sow the seeds in the garden as soon as the ground can be spaded and raked, and space the plants about 4 inches apart.

LANTANA

L. camara (common lantana). *L. montevidensis*, also called *L. sellowiana* or *L. delicatissima* (trailing lantana).

These two species of lantana are widely grown both in summer gardens and in pots as house plants. Common lantana ordinarily grows 3 feet high but is also available in dwarf varieties 12 to 18 inches tall. It is a stiff-branched shrub with 1- to 1½-inch clusters of tiny yellow, pink, white, red, orange or bicolored flowers. Both the flowers and the foliage have a pungent fragrance—pleasing to some but unpleasant to others. It was discovered in Jamaica in 1692 and grows wild from the southern United States southward. The more graceful trailing lantana has small clusters of rosy lilac, yellow-centered flowers borne on limber cascading stems; there is also a white variety.

USES. Many gardeners feel that common lantana is at its best when grown in individual pots to use as accent plants in gardens and on terraces. The dwarf varieties are ef-

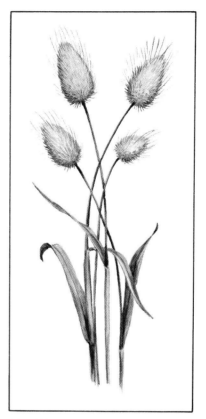

RABBIT-TAIL GRASS
Lagurus ovatus

COMMON LANTANA
Lantana camara

For climate zones and frost dates, see maps, pages 164-165.

fective in beds and borders. Trailing lantana is effective in hanging baskets or window boxes, or it can be grown upright by tying the canes to a stake and allowing the side branches to tumble downwards. In Zones 9-10, trailing lantana is used as a ground cover that flowers throughout the year. Both species do best in a rich soil in full sunshine.

HOW TO GROW. Most lantanas are cultivated from cuttings because plants grown from seeds do not blossom until late in the season; the seeds take six to eight weeks to germinate and need relatively high temperatures—65° to 75°. Outdoors, set the plants about 18 inches apart. They will become a carpet of flowers. Six to eight weeks before the first fall frost, plants can be cut back severely and potted. Kept indoors, they will flower during the winter and serve as a source of cuttings for next year's garden.

LARKSPUR See *Consolida*

LATHYRUS
L. odoratus (sweet pea).

All flower lovers know sweet peas and cherish their multiflowered stems of delicate, airy 1- to 2-inch blossoms, which come in almost all colors and have a delightful fragrance. Looking like miniature sunbonnets, the flowers may be bicolored, striped or mottled, and most have riffled, wavy petals. Though most sweet peas climb 5 to 10 feet high, attaching themselves to supports by means of tendrils, there are nonclimbing varieties such as Bijou and Little Sweethearts, which produce colorful mounds of flowers about 8 to 12 inches tall. Still another new type of sweet pea is aptly called Knee-Hi. It does not climb, but bears quantities of large colorful flowers on bushy plants 2 to 2½ feet tall. An intermediate strain known as Americana grows about 18 inches tall and bears 5 to 7 large flowers per stem. Sweet peas originated as Italian wild flowers.

USES. The many different varieties of sweet peas can be used as climbers for screens, as border or bedding plants and as cut flowers. The plants do best in rich, deep soil and cool temperatures; the roots particularly must be protected against heat and dryness. Southern gardeners grow excellent sweet peas during the winter months when temperatures are cool, and a gardener in a cool mountain area can have lovely summer plants without special effort, but those who live in mid-America, or other areas where summers are hot and dry, need every possible aid to attain satisfactory growth. Strains that endure heat particularly well include the Cuthbertson, Galaxy and Zvolanek types.

HOW TO GROW. In Zones 8-10, plant the seeds in late summer or early fall. Elsewhere, prepare the soil in the fall while it is easily workable and plant the seeds in the spring as soon as the frost has left the ground. The real secret of successful growth is proper preparation. A deep trench must be dug and refilled with fertilizer-enriched soil (for instructions, see page 41). The seeds, like those of other legumes, should be treated, or inoculated, with a specially purchased culture of nitrogen-fixing bacteria; to do this, shake the seeds around in a container with a bit of the culture until the seeds are coated. Several brands of the culture, such as Legume-Aid and Nitracin, are available at most seed stores. Soak the seeds in tepid water an hour or two before planting, to soften their coats. When the seedling is about 4 inches high, pinch it back as shown on page 42 so the plant will develop strong side branches. Provide a support of string or wire for the climbing varieties. Mulch the soil around the plants to help keep the ground cool, water regularly, and remove flowers as they die. Plants so treated will blossom all summer where night temperatures generally drop below 65°.

SWEET PEA
Lathyrus odoratus

LAVATERA

L. trimestris also called *L. rosea* (tree mallow).

You may find it difficult to get seeds of the tree mallow unless you order them from the catalogue of a seedsman in England, but the results are well worth the trouble, for it bears lovely pink or white flowers, cuplike and up to 3 inches in diameter. Tree mallows, which are native to the Mediterranean region, are related to the hibiscus but are shorter. Plants grow 2½ to 4 feet high and have hairy stems with maplelike leaves.

USES. Tree mallows make fine middle-height hedges or screens and provide striking, though short-lived, cut flowers. They are easy to grow and flourish in ordinary well-drained soil in sunny locations.

HOW TO GROW. Because tree mallows do not transplant easily, sow the seeds where you want them to blossom as early in the spring as the soil can be cultivated. Space the plants about 2 feet apart.

LAVENDER, SEA See *Limonium*

LAYIA

L. campestris, sometimes listed as *L. elegans* (tidy tips).

Although it is a wild flower in the western United States, tidy tips is more popular in England than in this country. Its solid mound of clear yellow, white-tipped daisylike flowers, 12 to 18 inches high, hides small, narrow leaves.

USES. The willowy stems of tidy tips belie the rugged nature of the plants. Given sufficient sun and well-drained soil, they thrive in window boxes as well as in the garden, where they are best suited as a front border. Tidy tips also produces exquisite flowers for cutting.

HOW TO GROW. As soon as the ground can be prepared in the spring, sow the seeds where they are to bloom and space the plants 4 to 5 inches apart.

LAZY DAISY See *Aphanostephus*
LEPTOSIPHON See *Gilia*

LIMONIUM

L. sinuatum (notchleaf statice). *L. bonduellii superbum* (Algerian statice). *L. suworowii* (rat-tail statice, Russian statice).

The name *Limonium* comes from the Greek *leimon,* meaning meadow, and refers to the fact that this genus often grows naturally in salt meadows, watered by tidal flooding or sea spray (all three species are sometimes called sea lavender). The plants have such decorative clusters of flowers that they are grown by florists. Notchleaf statice has clusters of ⅜-inch paper-textured blossoms of blue, lavender, rose or white on many-branched 18-inch stems, which rise out of a ground-hugging rosette of leaves. Algerian statice bears yellow blossoms of the same type. The beauty of rat-tail, or Russian, statice, which comes from Turkestan, lies in its 18-inch-long pencil-thin spires of tiny lilac-colored blossoms that last for many weeks in the garden or add airy grace to summer bouquets.

USES. Because of its affinity for salt meadows, statice is especially suitable for seaside gardens. For best results, it should be given plenty of sun and fairly dry, well-drained soil. All three species make excellent cut flowers. Notchleaf and Algerian statice can readily be dried; cut the flowers when they are fully expanded and hang them upside down in a shady place until they are completely dry.

HOW TO GROW. Statice seeds are imbedded within the dried flower clusters and are often sold in this manner. Pick them apart as much as possible and plant the sections on their sides to aid germination. Seeds sown outdoors

TREE MALLOW
Lavatera trimestris

TIDY TIPS
Layia campestris

STATICE
LEFT: *Limonium sinuatum*
RIGHT: *L. suworowii*

For climate zones and frost dates, see maps, pages 164-165.

131

as early as the seedbed can be worked will flower by mid-summer. Plants should be spaced 9 to 12 inches apart. For earlier flowers, sow the seeds indoors eight weeks before all danger of frost is past.

LINARIA
L. maroccana (Morocco toadflax, annual linaria).

A relative of the snapdragon, Morocco toadflax forms mounds of dainty ½-inch blossoms in shades of yellow, blue, lavender, pink, red, salmon and bronze as well as white and multicolors. Plants grow 9 to 12 inches tall.

USES. Morocco toadflax grows best where summers are relatively cool, but does well in nearly any soil if it receives full sun. It is particularly flattering to rock gardens and may be used as an edging plant. Cut flowers are lovely and long lasting in small indoor arrangements.

HOW TO GROW. Sow the seeds outdoors as soon as the ground can be spaded and raked, at 6-inch intervals.

LINUM
L. grandiflorum (flowering flax, scarlet flax). *L. usitatissimum* (common flax).

An attractive, easily grown annual from North Africa, flowering flax has 18-inch stems topped with a succession of colorful flowers that are nearly 2 inches in diameter. Most varieties bear red blossoms, but some have bluish purple, pink or white flowers. The leaves are narrow and grasslike. Common flax, from which linen and linseed oil are made, is rarely used as a garden flower, but it makes an attractive annual, growing 2 to 3 feet tall and bearing sky-blue, or occasionally white, flowers.

USES. Given plenty of sun and light, well-drained soil, flax can be used as a colorful border plant. It blooms most profusely where summers are cool.

HOW TO GROW. Flax is very difficult to transplant. Sow the seeds outdoors where you want them to grow any time in the fall, or as early in spring as you can prepare the soil; space the seeds so that the plants will stand 8 to 10 inches apart. Sow more seeds at intervals of three to four weeks to have successive crops of flowers; this is necessary because each plant blossoms only three to four weeks.

LIVINGSTON DAISY See *Mesembryanthemum*

LOBELIA
L. erinus (edging lobelia).

Introduced more than 200 years ago from the region around the Cape of Good Hope, the original wild forms of lobelia have been bred to bloom more profusely. There are both trailing varieties, with billowing masses of blossoms, and more compact bedding types, seldom exceeding 6 inches in height. The ½- to ¾-inch-wide flowers, borne along each stem, are blue on the common varieties, but white and carmine types have also been developed.

USES. Trailing varieties of lobelia are prized for window boxes, hanging baskets and planters. They are also used as ground covers. Other types are excellent for edges, beds and borders. Although the plants do best in full sun and moist, rich soil where summers are cool, they will grow surprisingly well in hot areas if given partial shade.

HOW TO GROW. Edging lobelia is not ordinarily sown directly in the garden because it does not begin to flower until two months after seed is planted. Start the seeds indoors 10 to 12 weeks before the last frost is due; since the seeds are very small, plant them on top of finely prepared soil without covering them. Or buy started plants already in blossom and set them in the garden after all danger of frost is past, spacing them 4 to 6 inches apart.

MOROCCO TOADFLAX
Linaria maroccana

FLOWERING FLAX
Linum grandiflorum

EDGING LOBELIA
Lobelia erinus

LOBULARIA

L. maritima, also called *Alyssum maritimum* (sweet alyssum).

Because it is covered with tiny flowers from late spring until frost, sweet alyssum, a native of the Mediterranean area, has been a garden-border favorite for generations. The old-fashioned variety is white, but clear pink and deep lavender types, sharing the honeylike fragrance of the white, have been developed. Though most varieties grow to only 3 or 4 inches, some reach 10 inches; all types become mounds of solid color broader than their height.

USES. Alyssum provides sweet-smelling flowers for window boxes and hanging baskets in addition to its primary role as an edging plant. Since the plants can be moved any time with a clump of soil around their roots, keep a few extra on hand to fill in empty spaces in your garden. They will do well in rock gardens and between flagstones, and are often planted in bulb beds to provide color after spring-flowering bulbs have faded. They prosper in almost any soil and do best in full sun but will tolerate light shade.

HOW TO GROW. Sow the seeds as early in spring as you can spade and rake the seedbed, or start plants indoors four to six weeks before the last frost is due, setting them in the garden 6 to 8 inches apart after all danger of frost is past. Sweet alyssum blossoms very quickly from seed and continues to flower until late fall. If the flower output wanes, shear the plants back part way and they will blossom again. They often seed themselves in gardens, and in Zones 9-10 sweet alyssum blooms the year around.

LOVE-IN-A-MIST See *Nigella*
LOVE-IN-A-PUFF See *Cardiospermum*
LOVE-LIES-BLEEDING See *Amaranthus*
LUPINE See *Lupinus*

LUPINUS

Hybrids derived chiefly from *L. luteus, L. pubescens, L. hartwegii* and *L. hirsutus* (annual lupines). *L. subcarnosus,* also called *L. texensis* (Texas bluebonnet).

The botanical name *Lupinus* is believed to be derived from the Latin *lupus,* or wolf, reflecting an erroneous belief that the deep-rooting plant rapaciously impoverishes the soil. Members of the pea family, annual lupines bear their blue, lavender, pink, yellow, white or bicolored flowers in midsummer on long, graceful spikes 1 to 3 feet tall, depending on the strain. Most seed catalogues list them as simply lupines, some as *L. hybridus.* In addition to the richly colored hybrid annual lupines, there is the beautiful Texas bluebonnet—the state flower—which is easily grown anywhere in the U.S.

USES. Both species of *Lupinus* make lovely cut flowers as well as garden plants, although their blossoming season is short. Flowers should be cut while the upper blossoms are still buds. Given good rich soil and full sun or light shade, they thrive in areas with cool springs and summers.

HOW TO GROW. As soon as the ground can be spaded and raked in spring, plant the seeds outdoors. They should be inoculated in the same manner as those of sweet peas (see *Lathyrus*). Set them 4 or 5 inches apart, then thin the seedlings to stand 8 to 10 inches apart to give them room to develop. If the flower stems are cut back to within 6 inches of the ground before seeds form, two to four smaller flower stems will develop where one was.

M

MACHAERANTHERA See *Aster*
MADAGASCAR PERIWINKLE See *Vinca*
MAIZE, STRIPED See *Zea*

SWEET ALYSSUM
Lobularia maritima

LEFT: ANNUAL LUPINE
Lupinus hybrid

RIGHT: TEXAS BLUEBONNET
L. subcarnosus

For climate zones and frost dates, see maps, pages 164-165.

VIRGINIA STOCK
Malcomia maritima

MALOPE
Malope trifida

COMMON STOCK
Mathiola incana annua

MALCOMIA

M. maritima, also called *Cheiranthus maritimus* (Virginia stock).

Once a common annual in the United States, Virginia stock is now more appreciated in Europe, where it grows wild, and its seeds must usually be ordered from English seedsmen. Its ¾-inch four-petaled blossoms—lilac, red, pink, white or, occasionally, yellow—are shaped much like those of single-flowered ordinary stock, which is a different genus entirely, *Mathiola.* The blossoms appear in great profusion on bushy 6- to 9-inch plants.

USES. Virginia stock thrives in any soil in full sun or light shade. It is useful for borders and edges, and for added color in rock gardens. Since it begins to flower only six weeks after seed is sown, it can be used in bulb beds for quick color when spring-flowering bulbs have faded.

HOW TO GROW. Sow seeds where you want them to grow, planting in the fall for spring flowering or, for summer flowerings, in the spring as soon as the ground can be worked. Space plants 4 inches apart. Virginia stock tends to reproduce itself, providing color in unexpected places.

MALLOW, ROSE See *Hibiscus*
MALLOW, TREE See *Lavatera*
MALLOW-WORT See *Malope*

MALOPE

M. trifida (malope, mallow-wort).

Descended from a Spanish wild flower, varieties of malope develop into bushy plants 2½ to 3 feet high, and have lavish clusters of rosy purple, pink, red or white flowers shaped like trumpets, each 3 inches across. They are common in Europe, but gardeners in the United States may have to order the seeds from English seedsmen.

USES. Malopes should be given light, sandy loam in full sun. They are excellent in garden beds and for cutting.

HOW TO GROW. Sow the seeds indoors four to six weeks before the last frost is due, and set the seedlings in the garden when all danger of frost is past. Alternatively, sow the seeds where you want them to grow as soon as a seedbed can be prepared, spacing them 9 to 12 inches apart.

MAPLE, FLOWERING See *Abutilon*
MARIGOLD See *Tagetes*
MARIGOLD, CAPE See *Dimorphotheca*
MARIGOLD, CORN See *Chrysanthemum*
MARIGOLD, FIG See *Mesembryanthemum*
MARIGOLD, POT See *Calendula*
MARTHA WASHINGTON GERANIUM See *Pelargonium*
MARVEL-OF-PERU See *Mirabilis*
MASK FLOWER See *Alonsoa*

MATHIOLA

M. bicornis (evening stock, Grecian stock). *M. incana annua* (common stock).

Descended from a species native to the Mediterranean region, these delicately fragrant stocks have stems covered with flowers ranging in color from snowy white through shades of cream and buff to pink, deep rose, lilac and purple. Evening, or Grecian, stock is a 1-foot-tall species with spikes of small four-petaled lilac-colored flowers that close during the day and open in the evening. Certain varieties of common stock, such as Column and Ten-Week, are 1 to 3 feet in height and bear inch-wide double flowers, although a certain percentage of singles always comes from any seeding. A new strain called Trysomic stock is profusely branched and also double-flowering. The Trysomics include both dwarf and tall strains from 12 to 30 inches high. They can withstand hot summers—a weakness in other stocks.

USES. At night, and on dull or rainy days, evening stocks send forth a captivating fragrance. Gardeners often plant them among more colorful, but unscented, flowers like Virginia stock (see *Malcomia*) so that the evening stocks' closed flowers will not be noticed during the day. Common stocks are excellent for beds; their densely flowered spikes also make splendid fragrant cut flowers. Stocks do best in moderately rich soil, full sun and cool temperatures (below 60° at night), but evening stocks will tolerate some shade. They require abundant moisture.

HOW TO GROW. Sow the seeds 8 inches apart outdoors as soon as the planting bed can be spaded and raked, or for earlier flowering start them indoors five to six weeks before the last frost is due. In Zones 9-10, sow stocks in early fall to blossom in late winter and early spring. After seedlings sprout, the double-flowering stocks, whose dense blooms provide richer color than single-flowered ones, can be favored during the thinning process. This is necessary even with the so-called double-flowering stock strains, for the breeding method provides seeds that rarely produce more than 50 per cent double flowers. Two ways may be used to select the singles to be discarded while they are in the seedling stage: the least vigorous seedlings are apt to be singles, and in strains such as Beauty of Nice, Giant Column and Large-Flowered Ten-Week, so are the dark-leaf seedlings. (Variations in leaf color, however, show up only when the plants are grown at about 50°.)

MATRICARIA See *Chrysanthemum*

MAURANDIA
M. barclaiana (maurandia).

This fast-growing vine from Mexico bears a wealth of white, rose or lavender to deep purple trumpet-shaped flowers about 3 inches long. A tender perennial in Zones 9-10, it is grown as an annual in cooler areas. The vines climb to a height of 6 to 10 feet.

USES. In addition to making fine hedges and screens when supported by a trellis or wires, maurandia will trail from a hanging basket. It requires abundant sun and rich soil.

HOW TO GROW. Sow the seeds indoors in midwinter or very early spring since the plants will not begin to flower until five months later. Transplant the seedlings to individual 3-inch peat pots. Set them outside, pots and all, when all danger of frost is past. For hanging baskets, transplant the seedlings into 5-inch flowerpots filled with potting soil and set the pots into the basket. The plants should be well watered and shaded until established, then placed in a light, well-ventilated place. They require plenty of water and occasional applications of liquid fertilizer.

MEALYCUP SAGE See *Salvia*

MENTZELIA
M. lindleyi, also called *Bartonia aurea* (blazing star).

Common wild flowers in many parts of the West, blazing stars are popular garden flowers because of their fragrant golden blossoms. The plants grow from 12 to 18 inches tall and produce flowers about 2½ inches across, which open in the evening and last until the next noon.

USES. Blazing stars make gaudy borders and also provide cut flowers (although they last only a short while in water, new buds quickly replace faded ones). They do well in windy spots if given full sun and well-drained soil.

HOW TO GROW. Sow the seeds where you want them to grow as soon as the ground can be worked, spacing plants 8 to 9 inches apart. They are difficult to transplant.

MAURANDIA
Maurandia barclaiana

BLAZING STAR
Mentzelia lindleyi

For climate zones and frost dates, see maps, pages 164-165.

LIVINGSTON DAISY
Mesembryanthemum criniflorum

MESEMBRYANTHEMUM

M. cordifolium variegatum, also called *Aptenia cordifolia variegata* (variegated heartleaf mesembryanthemum). *M. criniflorum*, also called *Dorotheanthus bellidiflorus* (Livingston daisy). *M. crystallinum*, also called *Cryophytum crystallinum* (ice plant). *M. gramineum*, also called *Dorotheanthus gramineus* or *M. tricolor* (tricolor mesembryanthemum). (All four species are called fig marigold.)

Thousands of species of South African succulents commonly known as fig marigolds are grouped together under the name *Mesembryanthemum*. The cultivated species listed above grow less than 6 inches tall and bear daisylike flowers ½ inch to 3 inches across. Flower colors cover a gamut from brilliant pink, red, white, lavender and yellow to more subtle hues, and some open only on sunny days. The Livingston daisy has 1-inch flowers of rose, buff, pink, crimson, apricot, orange or white colors. Ice plants and variegated heartleaf mesembryanthemums are noted more for their foliage than their flowers. The ice plant derives its name from its silver-flecked leaves, which look icy. The variegated heartleaf species has green and white leaves and rose-colored flowers. The tricolor species flowers profusely with pink, red or white blossoms.

USES. All species require full sun and do best in dry soil. They flourish in seaside gardens. The types listed here are excellent for windy places and can be used for window boxes and planters where their blossoms cascade over the edges. They also make fine edging plants since they seldom exceed a few inches in height. In Zones 9-10, particularly in dry areas of the West Coast, perennial species of fig marigolds are used as ground covers.

HOW TO GROW. Start the seeds indoors 10 to 12 weeks before the last frost or buy started plants late in the spring and set them 2 inches apart in the garden. If you plant the seeds outdoors, wait until all frost danger is past, then scatter the seeds and rake them into the soil. Thin seedlings to stand 2 inches apart. Plants started outdoors flower somewhat later than plants started indoors, but last longer.

MEXICAN FIRE PLANT See *Euphorbia*
MEXICAN PRICKLY POPPY See *Argemone*
MEXICAN SUNFLOWER See *Tithonia*
MEXICAN TULIP POPPY See *Hunnemannia*
MIGNONETTE See *Reseda*
MILKWEED, BLOODFLOWER See *Asclepias*

MIMOSA

M. pudica (sensitive plant, humble plant).

The sensitive plant's name comes from the startling ability of its leaves to fold up quickly upon being touched. Standing 2 feet high, the plant's foliage is graceful and fernlike, and the flowers of this Brazilian native are small puffs of pinkish lavender. (In some areas, the silk tree, *Albizia julibrissin,* and the true acacia, or Australian wattle, are erroneously called "mimosa.")

USES. Although sensitive plants can be used as edging or border plants, they are not particularly decorative. They are valued mainly as amusement, for their folding leaves. The plants require full sun and well-drained soil.

HOW TO GROW. Start the seeds indoors 10 to 12 weeks before the last frost. Sow the seeds in separate 3-inch peat pots so seedlings can be moved to the garden, pots and all, with a minimum of transplanting shock.

MIMULUS

Hybrids derived from *M. luteus, M. cupreus,* and *M. variegatus,* sometimes sold as *M. hybridus grandiflorus* and *M. tigrinus* (monkey flower).

SENSITIVE PLANT
Mimosa pudica

Monkey flowers get their name from the fancied resemblance of the blossoms to the faces of grinning monkeys. Actually the 2-inch flowers, borne on low, mound-shaped plants throughout the summer, look somewhat like small spotted gloxinias. Colors range mostly among bright shades of red as well as yellow with red spots. Plants grow 6 to 12 inches high. Most so-called annual monkey flowers are really delicate perennials that are treated as annuals; they originated in Chile.

USES. The brilliant monkey flower is one of the few annuals that does extremely well in shady spots and wet soil. Plants can also be brought indoors for winter flowering.

HOW TO GROW. Start the seeds indoors 10 to 12 weeks before the last frost is due and move the seedlings into the garden, spacing them 6 inches apart, when all danger of frost has passed.

MIRABILIS
M. jalapa (four-o'clock, marvel-of-Peru).

Four-o'clocks are so called because fresh blossoms open late in the afternoon. They remain open until the following morning—or longer on dull or rainy days. Their trumpet-shaped flowers are about 1 inch in diameter, 1 to 2 inches deep, and are borne on plants 2 to 3 feet tall. A dwarf strain grows to a height of only 18 to 20 inches. Colors range from white through pink, red, yellow and violet and often with more than one color appearing on a single plant. While four-o'clocks are perennials in tropical America, where they originated, they are treated as annuals in cold-winter climates.

USES. With four-o'clocks, you get a changed look for your garden every afternoon, when the flowers open to present a dazzling array of fresh color. They need a sunny location and well-drained soil.

HOW TO GROW. Sow seeds indoors four to six weeks before the last frost or outside when frost danger is past. In the garden, plants should be spaced at least 1 foot apart. Four-o'clocks can also be grown from the dahlialike tubers they produce, which can be dug up and stored over the winter if protected from freezing. Plants propagated in this way quickly develop into large and colorful specimens.

MOCK CUCUMBER See *Echinocystis*
MOLTEN FIRE See *Amaranthus*
MOLUCCA BALM See *Molucella*

MOLUCELLA
M. laevis (bells-of-Ireland, shell flower, Molucca balm, Irish bells).

The 1- to 2-inch, white-veined green bells that cling closely to the 2- to 3-foot stems of this annual are not really flowers but enlarged calyxes—the outer leaves that appear at the base of most flowers; the true flowers, tiny, fragrant and white, are deep within the bells. The popular names alluding to Ireland have been applied to this plant only because of the green color of the bells, not because the plant comes from Ireland; it is native to the eastern Mediterranean region. The name Molucca balm is also misleading since the Moluccas are a group of islands between Celebes and New Guinea in the South Pacific.

USES. Bells-of-Ireland grow well in average soil if given a sunny location. They make interesting and long-lasting cut flowers, and have additional value as dried flowers for winter arrangements. Dry them in a cool, dark, airy location and pick the sparse leaves off the stems so that the bells become more conspicuous.

HOW TO GROW. Since bells-of-Ireland are difficult to transplant, sow the seeds outdoors when there is no longer

MONKEY FLOWER
TOP: *Mimulus variegatus* hybrid
BOTTOM: *M. cupreus* hybrid

FOUR-O'CLOCK
Mirabilis jalapa

BELLS-OF-IRELAND
Molucella laevis

For climate zones and frost dates, see maps, pages 164-165.

137

BALSAM PEAR
Momordica charantia

WOODLAND FORGET-ME-NOT
Myosotis sylvatica

NEMESIA
Nemesia strumosa

any danger of frost, but while the weather is still cool. Space them 1 foot apart. They germinate best at 50°; germination takes 3 to 5 weeks.

MOMORDICA

M. balsamina (balsam apple). *M. charantia* (balsam pear).

Members of the gourd family, these are fast-growing African and Asian vines with distinctive ornamental fruit. The balsam apple's fruit is 2 to 3 inches long, egg-shaped, orange when ripe and somewhat warty in appearance. When mature, it splits open to exhibit a carmine interior. The balsam pear has 4- to 8-inch long, deeply furrowed, heavily warted fruit that is bright yellow. When ripe, it opens to reveal a bright red pulp. Both species have dark green, deeply lobed leaves 2 to 4 inches across and both species produce solitary yellow bell-shaped blossoms about an inch across.

USES. The vines of balsam apple and balsam pear thrive in rich moist soil and full sunlight. They make graceful covers for trellises, porches or fences, but will produce their decorative fruit only in areas with long, hot summers like those of the Gulf Coast and Southern California.

HOW TO GROW. For a head start on the growing season, begin the seeds indoors in individual 3-inch peat pots two to three weeks before the last frost is due. Or sow seeds directly into the garden when frost danger is past. Space plants to stand 8 to 12 inches apart in the garden.

MONARCH-OF-THE-VELDT See *Venidium*
MONKEY FLOWER See *Mimulus*
MOONFLOWER See *Calonyction*
MORNING GLORY See *Ipomoea*
MORNING GLORY, BUSH See *Convolvulus*
MORNING GLORY, DWARF See *Convolvulus*
MOROCCO TOADFLAX See *Linaria*
MOSS, ROSE See *Portulaca*
MOURNING BRIDE See *Scabiosa*

MYOSOTIS

M. sylvatica, also called *M. oblongata* (woodland forget-me-not).

A gardener might say that springtime is best exemplified by the sight of pink or golden tulips raising their pretty heads above an azure sea of forget-me-nots. But blue is not the only color of forget-me-nots—pink and white varieties are also available. The flowers, natives of Europe and North Asia, are tiny in themselves and are borne on plants only 9 to 12 inches tall.

USES. Forget-me-nots grow well in almost any soil in the sun or shade, but they do particularly well in cool places. They are incomparable for flower beds, make excellent edging and border plants, and provide lovely, long-lasting cut flowers for use in arrangements indoors.

HOW TO GROW. Forget-me-nots are often cultivated in much the same manner as pansies, with the seeds being sown outdoors in late summer or fall for plants that will begin to blossom early the following spring. In cold climates (Zones 3-8) special protection in cold frames is necessary to bring the plants through the winter. Seeds that are sown in early spring, if given partial shade during the hottest weather, will flower from late spring until midsummer. Forget-me-nots reproduce extremely easily from their own scattered seeds.

N

NASTURTIUM See *Tropaeolum*
NATAL GRASS See *Tricholaena*

NEMESIA

N. strumosa (nemesia).

A native of South Africa, nemesia grows to become about 1 foot tall, covered with masses of ¾-inch, cuplike flowers in 3-to-4-inch wide clusters. Their colors are white, yellow, bronze, pink, crimson or lavender-blue.

USES. Nemesia cannot tolerate much heat. It does best in cool coastal and mountainous regions, where night temperatures in summer can be expected to drop below 65°. There it thrives in full sun when set in moist soil enriched with compost or other organic matter. Given these conditions, it makes jewellike edging or borders and provides attractive cut flowers. It also is a fine plant for growing in pots and other containers.

HOW TO GROW. In Zones 3-8, nemesia is best started indoors or in cold frames four to six weeks before the last spring frost. In frost-free areas of Zones 9-10, sow the seeds any time in the fall for winter and spring flowering. Space the plants 6 inches apart.

NEMOPHILA

N. menziesii (baby blue-eyes).

Baby blue-eyes are wild flowers in California and serve as colorful annuals in gardens in the coastal and mountainous areas where night temperatures in summer can be expected to drop below 65°. The botanical name comes from the Greek words *nemos,* or grove, and *phileo,* to love, and alludes to the wild flower's preference for shady areas. The plants grow 6 to 8 inches high in mounds about 1 foot across. The flowers are about 1 to 1½ inches across, composed of five rounded petals arranged like an open cup; they are sky blue with white centers.

USES. Baby blue-eyes do well in light, well-drained soil either in the sun or in light shade. They are excellent for beds or borders and can be used effectively in rock gardens. Although they make attractive cut flowers, they do not last long in water.

HOW TO GROW. Sow the seeds outdoors as soon as the planting bed can be spaded and raked in the spring. Space them 6 inches apart; seedlings are difficult to transplant successfully. In frost-free areas of Zones 9-10, sow the seeds in the autumn in order to have flowers in the winter and early spring.

NICOTIANA

N. alata grandiflora, also called *N. affinis* (flowering tobacco).

With its heavy, pleasant fragrance—especially noticeable in the evening—and wide range of colors, this relative of commercially used tobacco is anything but hazardous to the health. Its masses of bright blossoms, including among many colors from white to scarlet such unusual offshades as wine, chartreuse and chocolate, are borne on trim 12- to 18-inch-tall plants. Each flower is about 2 inches across. Old-time varieties, natives of South America, did not open their blossoms until dusk, but modern strains are less recalcitrant and keep their flowers wide open throughout the hottest summer days.

USES. Flowering tobacco will grow in any garden soil in either full sun or light shade. The plants are particularly useful for flower borders and beds along the north side of a house, and they provide fragrant cut flowers for use in indoor arrangements.

HOW TO GROW. Sow the tiny seeds indoors four to six weeks before the last frost. Or buy young plants from a garden center, and set them in the garden 9 to 12 inches apart when all danger of frost is past. In Zones 9-10, the plants will sometimes survive more than one season.

BABY BLUE-EYES
Nemophila menziesii

FLOWERING TOBACCO
Nicotiana alata grandiflora

For climate zones and frost dates, see maps, pages 164-165.

CUPFLOWER
Nierembergia caerulea

LOVE-IN-A-MIST
Nigella damascena

SWEET BASIL
Ocimum basilicum (Dark Opal)

NIEREMBERGIA

N. caerulea, also called *N. hippomanica* (cupflower, nierembergia).

Cupflowers, which grow wild in Argentina, rank among the easiest to grow of the dwarf violet-blue edging plants. Plants grow about 6 inches tall and form mounds that bear continuous masses of 1-inch cup-shaped flowers.

USES. Given a sunny but not too hot location with plenty of moisture and rich soil, cupflowers make excellent edges and borders and can be used in window boxes and rock gardens. Where summers are hot and dry, the plants will do well in light shade if they are watered often.

HOW TO GROW. Sow the seeds indoors eight to 10 weeks before the last frost is due. Set seedlings in the garden 6 to 8 inches apart when all danger of frost has passed.

NIGELLA

N. damascena (love-in-a-mist, devil-in-a-bush, fennel flower, nigella).

This plant's 1½-inch blossoms, set in the fringe of threadlike foliage, resemble cornflowers in shape and color. They may be an intense blue or pure white as well as pink, rose, mauve and purple, and they grow about 1 foot tall. The plant is a native of the Mediterranean region.

USES. Nigellas do well in ordinary soil, if it is in full sun. They make fine cut flowers. The blooms are replaced by pale green seed pods with reddish brown markings, about 1 inch in diameter, excellent for winter arrangements. To preserve the pods, cut the stems when the pods are mature and hang them upside down in a shady place to dry.

HOW TO GROW. Sow the seeds outdoors as early in the spring as the ground can be cultivated, or in the fall for spring flowering. Space them 8 inches apart. Nigellas are difficult to transplant. Two or three sowings a month apart will extend nigella's short flowering season.

NONE-SO-PRETTY See *Silene*
NOTCHLEAF STATICE See *Limonium*

O

OAT, ANIMATED See *Avena*
OBCONICA PRIMROSE See *Primula*

OCIMUM

O. basilicum (sweet basil).

Both cooks and gardeners find sweet basil indispensable. Its fragrant leaves have been used for centuries as a flavoring for all sorts of dishes, but these bushy annuals, which grow wild in the Old World tropics, are also a visual treat in the garden. This is particularly true with the variety known as Dark Opal, which has deep purplish red leaves. Sweet basil grows about 15 inches tall and 1 foot wide and has 2-inch spikes of small white or purple-tinged flowers.

USES. Sweet basil is a striking foliage plant in beds and borders, and is effective in window boxes and planters. It does well in light sandy loam and full sun. While the plants are in blossom, cut a few plant tops and hang them upside down in a dry shady place to use as flavoring during the winter. Plants can also be pruned and moved into pots in the fall, to grow indoors on a sunny window sill.

HOW TO GROW. Start the seeds indoors two months before the last expected frost. Move the seedlings outdoors when all frost danger is past, setting them 12 inches apart.

OENOTHERA

O. deltoides, sometimes confused with *O. trichocalyx* (hairy-calyx sundrops).

Although there are about 200 species of sundrops, only

O. deltoides is readily available. The plant, which grows to a height of 12 to 18 inches, provides a constant supply of wide-open, sweetly scented 2½-inch cups throughout the summer. The flowers open as a pure white in the evening and stay open throughout the following day, turning pink as they fade. They grow wild in the Rocky Mountains.

USES. The plant does well in almost any well-drained soil in full sun or very light shade. The flowers are freshest at night and are prized for their evening fragrance.

HOW TO GROW. Start the seeds indoors six to eight weeks before the last frost is due, then set seedlings into the garden, 6 inches apart, when all frost danger is past.

ORACH See *Atriplex*
ORANGE CLOCK VINE See *Thunbergia*
ORCHID, POOR-MAN'S See *Schizanthus*
ORNAMENTAL CABBAGE See *Brassica*
ORNAMENTAL KALE See *Brassica*

OXYPETALUM

O. caeruleum (southern star, star-of-the-Argentine).

Southern star is seldom listed in seed catalogues, perhaps because the plant's dainty, blue, unscented flowers are not particularly noticeable. But viewed at close range they exhibit an exquisite starlike shape. Each silvery blue ½- to 1-inch blossom starts out as a pink bud, turns purple as it fades, and finally becomes lilac. The plant has heartshaped, downy leaves. A 3-foot shrub in its native Argentina, it rarely exceeds 18 inches as an annual.

USES. Southern stars do best in rich, well-drained soil and full sun. The plants may be dug from the garden six to eight weeks before the first frost and grown as house plants on sunny window sills during the winter. Trim them moderately in March to induce new growth and use this growth to root cuttings for the garden (*page 85*).

HOW TO GROW. Sow the seeds indoors six to eight weeks before the last frost is due; then set seedlings in the garden 6 to 8 inches apart when frost danger is past. The plants will begin to bloom eight weeks after the seed is planted. Seeds may be sown directly into the garden when temperatures no longer drop below freezing, but plants from such a seeding do not flower until late in the summer.

P

PAINTED TONGUE See *Salpiglossis*
PALMA CHRISTI See *Ricinus*
PANSY See *Viola*
PANSY GERANIUM See *Pelargonium*

PAPAVER

P. alpinum (Alpine poppy). *P. glaucum* (tulip poppy). *P. nudicaule* (Iceland poppy). *P. rhoeas* (Shirley poppy).

Some poppies grown as annuals are really perennials but because they seldom last more than two or three years, it is best to sow a new crop each season. Poppies are among the easiest of all flowers to grow. Their brilliantly colored flowers look like crinkled sheer silk and are often delightfully fragrant. The Alpine, a hardy dwarf species native to the high mountains of Europe, has wiry stems that rise 6 to 10 inches from gray-green foliage and produce sweetly perfumed 1- to 2-inch flowers in orange, yellow, apricot, pink, white and scarlet. Tulip poppies, natives of Asia Minor, grow to 20 inches tall and produce blossoms 4 to 5 inches across with scarlet petals that stay semierect, giving them the appearance of giant tulips. One plant may send out as many as 50 or 60 flowers in a two-month season. The foliage of Iceland poppies, which are found in many arctic and mountain regions, forms clumps 10 to 12 inches

HAIRY-CALYX SUNDROPS
Oenothera deltoides

SOUTHERN STAR
Oxypetalum caeruleum

TOP: CORN POPPY
BOTTOM: SHIRLEY POPPY
Papaver rhoeas

For climate zones and frost dates, see maps, pages 164-165.

wide and sends up 1½- to 2-foot slender stems topped by fragrant 2- to 4-inch blooms in the Alpine's range of colors including rose. The 1½- to 2½-foot Shirley poppy, with its 2- to 3-inch flower, is a cultivated version of the famous black-centered scarlet wild flower, the corn poppy of the fields of Flanders. It was named by the Reverend Mr. W. Wilks of Shirley, England, in 1880. Every Shirley poppy has white-based petals and the blooms range from white to shades of pink, orange and red.

USES. Poppies are most effective when massed in beds by themselves. Alpine poppies, which require good drainage, flourish in rock gardens. Icelands, Alpines and Shirleys make excellent cut flowers but must be handled properly. Cut them just as they lift their nodding buds erect but before the flowers open. To conserve their moisture, sear the stem ends immediately *(page 64)*. All poppies do best in full sun and light, well-drained soil that is not too fertile.

HOW TO GROW. Icelands are the only poppies that survive transplanting (and even they do not always), so most poppies are grown from seed outdoors. In Zones 3-7, sow seeds in the late fall so that no growth occurs during the winter. Even if the ground is frozen or covered with snow, the seeds require no covering. They drop into tiny crevices in the soil and sprout at the first sign of spring. In these zones, seeds can also be sown as early in the spring as the soil can be cultivated. In Zones 8-10, fall-sown seed will germinate in the fall and grow through the winter to blossom very early. In Southern California, for example, they come to full flower in February and March. Poppy seeds are exceptionally tiny—it takes over 200,000 to make an ounce. To sow them thinly yet hold a handful, mix them with fine dry sand. Plant the seeds in rows or broadcast them. Thin the plants as they emerge in early spring. Space Alpines about 6 inches apart, Icelands and Shirleys 8 to 12 inches apart and tulip poppies 12 inches apart. Spring-sown poppies are not as robust as fall-sown plants.

PATIENCE See *Impatiens*
PATIENT LUCY See *Impatiens*
PEAR, BALSAM See *Momordica*

PELARGONIUM

P. domesticum (Lady Washington geranium, also called Martha Washington, fancy, show, royal or pansy geranium). *P. peltatum* (ivy geranium). *P. hortorum* (common or zonal geranium, also called horseshoe or fish geranium). Scented-leaved varieties: *P. graveolens* (rose-scented geranium); *P. tomentosum* (peppermint-scented geranium); *P. odoratissimum* (apple-scented geranium); *P. fragrans* (nutmeg-scented geranium); *P. crispum* (lemon-scented geranium); and many others.

It has been said that geraniums, natives of South Africa, are known and loved by more people than any other flower in the world. Wherever there is a garden, chances are there is a geranium; they will grow almost anywhere with minimum care. Colors range from white, subtle pinks and brilliant reds to purplish black. In Zones 9-10, geraniums grow outdoors from year to year with little attention and become shrubby plants 4 to 5 feet tall, but in frost zones they are treated as small, delicate annuals. Lady Washington geraniums grow about 1 to 2 feet tall—except in Zones 9-10, where they may reach 3 feet—and have huge clusters of 2- to 4-inch single and double blossoms sometimes blotched with a darker shade on the two upper petals. Ivy and common geraniums produce single or double flowers. The ivy, so called for its ivy-shaped leaves and trailing growth, has graceful stems that extend sideways up to 4 feet. Common or zonal geraniums, the most popular spe-

TOP: LADY WASHINGTON GERANIUM
Pelargonium domesticum

LOWER LEFT: IVY GERANIUM
P. peltatum

LOWER RIGHT: COMMON GERANIUM
P. hortorum

cies, grow about 1 to 2 feet tall—except in Zones 9-10, where they may reach 6 feet. Zonal geraniums are named for the concentric markings on their leaves. The many species of scented geraniums have a variety of fragrances: rose, lemon, peppermint, apple, nutmeg and others. The perfumes emanate from the leaves, not the flowers.

USES. Ivy and common geraniums make superb bed, border and pot plants because they bloom throughout the garden season. The trailing stems of ivy geranium make it particularly effective in window boxes and hanging baskets or as a flowering ground cover. The Lady Washington is a less successful summer-flowering plant in many sections of the country since it needs temperatures below 60° to bud. It is usually grown by florists as a flowering pot plant for Mother's Day and Memorial Day. Most geraniums thrive in climates with dry summers, warm days and cool nights. They do best in full sun but grow well in partial shade if they have sun at least half of each day. The soil should be well drained and only medium rich.

HOW TO GROW. Home gardeners usually buy geraniums as budded or flowering pot-grown plants ready to set into the garden. Most plants are raised from cuttings (page 85) since common geraniums take five months to flower from seed. To start plants from seed, sow seeds indoors eight to 10 weeks before the last frost is due. Young seedlings should be transplanted into 2-inch pots when the first true leaves appear and shifted to 4-inch pots as they become larger. Keep the pots on a sunny window sill. The seeds germinate unevenly over a period of three to eight weeks. Transfer them to the garden outdoors after the danger of frost is past, setting them about a foot apart. When growing ivy geraniums in garden beds, place the plants 12 to 18 inches apart and pin the stems down with bent pieces of wire to train them to grow close to the ground.

PENNISETUM

P. ruppelii, also called *P. ruppelianum* and *P. setaceum* (fountain grass). *P. villosum,* also called *P. longistylum* (feathertop).

These ornamental grasses from Ethiopia add a special gracefulness to gardens and their seed heads are widely used in dried flower arrangements. Fountain grass grows as high as 4 feet and has slender flower stalks topped by tall, strikingly colored plumes of rose, purple and copper red. Feathertop's stems are 1 to 2 feet high with 2- to 4-inch plumes that are purplish white and very feathery. Both are tender perennials in mild and tropical climates.

USES. Fountain grass is usually placed against a wall or fence or used as an accent plant, while feathertop is used in edges and borders. Both species need well-watered fertile soil and full sunshine. For dried arrangements, cut flower heads when they are fully expanded, and hang them upside down to dry for a few days before handling them.

HOW TO GROW. Sow seeds indoors six to eight weeks before the last frost is due. Set plants outdoors 15 to 18 inches apart after all frost danger is past. Mature plants can be carried over from year to year if they are protected against freezing. In Zones 3-7, shield them in a deep cold frame. In Zone 8, simply cover the crowns with a thick layer of leaves; after frost danger is past, shear the plants to the ground, then dig them up, divide them into smaller clumps and replant. In Zones 9-10 they grow as perennials and need no winter protection.

PENSTEMON

P. gloxinioides (penstemon, beard tongue).

Most gardeners think of penstemons as perennials but the lesser-known hybrid varieties of *P. gloxinioides* flower

FOUNTAIN GRASS
Pennisetum ruppelii

PENSTEMON
Penstemon gloxinioides

For climate zones and frost dates, see maps, pages 164-165.

BEEFSTEAK PLANT
Perilla frutescens crispa

PETUNIA
Petunia hybrid

the first year and survive cold winters only with great difficulty, so it is safer to use them as annuals. The flowers have a nodding bell-like shape and flaring lips similar to those of gloxinias (hence their botanical name). Plants grow close to the ground in thick clumps of dark green foliage. Shooting up from the center are 2- to 3-foot stalks covered with white-throated blossoms about 2 inches across, in brilliant pink, red or scarlet as well as pale lavender and pure white. English plant breeders developed these hybrids by crossing *P. hartwegii,* which grows in cool regions of Mexico, and *P. cobaea,* which is found on prairies from Missouri to Texas. The name penstemon derives from the Greek *pente,* five, and *stemon,* stamen—each flower has five stamens. One of these stamens is covered with hairs and lies in the center of the flower—thus the name beard tongue.

USES. Penstemons are excellent cutting flowers and make graceful, long-lasting summer bouquets. Masses of one color create handsome flower borders. They need well-drained soil and grow in full sun or light shade.

HOW TO GROW. Penstemons may be sown outdoors but, because they require 12 to 14 weeks to flower from seeds, it is best to start them indoors at least six to eight weeks before the last frost is due. Keep the seedlings in full sunshine as much as possible during this period. Set seedlings into the garden after all frost danger is past. Space them 12 to 18 inches apart. Plant a few extra penstemons in a reserve or cutting garden and move them to fill vacancies in other plantings through the season; they transplant easily even in full blossom. To move a plant, water it well, then lift it with as much soil as possible and set it in the new spot. If this is done in cloudy weather and the plant is kept well watered, it will show little effect from the transfer.

PERILLA

P. frutescens crispa, also called *P. frutescens nankinensis* and *P. ocymoides crispa* (perilla, beefsteak plant).

The charm of perillas, which come from India and China, lies in their reddish purple foliage with its metallic bronzy sheen, but in the late summer, as a bonus of color, the 18- to 24-inch plants produce tiny pale lavender-pink or white flowers. The leaves grow in crisp, fringed pairs, each 2 to 3 inches long, and give off a spicy cinnamonlike fragrance when they are rubbed or bruised. Throughout the Orient perillas are grown commercially for their small nutlike seeds, which are pressed to yield a drying oil (perilla oil) used in the manufacture of paint and varnish.

USES. Perillas are excellent foils for white and brightly colored flowers in beds or borders. They can be used for hedges or for growing indoors or outdoors in pots. Tough and pest free, they withstand wind or driving rain and thrive in almost any dry to average soil in a sunny site.

HOW TO GROW. Sow seeds outdoors after the last frost. Or, for larger plants, start seeds indoors four to six weeks earlier. Space plants 12 to 15 inches apart in the garden. Six to eight weeks before the fall frosts arrive, take a few cuttings *(page 85)* to root for house plants.

PERIWINKLE See *Vinca*

PETUNIA

Many hybrids grouped under the name *Petunia* (petunia).

If an indispensable flower exists, it is probably the petunia, a native of South America, which adapts to almost every climatic condition and grows in an extraordinary variety of sizes, colors and shapes of blossoms. There are dwarf types 6 to 8 inches tall, and others that exceed 1 foot. Among their colors are solid red, crimson, blue, purple, pink, rose, coral, orange, salmon, cream and white as well as two-color combinations. The modern varieties provide larger and more vigorous blooms than could ever be obtained before, largely because of recent advances in flower hybridization. Until the mid-'50s, most petunia seeds came from established hybrid strains. These hybrids were inbred and standardized; their offspring, generation after generation, retained the same characteristics. Now seedsmen offer plants that are much better but are generally good only for a single generation. They come from seeds obtained by cross-pollinating two different inbred hybrids and are called F_1 hybrids (page 15). Petunia blossoms from F_1 seeds often are more than twice as large as those borne by either of the parent plants; they can be counted on to be the desired colors, and the plants have great vitality, known as hybrid vigor. These appealing qualities, however, seldom carry over to their offspring. Seeds produced from F_1 hybrid plants are F_2 hybrids, which are available at some seed stores; the flowers are generally better than those of inbred strains but not as good as those of F_1 plants. The splendid flowers of F_1 petunias, which now have almost replaced inbred strains in gardens, fall into four general categories: double multifloras, which have great quantities of double blossoms about 2 inches across; double grandifloras with fewer but larger double blossoms, some more than 3 inches across; single multifloras, with great numbers of 2- to 3-inch blossoms; and single grandifloras with huge blossoms sometimes almost 5 inches across, some with ruffled or fringed petals. Many petunias are fragrant, especially during the evening hours.

USES. Single grandifloras and multifloras are the best petunias to use in garden beds and borders since they withstand strong rain better than double varieties, whose heavy blossoms are apt to be knocked to the ground during showers. Double grandifloras and multifloras are most effective trailing from planters, window boxes and hanging baskets where they can be appreciated at eye level. Double petunias make stunning short-stemmed cut flowers. Try petunias as winter-flowering house plants; they do surprisingly well indoors. All petunias flower prolifically and thrive in a sunny location. They tolerate several hours of light shade provided they receive sunshine at least half of each day. They require loamy, well-fertilized soil and plenty of water during the summer.

HOW TO GROW. Sow seeds indoors in containers of potting soil covered with moist sphagnum moss eight to 10 weeks before the last frost is due. Since the seeds are tiny, some 300,000 to an ounce, they fall into crevices in the moss and need not be covered. When seedlings develop three or four leaves, transplant them to individual 2- to 3-inch pots. They may do better in a cold frame than in a warm room, for petunias are healthiest when they grow to the budding stage at a temperature of about 55°. Plant them outdoors 8 to 12 inches apart when all frost danger has passed.

PHACELIA

P. campanularia (California blue bells). *P. viscida,* also called *Eutoca viscida* (sticky phacelia). *P. tanacetifolia* (wild heliotrope, tansy phacelia).

The appeal of these flowers from the western United States is their striking range of shades of blue. California blue bells, which grow 8 to 9 inches tall, produce clusters of ¾- to 1-inch, bell-shaped blossoms of bright blue. Sticky phacelia, 18 to 24 inches tall, has hairy, viscous leaves (hence, the botanical name, *P. viscida*) and ½- to ¾-inch deep-blue flowers with blue-speckled white throats. The 18-

CALIFORNIA BLUE BELLS
Phacelia campanularia

For climate zones and frost dates, see maps, pages 164-165.

inch-tall wild heliotrope has lavender-blue flower heads.

USES. Phacelias are extremely effective in masses. They make handsome low borders and are suitable for rock gardens, too. Phacelias are not suitable as cut flowers because they last only a short while after being picked. The leaves may produce dermatitis when they are handled by people who are disposed to allergic reactions. All phacelias require hot, dry days and cool nights, and full sunshine is imperative. California blue bells do best in rather poor, sandy loam in a very dry location; the soil for sticky phacelia and wild heliotrope need not be quite so dry.

HOW TO GROW. In Zones 3-8, sow phacelia seeds outdoors in early spring after the last frost is due. They will flower in six or seven weeks. In Zones 9-10, sow them anytime in fall for spring flowering. They are difficult to transplant except when they are very small, so broadcast the seeds throughout the garden bed and rake them lightly into the soil or sow them in rows and cover them with $1/8$ inch of soil. As soon as the plants have grown an inch or two, thin California blue bells to stand 6 to 8 inches apart, sticky phacelia and wild heliotrope 12 to 15 inches apart. Phacelia will continue to blossom for 10 to 14 weeks under ideal conditions, but in areas where summer temperatures remain continuously in the 80s or 90s, they bloom only for a few weeks in the spring.

PHASEOLUS

P. coccineus, also known as *P. multiflorus* (scarlet runner bean). *P. c. albus* (white Dutch runner bean).

These old-fashioned twining climbers from the South American tropics still delight new generations with their brilliant red or white blossoms less than an inch across, borne in clusters like those of sweet peas. Most plants climb 6 to 8 feet high, although there are dwarf varieties that bear flowers from mounds of deep green leaves barely a foot tall. Beans follow the flowers and are edible.

USES. Runner beans make spectacular decorations, entwining the posts of a back porch or an arbor. They attractively cover walls, provided they have a trellis, strings or netting for support. The plants need full sun, plenty of water and moderately rich, well-drained soil.

HOW TO GROW. Plant runner bean seeds about a week before the last frost is due. Sow five or six seeds about 2 inches deep in moist soil around a pole or other support 6 or 8 feet high. Place the seeds no farther than 3 inches away from the support. When seedlings sprout, thin to three plants. The runners do not have to be trained around the support; they twine by themselves.

PHEASANT'S EYE See *Adonis*

PHLOX

P. drummondii (annual phlox, Texas pride, Drummond phlox).

Annual phlox is an abundantly flowering plant originally from Texas, where fields of the wild species still grow, and is a particularly good plant to use wherever the summer is long and hot. Although one strain of annual phlox becomes 15 to 18 inches tall, the dwarf plants, 6 to 8 inches high with individual blossoms 1 to $1/2$ inches across, are considered more desirable in a garden because they become solid mounds of flowers. Phlox supplies a remarkable color range: many shades of pink, red, scarlet, yellow, lavender and bicolored as well as pure white.

USES. Annual phlox makes handsome beds and wide borders, and serves well in rock gardens and window boxes. The large compact clusters of annual phlox make good short-stemmed flowers for low bouquets. The plants grow

SCARLET RUNNER BEAN
Phaseolus coccineus

ANNUAL PHLOX
Phlox drummondii

in any good, well-drained garden soil with full sun or very light shade.

HOW TO GROW. Sow annual phlox seeds outdoors, where you want the plants to grow, after the last frost is due. To have early-flowering plants, you can sow seeds indoors four to six weeks before the last frost and transplant the seedlings to the garden when the danger of frost is past. Space seedlings to stand 6 inches apart in the garden. To rejuvenate straggly plants, cut stems to about 2 inches from the ground; they will soon send out new flowers.

PIMPERNEL See *Anagallis*
PINCUSHION FLOWER See *Cenia; Scabiosa*
PINK, CHINA See *Dianthus*
PINK, FRENCH See *Centaurea*
PINK SAND VERBENA See *Abronia*
PLUMED THISTLE See *Cirsium*
POINSETTIA, ANNUAL See *Euphorbia*
POLYANTHUS PRIMROSE See *Primula*
POOR MAN'S ORCHID See *Schizanthus*
POPPY See *Papaver*
POPPY, CALIFORNIA See *Eschscholzia*
POPPY, MEXICAN TULIP See *Hunnemannia*
POPPY, PRICKLY See *Argemone*

PORTULACA

P. grandiflora (portulaca, rose moss, sun moss, wax pink).

This pretty little annual from Brazil grows about 6 inches tall and produces many flowers about an inch in size that open every morning in the sunshine and form a carpet of color. The shining petals of the roselike single or double blossoms appear in shades of rose, salmon, pink, scarlet, orange, yellow and white. Its narrow, fleshy leaves are almost hidden by the flowers, which open only in sunshine.

USES. In a hot, dry location where most flowers will not grow, portulaca will prosper—on banks, along a driveway, in a rock garden, as a ground cover or in patio planters. To thrive, they need little more than sunshine and soil, preferably rather poor soil.

HOW TO GROW. Sow seeds outdoors after the last frost or start them indoors four to six weeks earlier. Outdoors, broadcast the very fine seed mixed with dry sand. They need no thinning or spacing. Young plants transplant easily. Mature plants may spread their own seed, so once portulaca is planted, it often reappears from year to year.

POT MARIGOLD See *Calendula*
PRICKLY POPPY See *Argemone*

PRIMULA

P. malacoides (fairy or baby primrose). *P. obconica* (obconica primrose). *P. polyantha* (polyanthus primrose).

Fairy and obconica primroses, which come from China, are such tender plants that in Zones 3-8 gardeners usually think of them only as winter- and spring-flowering house plants. But in coastal California from San Francisco southward they are popular garden flowers, and even the perennial primrose, the polyanthus, is sometimes grown as an annual. The plants of all three species grow about 12 to 18 inches high, with masses of flowers. The pink, red and white flowers of fairy primrose bloom in tiers on slender stems, while obconica blossoms, which are white, pink, lavender or reddish purple, form great clusters at the tops of the stems. Polyanthus primroses, hybrids created in Europe, come in almost any color and the individual blossoms in a flower cluster are often the size of a silver dollar. Tiny hairs on the underside of the leaves of obconica primroses may produce a rash on the skin of allergy-prone people.

PORTULACA
Portulaca grandiflora

PRIMROSE
Primula polyantha

For climate zones and frost dates, see maps, pages 164-165

UNICORN PLANT
Proboscidea louisianica

KUDZU VINE
Pueraria lobata

USES. Since primroses cannot withstand extreme heat any better than they can frost, they must be protected from direct sun. They are often massed under the shade of high trees or used as container plants on shady patios. They are also useful in rock gardens and in borders. They require moist, fertile soil as well as light shade.

HOW TO GROW. Primroses are so fussy about growing conditions that they can be grown from seed only in the controlled weather of a greenhouse. Most home gardeners buy plants that are already started; in California, the seedlings are set outdoors in early fall and bloom from midwinter until late spring.

PRINCE'S FEATHER See *Amaranthus*

PROBOSCIDEA
P. louisianica, also known as *P. jussieui, Martynia louisiana, M. proboscidea* (unicorn plant, proboscis flower, devil's claw).

The unicorn plant is a rank-growing, ill-scented wild flower of the south-central United States that is cultivated in gardens for its strange seed pods. These are 4 to 6 inches long and bear a curious resemblance to an elephant's trunk. When they ripen, they split into two parts, giving the plant its name, devil's claw. The flowers of the unicorn plant are 1½ to 2 inches across and yellowish white, lavender or pink, with saffron and violet dots and lines. The leaves and young stems are covered with sticky hairs.

USES. Unicorn pods make decorative dried arrangements; dry the stems with pods attached by hanging them, upside down, in a dry, shady place.

HOW TO GROW. In Zones 3-7, start seeds indoors four to six weeks before the last frost is due, and set seedlings into the garden in rich soil in a sunny spot when all frost danger is past. In all zones, seeds can be sown outdoors as soon as the soil can be cultivated in the spring. Plants should stand about 5 feet apart in a site away from the regular flower garden to allow them to spread with their customary vigor and to keep their unpleasant scent from overwhelming more delicately perfumed plants.

PROBOSCIS FLOWER See *Proboscidea*

PUERARIA
P. lobata, also known as *P. hirsuta* and *P. thunbergiana* (kudzu vine).

Although the kudzu vine is a woody twiner from Asia whose above-ground stems are hardy in Zones 7-10, it may be treated as an annual in northern areas because of its rapid growth in its first season. In warm southern states, old, well-established kudzu vines grow as much as 50 feet tall and bear 6- to 10-inch spikes of small purple, pealike flowers that, though fragrant, are often hidden beneath the thick foliage. When grown as an annual in Zones 3-6, the vine grows 10 to 15 feet tall and does not usually bloom; flowers emerge only from two-year-old stems and most northern winters kill all the plant above ground, although the roots often survive to grow for many seasons.

USES. The kudzu vine is most valued for its large, hairy leaves that provide dense shade for an arbor or a splendid screen on a fence. In the South, the vine is sometimes cultivated for forage and for erosion control (and has spread to become a weed that covers large areas with impenetrable thickets). In its native Asia, the starchy kudzu roots are used as food. Kudzu vines will flourish in any garden soil provided they are given full sunlight.

HOW TO GROW. Sow the seeds outdoors after frost danger has passed, about 3 inches away from the support on which the vine is to climb. When seedlings emerge, thin to 3 or 4 at each support. The vines will twine without aid and need little attention.

PURPLE RAGWORT See *Senecio*
PYRETHRUM See *Chrysanthemum*

Q

QUAKING GRASS See *Briza*

QUAMOCLIT

Q. coccinea, also called *Ipomoea coccinea* and *Mina sanguinea* (scarlet star glory, star ipomoea). *Q. lobata,* also called *I. versicolor* and *M. lobata* (crimson star glory, Spanish flag). *Q. pennata,* also called *I. quamoclit* (cypress vine). *Q. sloteri,* also called *I. cardinalis* (Cardinal climber).

These graceful twining vines, natives of tropical South America, are extremely popular in the U.S. South and West. Their brilliant flowers and leaves of various shapes offer filtered shade from the sun and delightful touches of color on arbors or porches. Scarlet star glories usually grow about 10 feet tall and have deep green leaves in a sharply defined heart shape and funnellike, yellow-throated scarlet flowers about 1½ inches across that are shaped like miniature versions of their botanical cousin, the morning glory *(Ipomoea).* Crimson star glories, which may grow 15 to 20 feet tall, have similar flowers, except that their funnellike blooms are somewhat larger and their crimson color fades to yellow as they mature. Their leaves are deeply lobed. Cypress vines, which often grow about 15 feet tall, have delicate, finely divided foliage that is extremely attractive but provides relatively little shade. Its flowers are about 1½ inches across and each petal is pointed, creating the effect of a star. One variety called Hearts and Honey has scarlet blossoms with yellow centers, and still another variety, *Q. pennata alba,* produces white flowers. The cardinal climber is a hybrid of the scarlet star glory and the cypress vine and is larger than both progenitors. The vine can grow as tall as 20 feet; it sprouts fernlike leaves, and its white-throated crimson flowers, also resembling morning glories, are at least 1½ inches across.

USES. Since these vines grow quickly and bloom all summer long, they are excellent plants for a wall, trellis or arbor. The cypress vine is especially effective on a trellis, where its leaves as well as flowers may be displayed most handsomely. All species of the vine need well-drained, light, sandy loam. They take full sun or partial shade.

HOW TO GROW. Quamoclit seeds are hard and will germinate more quickly if they are softened. Soak the seeds overnight in tepid water before sowing to weaken the shell and permit water to enter the seed easily, or nick the seeds with a file. In any zone, sow outdoors after all frost danger has passed. Or start the plants indoors 4 to 5 weeks before the last frost is due, placing 2 seeds in each 3-inch pot. When the seedlings sprout, discard the weaker of the two to obtain a plant more likely to survive transplanting. Space the seedlings 1 foot apart, about 3 inches from their supports. They will entwine the supports as they grow.

R

RABBIT-TAIL GRASS See *Lagurus*
RAGGED SAILOR See *Centaurea*
RAINBOW CORN See *Zea*
RAT-TAIL STATICE See *Limonium*
RATTLE-BOX See *Crotalaria*
RED MAIDS See *Calendrinia*
RED MOROCCO See *Adonis*

TOP: SCARLET STAR GLORY
Quamoclit coccinea

CENTER RIGHT: CYPRESS VINE
Q. pennata

LOWER LEFT: CARDINAL CLIMBER
Q. sloteri

For climate zones and frost dates, see maps, pages 164-165.

MIGNONETTE
Reseda odorata

CASTOR BEAN
Ricinus communis

GLORIOSA DAISY
Rudbeckia hirta gloriosa

RESEDA
R. odorata (mignonette).

Mignonette, a native of North Africa, is probably the most fragrant of all garden annuals. Its sweet perfume atones for the plant's relatively drab appearance. Most mignonettes stand about 1 to 1½ feet tall and have thick stems and 6- to 10-inch spikes covered with small greenish yellow, yellowish brown, or brownish red blooms.

USES. Mignonettes planted by a doorstep, under windows or in pots on window sills can fill a house with their fragrance. They can also be planted in beds and borders or added to indoor arrangements. They prefer fertile soil, shade at least part of the day, and cool weather. In very hot, dry weather, they have a short flowering season.

HOW TO GROW. In all zones, seeds may be sown outdoors in early spring after all frost danger has passed. A planting three or four weeks later will extend the summer flowering season. In Zones 9-10, sow in the late fall or winter for bloom in early spring. Do not cover seeds; rake the soil lightly, drop the seeds sparingly on the surface, and pat the soil down firmly. Thin seedlings to stand 10 inches apart; crowded plants produce inferior flower spikes. Mignonette does not transplant well.

RHODANTHE See *Helipterum*

RICINUS
R. communis (castor bean, castor oil plant, palma christi).

Castor beans, thought to have originated in Africa, are tropical annuals whose huge palmlike leaves create an exotic effect. The plant may grow 10 or more feet tall in a single summer; leaves are generally 1 to 3 feet across, each leaf bearing five to 12 deeply cut lobes. Young leaves have a distinct red-and-bronze coloration. The unimpressive petalless reddish brown flowers are borne in 1- to 2-foot clusters both at the tops of the plant and on side stems. They are almost hidden by the foliage. The prickly seed husks contain large shiny seeds resembling ticks—hence the botanical name *Ricinus,* Latin for tick. The seeds are poisonous, so castor beans should never be planted where children play. Also, some people have allergic reactions to the foliage and the spiny seedpods. The beans yield castor oil, for which the plant is grown commercially in India.

USES. Castor beans are best used as quick-growing background plantings to hide unsightly areas. They need rich soil, good drainage, full sun, plenty of heat and moisture.

HOW TO GROW. In Zones 3-7, start the seeds indoors six to eight weeks before the last frost is due. Before sowing, soak the hard-coated seeds in water for 24 hours, or nick them with a file. Then plant them in individual pots. Set the seedlings in the garden 3 feet apart when frost danger is past. In Zones 8-10, where a plant may live for several years and become 20 feet or more tall, the seeds should be sown outdoors in spring after all frost danger has passed.

ROCK PURSLANE See *Calandrinia*
ROCKET CANDYTUFT See *Iberis*
ROCKY MOUNTAIN GARLAND See *Clarkia*
ROSE EVERLASTING See *Helipterum*
ROSE-OF-HEAVEN See *Silene*
ROSE MOSS See *Portulaca*
ROSE SUNRAY See *Helipterum*
ROYAL GERANIUM See *Pelargonium*
RUBY GRASS See *Tricholaena*

RUDBECKIA
R. hirta gloriosa, also called *R. hybrida* (gloriosa daisy).

These hybrid versions of black-eyed Susans, first developed in the United States, are grown in millions of gardens around the world. They could be called glorious brown-eyed Susans, after their brown centers, which are surrounded by yellow, gold or mahogany petals that form large flowers, many of which are double blossoms 6 inches across. One variety has green centers and is called Irish eyes. The 2- to 3-foot-tall plant is a perennial but can be used as an annual because it blooms the first year.

USES. Gloriosa daisies are superb, long-lasting cut flowers and cutting encourages the plants to send out more blossoms. They brighten beds and borders and require only ordinary soil. They do well in full sun or light shade.

HOW TO GROW. In all zones, sow the seeds outdoors anytime in the fall or as early in the spring as the ground can be cultivated. Plants can be moved easily and should be spaced 12 to 15 inches apart. They often reproduce by distributing their own seed.

RUNNER BEAN, SCARLET See *Phaseolus*
RUNNER BEAN, WHITE DUTCH See *Phaseolus*
RUSSIAN STATICE See *Limonium*

S

SAGE See *Salvia*

SALPIGLOSSIS
S. sinuata (painted tongue).

Painted tongues are relatives of the petunia that originated in Chile. They have slender, wiry stems usually 2 to 3 feet tall topped by trumpet-shaped flowers 2 to 2½ inches across. The blossoms have a rich velvety texture and appear in muted shades of gold, scarlet, rose, crimson, mahogany and blue, all decorated with delicate veining that enhances their beauty. Two hybrid strains, called Splash and Bolero, are bushy plants that retain the delicate color of older varieties but flower more abundantly.

USES. Painted tongues make excellent cut flowers. They are also useful as background plants in borders and go well between perennials in the garden. They require sun and protection from the wind, and do best in fertile soil.

HOW TO GROW. These plants grow slowly when they are small, so start the seeds indoors eight weeks before the last frost is due or buy plants that are already started. Set the seedlings 1 foot apart in the garden when all danger of frost has passed. Insert a few pieces of brush around them to help support the slender stems.

SALVIA
S. farinacea (mealycup sage). *S. horminum* (clary).
S. patens (gentian sage). *S. splendens* (scarlet sage, salvia).

Of the *Salvia* species listed above, one, clary, is a true annual, and three—scarlet sage, mealycup sage and gentian sage—are tender perennials that flower from seed their first season. The plants blossom in tiers around tall stems, sometimes with distinct spaces between the blooms, sometimes densely massed. Mealycup sage, a native of Texas, is one of the airy varieties. Each lavender flower, less than an inch across, is held in a calyx (the leafy cup under the petals) that looks as though it had been dusted with flour; hence the name mealycup. Flower stems rise from mounds of silvery foliage and generally reach 3 feet in height. Clary sage, from southern Europe, may be a foot shorter and produces blue, pink, purple or white bracts beneath tubular flowers less than an inch long; the flowers appear at the top of the stems in spike-shaped clusters. Gentian sage, from Mexico, usually grows less than 2 feet tall with spikes of delicately drooping indigo-blue tubular flowers, gener-

PAINTED TONGUE
Salpiglossis sinuata

LEFT TO RIGHT: SCARLET SAGE, *Salvia splendens;* MEALYCUP SAGE, *S. farinacea;* CLARY, *S. horminum;* GENTIAN SAGE, *S. patens*

For climate zones and frost dates, see maps, pages 164-165.

CREEPING ZINNIA
Sanvitalia procumbens

PINCUSHION FLOWER
Scabiosa atropurpurea

ally about 2 inches long. Scarlet sage, from Brazil, is available in assorted strains that grow from 8 to 30 inches in height. The flowers are firm, dense tubes of magnificent scarlet with equally vivid scarlet bracts and are ¾ to 1 inch in size. Some strains of "scarlet" sage produce flowers in other colors, including pink, purple and white.

USES. Sage plants are handsome in flower beds or foundation plantings. Two mealycup varieties, Blue Bedder and White Bedder, are especially attractive massed in gardens and are excellent for cutting. Clary sage may be used as cut flowers or dried for winter arrangments; to dry, cut flowers at their peak and hang them upside down in a cool, shady place. The vivid red of scarlet sage may be overpowering if mixed with other colors; give the plants a corner of their own or use white flowers as a foil. Scarlet sage does not retain its color when cut. All species need fertile, well-drained soil and full sun or very light shade.

HOW TO GROW. In Zones 3-8, sow sage seeds indoors four to six weeks before the last frost is due and set seedlings outdoors when frost danger has passed, or sow outdoors when night temperatures will not drop below 50°. For indoor germination, maintain a 65° to 70° temperature until the seedlings sprout; then grow them at a 55° night temperature. Set them in the garden 12 inches apart. They will generally bloom from July until frost. In Zones 3-8, the roots of gentian sage may be stored indoors in sand in a cool place for replanting in spring. In Zones 9-10, all species are usually sown outdoors in February or March.

SAND VERBENA See *Abronia*

SANVITALIA
S. procumbens (creeping zinnia).

This pretty little plant from Mexico produces its daisylike flowers—yellow, single or double, with purple centers—throughout the summer and fall. Rarely topping 6 inches in height, it bears many flowers, each about 1 inch across. Its stems tend to trail along the ground.

USES. Creeping zinnias are fine for edgings and rock gardens. They need light, well-drained soil and sun.

HOW TO GROW. Creeping zinnia seedlings do not transplant easily, so sow the seeds in the area where the plants are to grow. In Zones 3-8, sow in the spring, as soon as the ground can be spaded and raked. Space plants 5 or 6 inches apart to allow plenty of room for the stems to creep. In Zones 9-10, seeds sown any time in the fall will produce flowers from early spring throughout the summer and fall.

SATINFLOWER See *Godetia*

SCABIOSA
S. atropurpurea (pincushion flower, sweet scabious, mourning bride).

The name pincushion flower describes this native of southern Europe accurately. The huge rounded flower head, as much as 3 inches across, does resemble a pincushion with dozens of silvery stamens poking out like pins. Sweet scabious has a sweet fragrance; scabious, from the Latin *scabiosus,* an itch, indicates it was once thought to cure itching. The name "mourning bride" describes the effect of a white wedding bouquet carried at the center of blooms of one variety that are almost black. The plant may grow 1½ to 2½ feet tall. In addition to a near-black color and white, flowers come in shades of pink, blue, salmon, coral, rose, red and maroon.

USES. With their unusual color range, pincushion flowers are handsome and long lasting in bouquets. They are beautiful in flower beds among other flowers or massed alone.

They require full sunlight and fertile, well-drained soil.

HOW TO GROW. Sow pincushion flower seeds indoors five or six weeks before the last frost is due. Acclimate the seedlings to outdoor conditions by placing them in a cold frame for a week or two. Transplant to the garden when all frost danger has passed. Space them about 9 inches apart. In Zones 3-7, seeds may be sown directly in the garden when frost danger has passed. In Zones 8-10, sow the seeds in the fall for early summer flowering.

SCABIOUS, SWEET See *Scabiosa*
SCARLET FLAX See *Linum*
SCARLET RUNNER BEAN See *Phaseolus*
SCARLET SAGE See *Salvia*
SCARLET STAR GLORY See *Quamoclit*
SCENTED-LEAVED GERANIUMS See *Pelargonium*

SCHIZANTHUS
S. wisetonensis (butterfly flower, poor man's orchid).

The odd botanical name of this lovely plant from Chile derives from the Greek *schizo*, to split, and *anthos*, flower, and refers to the deeply cleft segments of the bloom. Some varieties may grow 2 feet tall, others only half as high. The flowers, about 1½ inches across, are usually bicolored in brilliant combinations of pink, crimson, violet and purple, as well as white, all heavily veined with gold.

USES. Butterfly flowers are highly effective in flower beds because of their surprising colors and profuse flowering. In window boxes and hanging baskets, they cascade over the edges in a brilliant display. They also make good cut flowers. They do best in cool weather, full sun or light shade, and a moist soil, and flourish especially well in regions where night temperatures in summer drop below 65°.

HOW TO GROW. In Zones 3-8, start seeds indoors six to eight weeks before the last frost is due, or sow them outdoors when all danger of frost is past. Move seedlings started indoors into the garden when all frost danger has passed, spacing them 1 foot apart. In Zones 9-10, start the seeds outdoors any time in the fall for flowers in late winter and spring. Though the plants bloom profusely, the flowering season is short; extend it in all zones by sowing outdoors every two weeks for six weeks. Taller strains require twigs or brush to hold them upright (*page 43*).

SEA LAVENDER See *Limonium*
SEA PURSLANE See *Atriplex*

SENECIO
S. cineraria, also known as *Cineraria maritima* (dusty miller). *S. cruentus*, also known as *C. hybrida* and *C. grandiflora* (cineraria). *S. elegans*, also known as *Jacobaea elegans* and *J. erecta* (purple groundsel, purple ragwort).

Senecio is a large, diverse genus of some 1,300 species. Its name derives from the Latin *senex*, old man, because its seeds sprout hairlike appendages as white as an old man's whiskers. Dusty miller, native to southern Europe and a perennial in Zones 9-10, is grown as an annual in Zones 3-8 because of its handsome woolly-white first-year foliage. Modern varieties become 8 to 15 inches tall as annuals, but in Zones 9-10 some varieties grow 2 to 2½ feet tall, spreading the blunt-tipped lobes of their 6- to 8-inch leaves equally wide and sending up 2½- to 3-inch flat-topped clusters of tiny yellow flowers the second year. The plant's names are confusing. Its common name, dusty miller, is shared with other plants (see *Centaurea*). Worse, its species name, *cineraria*, is the common name for a different species of the same genus. The plant popularly called cineraria is a perennial from the Canary Islands

BUTTERFLY FLOWER
Schizanthus wisetonensis

LEFT: CINERARIA
Senecio cruentus

TOP RIGHT: GROUNDSEL
S. elegans

BOTTOM RIGHT: DUSTY MILLER
S. cineraria

For climate zones and frost dates, see maps, pages 164-165.

known to northern gardeners primarily as a house plant, but in cool, moist, frost-free areas of Zones 9-10, it can be planted outdoors as an annual. It usually grows 12 to 15 inches tall with lush green leaves and large clusters of 1- to 2-inch velvety daisylike flowers. Colors range from pink, red and lavender to deep purple and blue, with white, blush and two-color combinations. Purple groundsel, from South Africa, has single or double daisylike blossoms 1½ to 2 inches across, on 18-inch stems. They are mauve, purple, crimson, rose or white, with yellow centers.

USES. Dusty miller lends distinctive beauty to flower beds and window boxes with its shimmer of silvery leaves. Cineraria is effective too for shaded patios and terraces. Purple groundsel provides masses of color in the garden and fine cutting flowers. Dusty miller flourishes in dry to average soil and full sun; cineraria needs rich, moist soil in a cool, lightly shaded site; purple groundsel grows best in light, sandy loam and full sun.

HOW TO GROW. In Zones 3-8, sow dusty miller seeds indoors 10 to 12 weeks before the last frost is due. Set seedlings into the garden 10 to 12 inches apart after all frost danger has passed. In Zones 9-10, it can be planted any time in the winter or spring. Cineraria requires cool, moist conditions but cannot stand even light frost. In Zones 9-10, sow seeds indoors in fall or early spring; plant seedlings, 8 to 10 inches apart, in sheltered areas outdoors when danger of frost is past. Water them frequently. Purple groundsel is sown indoors in Zones 3-8, eight to 10 weeks before the last frost is due. Set the young plants outside 6 inches apart when all danger of frost has passed. In Zones 9-10, sow purple groundsel in the garden in the fall for spring flowers or in early spring for summer flowers.

SENSITIVE PLANT See *Mimosa*
SHELL FLOWER See *Molucella*
SHEPHERD'S CLOCK See *Anagallis*
SHIRLEY POPPY See *Papaver*
SHOW GERANIUM See *Pelargonium*
SIBERIAN WALLFLOWER See *Cheiranthus*
SIGNET MARIGOLD See *Tagetes*

SILENE

S. armeria (none-so-pretty, sweet William catchfly). *S. pendula,* also known as *S. graeca* and *S. rosea* (drooping catchfly). *S. oculata,* also known as *S. coeli-rosa, Lychnis coeli-rosa* and *Viscaria cardinalis* (rose-of-heaven).

On the leaves of some varieties of *S. armeria* is a sticky fluid that flies can get entangled in; hence, the common name sweet William catchfly. The plant, a native of Europe, usually grows about 15 inches tall. Its pink flowers are each generally less than an inch across but grow in 2- to 3-inch clusters. Most drooping catchfly grows only about 6 inches tall. Its great quantities of flowers, usually ½ inch across, are borne in drooping sprays of pink, salmon, scarlet or white. Rose-of-heaven is a lovely annual generally about 1 foot tall with abundant 1-inch cup-shaped red, pink, purple, lavender, blue or white flowers that face upward. Few American seed catalogues list the species, but it can be ordered from England.

USES. These species are good in beds, borders and rock gardens because of their long flowering season as well as their moderate size. Rose-of-heaven is fine for cut flowers but none-so-pretty and drooping catchfly are not long lasting. The plants do best in full sun and well-drained soil.

HOW TO GROW. For early summer flowering in all zones, sow *Silene* seeds any time in the fall where the plants are to grow, spaced 6 to 9 inches apart. For midsummer blooms, sow as soon as the ground is workable in the spring.

TOP: NONE-SO-PRETTY
Silene armeria

BOTTOM: DROOPING CATCHFLY
S. pendula

SNAPDRAGON See *Antirrhinum*
SNOW-ON-THE-MOUNTAIN See *Euphorbia*
SOUTHERN STAR See *Oxypetalum*
SPIDER FLOWER See *Cleome*
SPURGE See *Euphorbia*
SQUIRRELTAIL GRASS See *Hordeum*
STAR GLORY, SCARLET See *Quamoclit*
STAR IPOMOEA See *Quamoclit*
STARDUST See *Gilia*
STAR-OF-TEXAS See *Xanthisma*
STAR-OF-THE-VELDT See *Dimorphotheca*
STATICE See *Limonium*
STOCK See *Mathiola*
STOCK, VIRGINIA See *Malcomia*
STRAWBERRY, ALPINE See *Fragaria*
STRAWFLOWER See *Helichrysum*
SUCCORY, BLUE See *Catananche*
SUMMER ADONIS See *Adonis*
SUMMER CYPRESS See *Kochia*
SUMMER FORGET-ME-NOT See *Anchusa*
SUMMER POINSETTIA See *Amaranthus*
SUN MOSS See *Portulaca*
SUNDROPS, HAIRY-CALYX See *Oenothera*
SUNFLOWER See *Helianthus*
SUNFLOWER, MEXICAN See *Tithonia*
SUNRAY, ROSE See *Helipterum*
SUNSET HIBISCUS See *Hibiscus*
SUNSHINE DAISY See *Gamolepis*
SWAN RIVER DAISY See *Brachycome*
SWAN RIVER EVERLASTING See *Helipterum*
SWEET ALYSSUM See *Lobularia*
SWEET BASIL See *Ocimum*
SWEET PEA See *Lathyrus*
SWEET PEA, GOLDEN YELLOW See *Crotalaria*
SWEET SCABIOUS See *Scabiosa*
SWEET SULTAN See *Centaurea*
SWEET WILLIAM, ANNUAL See *Dianthus*
SWEET WILLIAM CATCHFLY See *Silene*

T

TAGETES

T. erecta (African or Aztec marigold). *T. patula* (French marigold). Hybrids of *T. erecta* and *T. patula* (African-French hybrid marigolds). *T. tenuifolia pumila*, also known as *T. signata pumila* (dwarf marigold, sometimes called signet marigold).

Marigolds are among the most popular flowers in American gardens, in all zones, because they reward gardeners with immense quantities of bright color and they are exceedingly easy to grow. Marigold colors range from near-white and cream through vivid yellow and orange to brownish red and maroon. Most marigolds have a pungent fragrance, but several varieties have foliage and flowers with no scent. All garden marigolds are descended from wild Mexican species that have been developed and hybridized to produce four separate types. The tallest one is the African or Aztec marigold. These plants generally grow 18 inches to 3 feet tall and bear globe-shaped 3½- to 5-inch double blossoms, mostly in off-white, yellow or shades of orange. There are many flower types among African or Aztec marigolds, some resembling chrysanthemums, others carnations. French marigolds are relatively low-growing; most stand 6 to 18 inches tall and have 1- to 2-inch single or double flowers in many shades of yellow, orange, mahogany red or combinations of these colors. African-French hybrids combine the colors of both species with 2- to 3-inch double flowers; they are sturdy plants whose height and spread varies from 12 to 18 inches. Dwarf marigolds are

TOP: AFRICAN MARIGOLD   CENTER: FRENCH MARIGOLD
Tagetes erecta   *T. patula*

BOTTOM RIGHT: DWARF MARIGOLD
T. tenuifolia pumila

For climate zones and frost dates, see maps, pages 164-165.

BLACK-EYED SUSAN VINE
Thunbergia alata

DAHLBERG DAISY
Thymophylla tenuiloba

generally about 12 inches tall and have fernlike foliage much finer than that of the other three types. Stems are topped by masses of single yellow or golden-orange flowers about an inch across.

USES. Marigolds serve every garden purpose—they show off their colors in beds, borders and terrace pots, mixed with other flowers or massed alone. Even the taller types stand up well to wind and heavy rain, and all have vivid beauty and long life as cut flowers. (Their versatility extends beyond garden uses. In Mexico, acres of orange-flowered marigolds are grown for chicken feed; when the blossoms are fed to hens, the eggs have the dark yellow yolks that Mexican housewives demand. Scientists have also observed that parasitic worms called nematodes disappear from soil in which marigolds have grown.) Marigolds flourish in ordinary garden soil in sunny locations.

HOW TO GROW. Marigold seed is very easy to start; sow indoors from four to six weeks before the last frost is due. Set the plants in the garden after the last frost is due. Or, at this time, sow seeds outdoors or buy started plants and set them out. Space taller varieties 12 to 18 inches apart, dwarf varieties about 6 inches apart. In Zones 9-10, marigolds can be sown outdoors at any time.

TAHOKA DAISY See *Aster*
TASSEL FLOWER See *Amaranthus* and *Emilia*
TELANTHERA See *Alternanthera*
TEXAS BLUEBONNET See *Lupinus*
TEXAS PRIDE See *Phlox*
THIMBLE FLOWER, BLUE See *Gilia*
THISTLE, PLUMED See *Cirsium*
THROATWORT See *Trachelium*

THUNBERGIA

T. alata (black-eyed Susan vine). *T. gibsonii* (orange clock vine).

These vines from tropical Africa are tender perennials that can be treated as annuals since they flower abundantly the first year. Black-eyed Susan vines are low, twining climbers; they seldom grow more than 6 feet high. They bear arrowhead-shaped leaves. Flowers are generally between 1 and 2 inches across; each stands separately. Most, but not all, have a black center and five clearly defined petals of white, buff, yellow or orange. The orange clock vine bears somewhat larger blossoms in a glowing orange.

USES. These vines are excellent for window boxes, hanging baskets and ground cover. They can be trained to a low trellis, wall or fence. They will grow in light shade as well as full sun and require fertile, moist soil.

HOW TO GROW. Start seeds indoors four to six weeks before the last frost is due. Seeds take two to three weeks to sprout and grow very slowly as young seedlings. Set seedlings outdoors when you can be sure night temperatures will not drop below 50°; a slight frost will kill even mature plants. Place seedlings about 3 inches away from the supports they will be climbing. Since *Thunbergia* vines climb by twining, strings or netting make suitable trellises.

THYMOPHYLLA

T. tenuiloba, also called *Hymenatherum tenuilobum* (Dahlberg daisy, golden fleece).

The Dahlberg daisy is a little-known but attractive annual from Texas and Mexico that seldom grows more than 8 inches tall and produces finely divided aromatic foliage. The leaves are almost hidden by great numbers of daisy-like golden-yellow flowers, usually about ½ inch in size.

USES. Dahlberg daisies are especially good in southern gardens because they continue to thrive even during long spells of hot weather. They make good edgings for borders and brighten rock gardens. The flowers are excellent for small indoor bouquets. Dahlberg daisies do best in full sun and well-drained, light, sandy loam.

HOW TO GROW. In Zones 3-8, sow seeds indoors 10 to 12 weeks before the last frost is due—plants often take four months to begin to flower. Set them in the garden 6 inches apart when all frost danger is past. In Zones 9-10, sow seeds outdoors any time in the fall or very early spring; they will bloom from early summer into winter.

TICKSEED See *Coreopsis*
TIDY TIPS See *Layia*

TITHONIA

T. rotundifolia, also known as *T. speciosa* (tithonia, Mexican sunflower, golden-flower-of-the-Incas).

Mexico and Central America are the sources of this flower and its graphic common names. In the sun, the flowers glow the orange-red of rough gold. The plant grows very tall, the original species sometimes reaching a towering 6 feet. However, varieties for garden use generally grow about 4 feet tall and bear blossoms approximately 3 inches in diameter.

USES. Tithonia flowers are good for cutting, provided the hollow stems are carefully seared *(page 64)* and put in a vase of warm (100°) water. The plants are large and vigorous enough to serve as a temporary hedge. As background plantings in a garden, their height allows them to be seen and appreciated from a distance. Tithonia needs full sun and grows in nearly any kind of soil. Since it is drought- and heat-resistant, it is good for desert gardens.

HOW TO GROW. Sow seeds outdoors when you can be sure night temperatures will not drop below 50°, or start them indoors about six weeks before the last frost is due. Set indoor-started plants in the garden about 2 feet apart after all frost danger has passed. They are fast growers and will soon fill the gaps solidly, but it may be three to four months from sowing before the plants produce flowers.

TOADFLAX See *Linaria*
TOBACCO, FLOWERING See *Nicotiana*

TORENIA

T. fournieri (wishbone flower, torenia).

In the throat of torenia flowers are a pair of stamens, or pollen-bearing filaments, bent to the shape of a chicken's wishbone, hence its common name, wishbone flower. This Vietnamese plant, common in the tropics and subtropics, is welcome in American gardens as one of the few annuals that thrive in shade. Most wishbone flower plants grow about 1 foot tall and bear hosts of trumpet-shaped bicolored blossoms about an inch across; the upper lip is light violet and the lower lip dark purple. Some types are white with yellow throats or yellow with purple throats.

USES. These little plants are attractive in garden borders, pots and hanging baskets. In Florida and along the Gulf Coast, they are sometimes used to edge walks and patios. They make unusual and attractive house plants. Wishbone flowers require warm, moist soil and partial shade. They will take full sun only in regions where night temperatures in summer usually drop below 65°.

HOW TO GROW. Start seeds indoors 10 to 12 weeks before the last frost is due, moving seedlings outdoors when night temperatures will not drop below 60°. Or sow them outdoors when all danger of frost has passed. Space plants 6 to 8 inches apart in the garden. Pot a few for house plants six to eight weeks before the first frost is due.

TITHONIA
Tithonia rotundifolia

WISHBONE FLOWER
Torenia fournieri

For climate zones and frost dates, see maps, pages 164-165.

THROATWORT
Trachelium caeruleum

BLUE LACE FLOWER
Trachymene caerulea

RUBY GRASS
Tricholaena rosea

TOUCH-ME-NOT See *Impatiens*

TRACHELIUM

T. caeruleum (throatwort).

The appeal of throatwort lies in its large cloudlike clusters of faintly fragrant, tiny, star-shaped violet or blue blossoms, which generally grow to a size of 3 to 5 inches above serrated foliage on wiry stems 2 to 3 feet tall. The common name, which sounds more like an infection than a pretty cluster of flowers, comes from the Greek, *trachelos,* meaning neck; the plant, a native of the Mediterranean area, once was believed to heal diseases of the trachea. Throatwort is a perennial in frost-free areas of Zones 9-10, but elsewhere it is grown as an annual.

USES. The flower clusters are fine for cutting and appear like pale blue froth among other flowers in beds. They require little care and will grow in average garden soil with either full sun or partial shade.

HOW TO GROW. Sow seeds indoors eight to 10 weeks before the last frost is due. Move seedlings into the garden after all frost danger has passed, spacing them 12 inches apart. Early sowing is essential; plants may not begin to blossom until five months after they are sown. Late-sown plants produce only foliage the first season and flower the following season in Zones 9-10; otherwise seeds sown indoors in midwinter will blossom by midsummer.

TRACHYMENE

T. caerulea, also known as *Didiscus caerulea* (blue lace flower).

The blue lace flower, a plant from Australia, may be described as a glorified version of the wild flower Queen Anne's lace. Its tiny sky-blue flowers, and the flowers of its white counterpart, Lace Veil, blossom in sweet-scented clusters resembling 2- to 3-inch umbrellas at the top of stems that are usually about 2½ feet tall.

USES. Blue lace flowers are good for bouquets because they last a long time after being cut. They make decorative additions to a flower bed. They do best in light soil and full sun, but they require night temperatures in summer below 70°. They do not do well in hot weather.

HOW TO GROW. Sow the seeds outdoors, where you intend the plants to grow, as early in spring as the ground can be cultivated, or start them indoors six to eight weeks before the last frost is due and move seedlings outdoors when all danger of frost has passed. In the garden, space plants 12 inches apart. When they are half-grown, insert some brush among them to keep them from toppling over in a strong wind.

TRAILING LANTANA See *Lantana*
TREASURE FLOWER See *Gazania*
TREE MALLOW See *Lavatera*

TRICHOLAENA

T. rosea, also known as *Rhynchelytrum repens* (ruby grass, Natal grass).

This African grass is a perennial that is customarily grown from seed and treated as an annual. It usually grows 3 to 4 feet tall and bears pyramidal clusters of silky spikelets that first are the color of red wine and then, with age, turn purple.

USES. The plants are handsome when used as a background for a border. Stems may be dried for use in winter bouquets upright in a vase, to achieve a graceful curve, or hung upside down in a dry, shady place for straight stems. Ruby grass will grow in any sunny garden but does best when given a light, well-drained soil.

HOW TO GROW. Sow the seeds outdoors as early in the spring as the ground can be cultivated, 12 to 18 inches apart. The grass will quickly grow into attractive clumps.

TRICOLOR CHRYSANTHEMUM See *Chrysanthemum*

TROPAEOLUM

T. majus (common nasturtium). *T. peregrinum* (canary-bird flower). *T. speciosum* (flame flower).

"Be nasty to nasturtiums" is an old gardening adage. The advice is sound, for kindness, in the form of frequent feeding and watering, often produces luxuriant leaves but few flowers. Nasturtiums are, therefore, excellent plants for beginning or forgetful gardeners, who can cultivate them with every assurance of success. They grow as wild flowers from Mexico south to Chile and come in double- and single-flowering varieties of both climbing vines and bushy plants. Dwarf types seldom grow more than 1 foot tall; climbers can grow as high as 6 to 10 feet. The spurred flowers of the common nasturtium, generally about 2 inches across, blossom in a wide variety of colors: creamy white, salmon, golden yellow, orange, scarlet, cerise, mahogany and deep red. They all have a tart fragrance, but the scent of the double-flowered varieties is stronger than that of the single-flowered ones. The bright green leaves of the common nasturtium are shaped like little shields. The canary-bird flower, a vine, has five-lobed leaves and bears smaller yellow flowers distinguished by feathery petals. Flame flower, another vine of this genus, produces flowers 1 to 1½ inches across in brilliant scarlet.

USES. Common nasturtiums make excellent cut flowers, especially when they are arranged with their distinctively shaped leaves. Dwarf varieties are good as edging plants for flower beds or vegetable gardens and trail attractively from hanging baskets or planters. Vines will decoratively cover fences, trellises, stumps and rocks. Young nasturtium leaves have a flavor like watercress and may be used in salads. Any light, sandy loam that is poor in nutrients, and sun at least part of the day, are all nasturtiums require in order to thrive. Common nasturtiums do well in dry soil; canary-bird flowers and flame flowers prefer average to moist soil. Canary-bird flowers and flame flowers do best in regions with cool summers where night temperatures usually fall below 65°; in hot areas, they need light shade at midday.

HOW TO GROW. Since the plants are not easy to transplant, sow seeds outdoors where plants are desired when all danger of frost has passed. Space dwarf varieties 6 inches apart, vines 12 inches apart. Aphids, tiny insect pests, are fond of nasturtiums and, given the opportunity, cluster under the leaves and buds *(pages 50-51)*. Nicotine sulfate, used according to the directions on the container, is the best remedy.

TRUMPET FLOWER See *Datura*
TULIP POPPY See *Papaver*
TULIP POPPY, MEXICAN See *Hunnemannia*
TWINSPUR See *Diascia*

U

UNICORN PLANT See *Proboscidea*

URSINIA

U. anethoides, also known as *Sphenogyne anethoides* (dill-leaf ursinia).

Ursinias, which are native to South Africa, are not always easy to obtain in the United States, but you can generally send to England for seeds. The effort is worth it; the plant

LEFT: COMMON NASTURTIUM
Tropaeolum majus

RIGHT: CANARY-BIRD FLOWER
T. peregrinum

URSINIA
Ursinia anethoides

For climate zones and frost dates, see maps, pages 164-165.

MONARCH-OF-THE-VELDT
Venidium fastuosum

GARDEN VERBENA
Verbena hortensis

GOLDEN CROWNBEARD
Verbesina encelioides

is a pretty combination of richly scented, feathery foliage and vividly colored flowers. The daisylike blooms, 2 to 3 inches across, are orange or yellow with a center ring of purple. They top thin, wiry stems that grow about 18 inches tall. Sometimes the plant blossoms so profusely the foliage is totally hidden. Like many South African plants, the flowers close at night and on cloudy days.

USES. Ursinias are colorful additions to borders and provide splendid cut flowers. They will also flower indoors as house plants. They require light, well-drained, rather poor soil and much sunshine.

HOW TO GROW. Sow seeds indoors four to six weeks before the last frost is due. Move seedlings outdoors when all frost danger has passed, spacing them 6 to 9 inches apart in the garden.

V

VENIDIUM

V. fastuosum (monarch-of-the-veldt).

This South African plant grows about 2 feet tall and comes vibrantly alive when its buds open into 4- to 5-inch daisylike flowers of brilliant orange with an inner zone of purplish black and a center of shiny black. Pale varieties of the flower are also available: white, ivory, cream and shades of lemon. As striking as the big flowers are the plant's silver-white, featherlike, hairy leaves, which shimmer as though they were covered with finely spun cobwebs.

USES. The monarch-of-the-veldt makes colorful contributions to borders and is an excellent cutting flower although the blossoms close at night and on cloudy days. It thrives only in well-drained, light, sandy loam and needs abundant sunshine.

HOW TO GROW. Sow seeds indoors six to eight weeks before the last frost is due. As soon as night temperatures remain above 50°, set seedlings in the garden 1 foot apart. In Zones 9-10, sow outdoors any time from midsummer to late winter and early spring.

VERBENA

V. hortensis, also known as *V. hybrida* (garden verbena).

These tender hybrid perennials, treated as annuals, spread as they grow and produce a multitude of flowers in their first season. Upright-growing strains make mounds about a foot high, while carpeting varieties creep along the ground. The delightfully fragrant verbena flowers bloom in flat clusters 2 to 3 inches across and range in color from snowy white to pink, red, blue, lavender and purple. Many of the colored flowers have contrasting white centers.

USES. Since verbenas provide solid masses of color they are good choices for ground covers, for garden beds and edgings, or for any location where a low carpet of color is needed. Verbena is also attractive in rock gardens and in window boxes. Plants require full sun and fertile soil.

HOW TO GROW. Sow verbena seeds indoors about three months before the last frost is due. Move seedlings into the garden when night temperatures remain above 50°, spacing them 1 foot apart. Or buy started plants. In frost-free areas of Zones 9-10, garden verbenas may act as perennials, but they are usually renewed from seeds each year because old plants become straggly.

VERBENA, PINK SAND See *Abronia*

VERBESINA

V. encelioides, also known as *Ximenesia encelioides* (golden crownbeard, butter daisy).

The golden crownbeard is a native of the West, growing wild from Montana to Mexico. It ranges in height from 2 to more than 3 feet and bears its golden flowers, which are about 2 inches across, like flamboyant daisies.

USES. Since the plants become so large, they are best planted toward the back of a border or in a wild-flower garden. They are fine for cutting. If soil is well drained, they will thrive in any sunny garden.

HOW TO GROW. As soon as the ground can be cultivated, sow the seed outdoors where the plants are to grow, since they are difficult to transplant successfully. Space so seedlings will be 18 inches apart.

VINCA

V. major variegata (variegated periwinkle). *V. rosea*, also known as *Catharanthus roseus* (Madagascar periwinkle).

The pert variegated periwinkle, native to Europe, is a tender perennial evergreen vine that is treated as an annual except in Zones 9-10 because it flowers the first year and has poor resistance to frost. The plant has trailing stems that root as they spread and carry dark green 1- to 3-inch leaves that are marked with white. The plants put forth 1- to 2-inch lavender-blue flowers with five flat, round-edged petals. Madagascar periwinkles, native to tropical areas, are a bushier species, growing 10 to 18 inches tall with glossy leaves and 1- to 2-inch flowers; these blossom in rose, pink and white, or white with a pink center.

USES. Variegated periwinkles are often planted in window boxes and terrace pots, where they trail attractively over the edge of the container. In Zones 9-10, the plant makes an excellent ground cover, especially when it is sheared occasionally to bring on new growth. Madagascar periwinkles are valued for the summer and fall color they provide everywhere, but are especially welcome in desert regions of the West. Periwinkles thrive in almost any soil and prefer some shade, although they will grow in sunny sites provided they are well watered.

HOW TO GROW. Start Madagascar periwinkle seeds indoors three or four months before the last frost is due, or buy started plants. Set the seedlings in the garden 8 to 10 inches apart after all danger of frost has passed. This plant is a perennial in Zones 9-10. New plants are usually started from seeds early each spring, however, because old plants become unkempt in appearance. They flower most freely in hot weather. The variegated periwinkle must be started from cuttings rather than seeds. These will root at any season, but usually they are taken during winter months so that good-sized plants will be available to set out when night temperatures remain above 50°.

VIOLA

V. wittrockiana, also known as *V. tricolor hortensis*, *V. tricolor maxima*; *V. tricolor* (both called pansy). *V. williamsii*, descended from *V. cornuta* and other species (viola, tufted pansy).

The wonderful diversity of the colors and markings of pansies, hybrids originally created in Europe, has made them one of the best loved and most widely known of all cultivated flowers. Although they are tender perennials, pansies are at their best the first year from seed, and deteriorate rapidly thereafter, so they are usually grown as annuals or biennials. Pansies are low plants, growing about 8 inches tall. They are distinguished by delicately fragrant 2- to 3-inch flowers of five overlapping petals looking like gigantic violets, except that the colors are purple, white, blue, dark red, rose or yellow combined in almost endless variations of stripes and blotches. Often the patterns look like small, smiling faces. Violas, which grow 6 to 8 inches tall, bear flowers about 1½ inches across, each with a slender spur. These come in a variety of solid colors: blue, yel-

PERIWINKLE
Vinca rosea

PANSY
TOP LEFT: *Viola wittrockiana*
TOP RIGHT: *V. tricolor*
BOTTOM RIGHT: *V. wittrockiana*
CENTER LEFT AND RIGHT: *V. williamsii*

For climate zones and frost dates, see maps, pages 164-165.

STAR-OF-TEXAS
Xanthisma texanum

COMMON IMMORTELLE
Xeranthemum annuum

low, apricot, ruby red and white. Violas usually flower longer than pansies, but their blossoms are smaller.

USES. Pansies and violas provide brilliant masses of velvety color in borders and edgings. They are handsome in pots and window boxes and make delightful small bouquets of cut flowers. Frequent picking keeps new flowers coming. They do best in full sun in most localities; where summer temperatures often exceed 90° they need light shade. Soil should be moist and fertile.

HOW TO GROW. There are several ways to obtain pansies and violas for your garden. Most gardeners buy started plants and set them out in the spring; often such plants have already started to bloom. Seeds started indoors 10 to 12 weeks before the last frost is due will produce flowering plants by late spring. Seeds sown outdoors in late summer or early fall will produce plants that can be protected in a cold frame over the winter; set in the garden after the last frost in the spring, they will quickly start to bloom. In Zones 9-10, summer-planted pansies and violas grow through the winter and produce masses of color in late winter and spring, though they need to be replaced by other flowers when hot summer weather arrives.

VIPER'S BUGLOSS See *Echium*
VIRGINIA STOCK See *Malcomia*

W

WALLFLOWER See *Cheiranthus*
WAX BEGONIA See *Begonia*
WILD CUCUMBER See *Echinocystis*
WINGED EVERLASTING See *Ammobium*
WISHBONE FLOWER See *Torenia*
WOODLAND FORGET-ME-NOT See *Myosotis*
WOODRUFF, ANNUAL See *Asperula*
WOOLFLOWER See *Celosia*

X

XANTHISMA
X. texanum (star-of-Texas).

Star-of-Texas, a native of that state, is a little-known annual that grows 18 to 30 inches tall and bears 2- to 3-inch citron-yellow flowers with daisylike petals fanning out from the center.

USES. The blossoms make excellent cut flowers. They also brighten dry open spaces or wild gardens. The plant does very well in poor, dry soil under a hot sun.

HOW TO GROW. Sow the seeds of the star-of-Texas outdoors where the plant is to grow. In all zones, seeds may be planted any time in the fall or early spring. Space plants 6 inches apart. Staking is usually necessary to hold the flowers upright.

XERANTHEMUM
X. annuum (common immortelle).

The common immortelle, a native of fields around the Mediterranean, is usually grown because it makes a striking addition to an arrangement of dried flowers. The plants reach a height of 2 to 3 feet and produce 1½-inch single and double flowers about 1½ inches across that are, at first glance, similar to daisies. But the petals have an unusual, attractive, papery texture. The colors range through shades of rose, pink and purple as well as white.

USES. These flowers are eye-catching in a garden border and are excellent for use in fresh-flower arrangements as well as for drying. For use in winter bouquets, blossoms should be cut when they are fully opened and hung upside down in bunches in a cool, airy location until dry. The plants need light garden soil and abundant sunlight.

HOW TO GROW. Since common immortelle is very difficult to transplant, sow the seeds where the plant is to grow in the spring after all danger of frost has passed. Space plants 1 foot apart. Place twiggy brush among the half-grown plants to keep them upright.

Y

YELLOW COSMOS See *Cosmos*

Z

ZEA

Z. mays japonica (rainbow corn, striped maize).

A novelty annual for a garden is this ornamental corn, which grows about 5 to 6 feet tall and has leaves that are striped green, pink, yellow and white. The ears, which are 6 to 8 inches long, are not edible by humans. The origin of corn plants in general is a matter of controversy. Although corn was a basic food for Indians of North and South America long before white men arrived, no wild corn has ever been discovered. One theory is that corn originated as a natural hybrid between grasses in Mexico; another theory claims that it is a species of plant kept in cultivation by men after its wild progenitors became extinct.

USES. Rainbow corn, with its colorful variegated foliage, is used primarily as a garden ornament and is tall enough to serve as a screen. It requires fertile soil and full sun.

HOW TO GROW. Sow seeds where you want the plants to grow after all frost danger has passed; seedlings are readily nipped by a late cold spell. Space seeds so plants will stand 8 to 12 inches apart.

ZINNIA

Z. elegans (zinnia). *Z. linearis* (narrow-leaf zinnia).

Zinnias, invariably the last flower in an alphabetical listing of annuals, often come first in preference among gardeners because they are so easy to grow and because their brilliant flowers are so handsome. Zinnias come in many heights and flower sizes and forms. Some are less than 1 foot tall with round flower heads less than 1 inch across, while others tower 3 feet tall and bear 7-inch blossoms on strong, wiry stems. Zinnia colors once were harsh and their petals coarse, a double heritage from their wild Mexican progenitors, but the plants have been subject to much development and improvement. The color range has softened; modern varieties include such colors as apricot, rose, cream, white, violet, pale yellow and even green, as well as the familiar bright red and orange. Multicolored and striped varieties are also available. The narrow-leaf zinnia, which grows about a foot tall, has flowers usually 2 inches in diameter that are golden yellow with petal tips of a darker shade.

USES. The many varieties of zinnia are decorative in borders, in edgings, in garden beds and in arrangements of cut flowers—in short, they are the all-purpose garden annual. They add much color to late-summer gardens when most annuals are past their prime. Any good garden soil and a sunny location are all that zinnias require to flourish.

HOW TO GROW. Start zinnia seeds indoors four to six weeks before the last frost is due, and move seedlings outdoors when all frost danger has passed. Seeds may also be sown outdoors, where the plants are to grow, when night temperatures remain above 50°. Zinnias like hot weather, and when temperatures are cool they simply stand still. In the garden, space plants 6 to 12 inches apart, depending on their expected height.

ZINNIA, CREEPING See *Sanvitalia*
ZONAL GERANIUM See *Pelargonium*

RAINBOW CORN
Zea mays japonica

ZINNIA
Zinnia elegans

For climate zones and frost dates, see maps, pages 164-165.

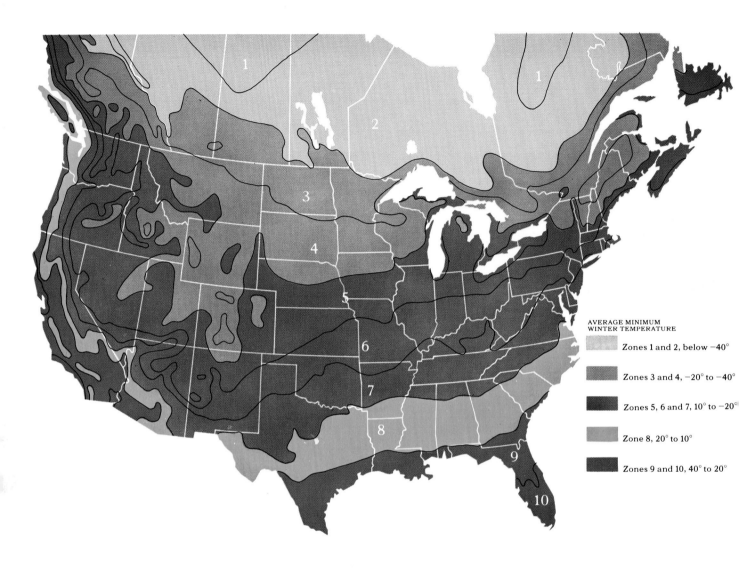

AVERAGE MINIMUM
WINTER TEMPERATURE

Zones 1 and 2, below −40°

Zones 3 and 4, −20° to −40°

Zones 5, 6 and 7, 10° to −20°

Zone 8, 20° to 10°

Zones 9 and 10, 40° to 20°

Winter cold and annuals—climate zones

Almost any annuals can be grown anywhere, but how and when they are to be started depends on two aspects of winter conditions indicated on the maps on these pages and specified in the plant encyclopedia, Chapter 5. The map above shows a simplified version of the climate zones worked out by Donald Wyman of the Arnold Arboretum of Harvard University. This severity of winter determines whether plants instead of seeds must be set into the garden, whether seeds can be sown in the fall, and whether some frost-susceptible perennials can be cultivated as annuals.

In Zones 1 and 2 *(top color band)* winters are so cold—and summers so short—that all annuals must be started indoors and transplanted into the garden as well-established plants; otherwise there may not be enough time for flowers to appear before fall frost kills the plants. Even in Zones 3 and 4, tender annuals such as torenias and verbenas may not produce flowers from seeds sown outdoors. In Zones 5-7, almost every annual listed in the encyclopedia can be grown from seed outdoors, and in Zones 3-7 frost-susceptible perennials such as wax begonias and geraniums can be grown as annuals if started indoors. In the warm Zones 9 and 10, and with some risk in Zone 8, annuals may be started outdoors any time, but fall planting for winter and spring flowers is favored.

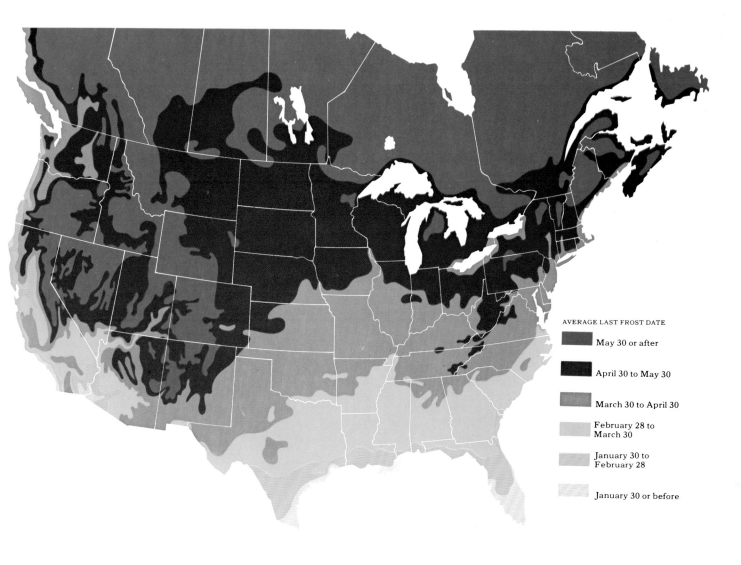

AVERAGE LAST FROST DATE

May 30 or after

April 30 to May 30

March 30 to April 30

February 28 to March 30

January 30 to February 28

January 30 or before

Spring planting times — average dates of last frost

While climate zones *(left)* supply general guidance for starting annuals, specific times are best gauged by the date of the last frost. The time when this critical change in seasonal weather conditions comes to various regions is indicated by the color bands on the map above and is used as a reference point in the planting instructions given for the annuals in the encyclopedia section of this book, Chapter 5.

Because some annuals germinate and grow slowly, they are best started indoors before frost ends and afterward transplanted into the ground outdoors, as indicated in the encyclopedia. Others—the so-called half-hardy plants such as hollyhocks and larkspur—may be started from seed outdoors even before the last frost, but if they are started indoors, seedlings should not go into the ground until the frost danger has passed. In most regions (see climate-zone data), however, most annuals can be grown from seeds sown outdoors after the date of the last frost.

The dates given on the maps are long-term averages; actual dates may vary from the averages by at least a week or two. Also, both frost and minimum temperatures within a zone are affected by local conditions of terrain, wind and nearness to bodies of water. For specific local data, consult the nearest office of the U.S. Weather Bureau.

Characteristics of 249 annuals and plants treated as annuals

Plant	FLOWER COLOR							PLANT HEIGHT				LIGHT AND SOIL REQUIREMENTS						USES							
	White	Yellow-orange	Pink-rose	Red	Blue-purple	Multicolor	Colored foliage	6 to 12 inches	1 to 2 feet	2 to 3 feet	Over 3 feet	Sun-average soil	Sun-dry soil	Sun-moist soil	Partial shade-average soil	Partial shade-dry soil	Partial shade-moist soil	Cut flowers	Fragrance	Dried flowers (everlastings)	Ornamental grasses	Climbing vines	Hedges, screens	Window boxes, planters	Hanging baskets
ABRONIA UMBELLATA (pink sand verbena)			●					●				●	●					●	●					●	●
ABUTILON HYBRIDUM (flowering maple)	●	●	●		●				●			●			●									●	●
ADONIS AESTIVALIS (summer adonis)				●					●			●			●	●	●								
ADONIS AUTUMNALIS (autumn adonis)				●					●			●			●	●	●								
AGERATUM HOUSTONIANUM (ageratum)	●		●		●	●	●	●				●											●		
AGROSTEMMA GITHAGO (corn cockle)			●							●		●		●											
AGROSTIS NEBULOSA (cloud grass)	●							●				●	●	●				●		●	●				
ALONSOA WARSCEWICZII (mask flower)		●	●					●	●			●													
ALTERNANTHERA AMOENA (Tom Thumb alternanthera)							●	●				●	●										●		
ALTERNANTHERA BETTZICHIANA (garden alternanthera)							●	●				●	●										●		
ALTERNANTHERA VERSICOLOR (copper alternanthera)							●	●				●	●										●		
ALTHAEA ROSEA (hollyhock)	●	●	●	●						●	●	●											●		
* AMARANTHUS CAUDATUS (love-lies-bleeding)			●				●			●	●	●								●					
* AMARANTHUS HYPOCHONDRIACUS (prince's feather)			●				●			●	●	●								●					
* AMARANTHUS SALICIFOLIUS (flaming fountain)							●			●		●	●												
* AMARANTHUS TRICOLOR (Joseph's coat)							●			●		●	●												
AMMOBIUM ALATUM (winged everlasting)	●									●		●	●							●					
ANAGALLIS ARVENSIS (pimpernel)	●		●	●				●				●	●											●	
ANAGALLIS LINIFOLIA (flaxleaf pimpernel)				●	●			●	●			●	●											●	
ANCHUSA CAPENSIS (summer forget-me-not)					●				●			●			●	●									
ANCHUSA CAPENSIS ALBA (white summer forget-me-not)	●								●			●			●	●									
ANTIRRHINUM MAJUS (snapdragon)	●	●	●	●	●	●		●	●	●	●	●						●	●						
APHANOSTEPHUS SKIRRHOBASIS (lazy daisy)	●							●				●	●					●							
ARCTOTIS GRANDIS (arctotis)	●	●	●			●			●			●	●					●							
ARGEMONE GRANDIFLORA (prickly poppy)	●									●			●												
ARGEMONE MEXICANA (Mexican prickly poppy)		●								●			●												
ASCLEPIAS CURASSAVICA (blood flower)			●						●	●	●	●							●						
ASPERULA ORIENTALIS (annual woodruff)					●			●				●			●	●	●		◉						
* ASTER TANACETIFOLIUS (Tahoka daisy)					●					●		●			●										
ATRIPLEX HORTENSIS (orach)				●			●				●	●											●		
* AVENA STERILIS (animated oat)										●		●	●	●						●	●				
BEGONIA SEMPERFLORENS (wax begonia)	●		●	●			●	●				●			◉		●							●	
BELLIS PERENNIS (English daisy)	●		●	●				●				●			●	●									
BRACHYCOME IBERIDIFOLIA (Swan River daisy)	●		●		●			●				●						●	●					●	
BRASSICA OLERACEA ACEPHALA (ornamental kale)						●	●	●				●													
BRASSICA OLERACEA CAPITATA (ornamental cabbage)						●	●	●				●													
BRIZA MAXIMA (large quaking grass)									●			●	●							●	●				
BRIZA MINOR (lesser quaking grass)								●				●	●							●	●				
BROWALLIA SPECIOSA MAJOR (browallia)	●				●				●			●			●	●								●	●
BROWALLIA VISCOSA COMPACTA (sticky browallia)					●			●	●			●			●	●		●						●	●
CALANDRINIA GRANDIFLORA (rock purslane)			●						●			●	●												●
CALANDRINIA MENZIESII (red maids)			●					●				●	●											●	●
CALANDRINIA UMBELLATA (rock purslane)			●					●				●	●											●	●
CALENDULA OFFICINALIS (calendula)	●	●							●			●						●							
CALLISTEPHUS CHINENSIS (China aster)	●	●	●	●	●				●	●		●			●			●							
CALONYCTION ACULEATUM (moonflower)	●										●	●							◉			●	●		
CAMPANULA MEDIUM (Canterbury bells)	●		●		●					●		●			●			●							
CARDIOSPERMUM HALICACABUM (balloon vine)	●									●	●	●										●	●		
CATANANCHE CAERULEA (Cupid's dart)					●				●			●	●							●					
CATANANCHE CAERULEA ALBA (white Cupid's dart)	●								●			●	●												

✱ *Indicates species that are relatively easy to grow from seed outdoors anywhere in the United States or southern Canada.*

◉ *Indicates a characteristic for which the plant is especially noted.*

Name	White	Yellow-orange	Pink-rose	Red	Blue-purple	Multicolor	Colored foliage	6 to 12 inches	1 to 2 feet	2 to 3 feet	Over 3 feet	Sun-average soil	Sun-dry soil	Sun-moist soil	Partial shade-average soil	Partial shade-dry soil	Partial shade-moist soil	Cut flowers	Fragrance	Dried flowers (everlastings)	Ornamental grasses	Climbing vines	Hedges, screens	Window boxes, planters	Hanging baskets
CATANANCHE CAERULEA BICOLOR (bicolor Cupid's dart)					●				●			●	●							●					
CELOSIA ARGENTEA CRISTATA (cockscomb)		●	●	●				●	●			●	●					●							
CELOSIA ARGENTEA PLUMOSA (feather cockscomb)	●	●	●	●				●	●	●		●	●					●		●				●	
CENIA BARBATA (pincushion flower)		●						●				●	●												
CENTAUREA AMERICANA (basket flower)	●		●		●					●	●	●						●						●	
CENTAUREA CINERARIA (dusty miller)			●				●		●			●	●											●	●
CENTAUREA CYANUS (cornflower)	●		●	●	●			●	●	●		●	●					●							
* CENTAUREA GYMNOCARPA (velvet centaurea)			●				●		●			●	●											●	●
* CENTAUREA MOSCHATA (sweet sultan)	●	●	●		●				●	●		●						●	◉						
CERINTHE ASPERA (honeywort)						●			●			●	●												
CHARIEIS HETEROPHYLLA (charieis)					●			●				●	●					●	●					●	●
CHEIRANTHUS ALLIONII (Siberian wallflower)		●						●				●	●		●	●		●	◉						
CHEIRANTHUS CHEIRI (English wallflower)		●	●	●		●		●	●			●	●		●	●		●	◉						
CHRYSANTHEMUM, hybrids (annual chrysanthemum)	●	●	●	●	●	●			●			●						●							
CHRYSANTHEMUM PARTHENIUM (feverfew)	●	●						●	●			●	●		●			●							
CIRSIUM JAPONICUM (plumed thistle)			●							●		●	●	●											
CLADANTHUS ARABICUS (cladanthus)		●								●		●	●												
CLARKIA ELEGANS and C. PULCHELLA (clarkia)	●		●	●	●				●	●		●	●	●				●							
CLEOME HASSLERANA (cleome)	●		●		●					●	●	●	●					●							
CLEOME LUTEA (yellow cleome)		●								●		●	●					●							
COBAEA SCANDENS (cup-and-saucer vine)	●				●					●	●	●										●	●		
COIX LACRYMA-JOBI (Job's tears)										●		●	●							●	●				
COLEUS BLUMEI (coleus)							●	●	●	●		●	●		◉	●								●	
COLLINSIA HETEROPHYLLA (collinsia)						●			●						●	●	●	●							
CONSOLIDA AMBIGUA (larkspur)	●		●		●				●	●		●						●							
* CONVOLVULUS TRICOLOR (dwarf morning glory)	●		◉	●	●	●		●				●	●	●										●	●
* COREOPSIS DRUMMONDII and C. TINCTORIA (coreopsis)		●		●				●	●	●	●	●	●	●				●							
* COSMOS BIPINNATUS (cosmos)	●		●	●						●	●	●	●		●	●		●						●	
* COSMOS SULPHUREUS (yellow cosmos)		●		●						●		●	●		●	●		●							
CREPIS RUBRA (hawk's beard)			●					●				●	●												
CROTALARIA RETUSA (crotalaria)		●				●			●			●	●					●							
CUPHEA IGNEA and C. MINIATA (cigar plant)		●	●	●				●	●			●						●						●	●
CYNOGLOSSUM AMABILE (Chinese forget-me-not)					●	●			●			●			●	●	●	●				●			
* DAHLIA, hybrids (dahlia)			●	●	●	●			●	●		●			●							●			
DATURA METEL (trumpet flower)	●	●	●	●	●				●	●	●	●						●							
* DIANTHUS BARBATUS (sweet William)	●		●	●	●	●		●				●						●							
DIANTHUS CARYOPHYLLUS (annual carnation)	●	●	●	●		●		●	●			●						●	◉						
* DIANTHUS CHINENSIS (China pink)	●		●	●		●		●				●						●							
DIASCIA BARBERAE (twinspur)		●	●					●				●													
DIGITALIS PURPUREA, annual type (annual foxglove)	●	●	●		●					●	●				●										
DIMORPHOTHECA, hybrids (cape marigold)	●	●	●			●		●				●	●												
DOLICHOS LABLAB (hyacinth bean)	●				●						●	●										●	●		
* ECHINOCYSTIS LOBATA (wild cucumber)	●										●	●	●	●								●	●		
ECHIUM PLANTAGINEUM (viper's bugloss)	●		●		●			●				●	◉												
EMILIA FLAMMEA (tassel flower)		●		●					●			●	●					●							
* ESCHSCHOLZIA CALIFORNICA (California poppy)	●	●	●	●		●		●				●	●											●	
EUPHORBIA HETEROPHYLLA (annual poinsettia)							●			●		●	◉					●							
* EUPHORBIA MARGINATA (snow-on-the-mountain)							●		●			●	◉					●							
FELICIA AMELLOIDES (blue daisy)					●			●				●						●							
FELICIA BERGERIANA (kingfisher daisy)					●			●				●						●							

167

	FLOWER COLOR							PLANT HEIGHT				LIGHT AND SOIL REQUIREMENTS						USES							
	White	Yellow-orange	Pink-rose	Red	Blue-purple	Multicolor	Colored foliage	6 to 12 inches	1 to 2 feet	2 to 3 feet	Over 3 feet	Sun-average soil	Sun-dry soil	Sun-moist soil	Partial shade-average soil	Partial shade-dry soil	Partial shade-moist soil	Cut flowers	Fragrance	Dried flowers (everlastings)	Ornamental grasses	Climbing vines	Hedges, screens	Window boxes, planters	Hanging baskets
FRAGARIA VESCA (Alpine strawberry)	●						●					●			●										
GAILLARDIA AMBLYODON and G. PULCHELLA (gaillardia)		●	●		●				●			●	◉	●				●						●	
GAMOLEPIS TAGETES (sunshine daisy)		●	●						●			●	◉					●						●	
GAZANIA LONGISCAPA (gazania)		●	●	●					●			●	◉												
GILIA CAPITATA (blue thimble flower)					●				●			●						●							
GILIA HYBRIDA (stardust)		●	●	●					●			●													
GODETIA AMOENA (farewell-to-spring)	●		●	●	●			●	●	●		●			●			●							
GODETIA GRANDIFLORA (satinflower)	●		●	●				●	●			●			●			●							
* GOMPHRENA GLOBOSA (globe amaranth)	●	●	●		●			●	●			●	●					●		●			●		
* GOURDS										●	●	●										●	●	●	
* GYPSOPHILA ELEGANS (annual babies'-breath)	●		●						●			●	●					●							
* HELIANTHUS ANNUUS (common sunflower)		●							●	●		●											●		
* HELIANTHUS DEBILIS (cucumberleaf sunflower)	●	●	●	●		●			●	●	●	●	◉					●			◉		●		
* HELICHRYSUM BRACTEATUM (strawflower)	●	●	●	●	●					●		●						●		◉					
HELIOTROPIUM CORYMBOSUM (big heliotrope)	●				●				●			●						●	◉					●	
HELIOTROPIUM PERUVIANUM (common heliotrope)	●				●				●			●						●	◉					●	
HELIPTERUM MANGLESII (Swan River everlasting)	●		●		●			●				●	●					●		◉					
HELIPTERUM ROSEUM (rose everlasting)	●		●						●			●	●					●		◉					
HIBISCUS MANIHOT (sunset hibiscus)		●								●	●	●		●									●		
HIBISCUS TRIONUM (flower-of-an-hour)		●							●			●		●											
HORDEUM JUBATUM (squirreltail grass)								●	●	●		●	◉					●		●	●				
HUMULUS SCANDENS (Japanese hop vine)										●	●	●		●								●	●		
HUNNEMANNIA FUMARIAEFOLIA (Mexican tulip poppy)		●							●			●	◉												
* IBERIS AMARA CORONARIA (hyacinth-flowered candytuft)	●								●						●			●	◉						
* IBERIS UMBELLATA (globe candytuft)	●		●	●					●						●			●							
* IMPATIENS BALSAMINA (garden balsam)	●		●	●	●	●		●	●	●		●			●										
IMPATIENS WALLERANA (patient Lucy)	●	●	●	●	●	●		●	●						◉		●							●	●
* IPOMOEA PURPUREA and I. TRICOLOR (morning glory)	●		●	●	●	●					●	●										●	●		
IRESINE HERBSTII and I. LINDENII (bloodleaf)							●		●			●		●										●	
* KOCHIA SCOPARIA TRICHOPHILA (burning bush)							●			●		●	●										●		
LAGURUS OVATUS (rabbit-tail grass)								●				●	●					●		●	●				
LANTANA CAMARA (common lantana)	●	●	●	●		●			●			●	●						●					●	
LANTANA MONTEVIDENSIS (trailing lantana)					●				●			●	●						●					●	●
LATHYRUS ODORATUS (sweet pea)	●	●	●	●	●	●		●	●			●		●				●	◉			●			
LAVATERA TRIMESTRIS (tree mallow)	●		●							●	●	●						●					●		
LAYIA CAMPESTRIS (tidy tips)		●							●			●						●					●		
LIMONIUM BONDUELLII SUPERBUM (Algerian statice)		●							●			●	●					●		●					
LIMONIUM SINUATUM (notchleaf statice)	●		●		●				●			●	●					●		●					
LIMONIUM SUWOROWII (rat-tail statice)			●						●			●	●					●							
LINARIA MAROCCANA (Morocco toadflax)	●	●	●	●	●	●		●				●						●							
LINUM GRANDIFLORUM (flowering flax)	●		●	●					●			●						●							
LINUM USITATISSIMUM (common flax)	●				●					●		●													
LOBELIA ERINUS (edging lobelia)	●		●	●				●							●									●	●
* LOBULARIA MARITIMA (sweet alyssum)	●		●		●			●							●				●					●	●
* LUPINUS, hybrids (annual lupines)	●	●	●		●	●			●	●		●			●			●							
LUPINUS SUBCARNOSUS (Texas bluebonnet)					●				●			●			●			●							
MALCOMIA MARITIMA (Virginia stock)	●	●	●	●	●			●				●	●	●	●	●	●								
MALOPE TRIFIDA (malope)	●		●	●						●		●	●					●							
MATHIOLA BICORNIS (evening stock)			●		●				●			●			●	●		●	◉						
MATHIOLA INCANA ANNUA (common stock)	●	●	●	●	●				●	●		●		●				●	◉						

* *Indicates species that are relatively easy to grow from seed outdoors anywhere in the United States or southern Canada.*

◉ *Indicates a characteristic for which the plant is especially noted.*

Plant	FLOWER COLOR							PLANT HEIGHT				LIGHT AND SOIL REQUIREMENTS						USES							
	White	Yellow-orange	Pink-rose	Red	Blue-purple	Multicolor	Colored foliage	6 to 12 inches	1 to 2 feet	2 to 3 feet	Over 3 feet	Sun-average soil	Sun-dry soil	Sun-moist soil	Partial shade-average soil	Partial shade-dry soil	Partial shade-moist soil	Cut flowers	Fragrance	Dried flowers (everlastings)	Ornamental grasses	Climbing vines	Hedges, screens	Window boxes, planters	Hanging baskets
MAURANDIA BARCLAIANA (maurandia)	●		●		●						●	●										●	●	●	
MENTZELIA LINDLEYI (blazing star)		●						●				●	●					●							
MESEMBRYANTHEMUM CORDIFOLIUM VARIEGATUM (variegated heartleaf mesembryanthemum)			●			●	●	●				●	◎												●
MESEMBRYANTHEMUM CRINIFLORUM (Livingston daisy)	●	●	●	●			●	●				●	◎												●
MESEMBRYANTHEMUM CRYSTALLINUM (ice plant)	●					●	●	●				●	◎												●
MESEMBRYANTHEMUM GRAMINEUM (tricolor mesembryanthemum)	●		●	●			●	●				●	◎												●
MIMOSA PUDICA (sensitive plant)					●			●				●	●												
MIMULUS, hybrids (monkey flower)		●		●		●		●							●		◎								
* MIRABILIS JALAPA (four-o'clock)	●	●	●	●	●	●			●	●		●	●												
MOLUCELLA LAEVIS (bells-of-Ireland)	●								●		●						●		●	●				
MOMORDICA BALSAMINA (balsam apple)		●								●	●	●		●								●	●		
MOMORDICA CHARANTIA (balsam pear)		●								●	●	●		●								●	●		
MYOSOTIS SYLVATICA (woodland forget-me-not)	●		●		●			●							●	●	●	●							
NEMESIA STRUMOSA (nemesia)	●	●	●	●	●	●		●				●						●							
NEMOPHILA MENZIESII (baby blue-eyes)					●			●							●			●							
* NICOTIANA ALATA GRANDIFLORA (flowering tobacco)	●	●	●	●					●			●			●			●	◎						
NIEREMBERGIA CAERULEA (cupflower)			●			●		●				●			●	●								●	
* NIGELLA DAMASCENA (love-in-a-mist)	●		●		●			●				●						●		●					
OCIMUM BASILICUM (sweet basil)	●			●			●	●				●	●						●					●	
OENOTHERA DELTOIDES (hairy-calyx sundrops)	●								●			●			●			●							
OXYPETALUM CAERULEUM (southern star)					●				●			●													
PAPAVER ALPINUM (Alpine poppy)	●	●	●			●		●				●						●	●						
PAPAVER GLAUCUM (tulip poppy)				●					●			●													
* PAPAVER NUDICAULE (Iceland poppy)	●	●	●	●					●			●						●	●						
* PAPAVER RHOEAS (Shirley poppy)	●	●	●	●		●			●			●						●							
PELARGONIUM DOMESTICUM (Lady Washington geranium)	●		●	●	●	●			●			●		●	●	●								●	
PELARGONIUM HORTORUM (common geranium)	●		●	●	●	●	●		●	●		●		●	●	●								●	
PELARGONIUM PELTATUM (ivy geranium)	●		●	●	●	●			●			●		●	●	●								●	●
* PENNISETUM RUPPELII (fountain grass)			●	●						●	●	●		●						●	●		●		
* PENNISETUM VILLOSUM (feathertop)	●									●		●								●	●		●		
PENSTEMON GLOXINIOIDES (penstemon)	●		●	●	●					●		●			●			●							
PERILLA FRUTESCENS CRISPA (beefsteak plant)	●		●				●		●			●	●											●	
PETUNIA, hybrids (petunia)	●	●	●	●	●	●		●	●			●			●			●	●					●	●
PHACELIA CAMPANULARIA (California blue bells)					●		●					●	◎												
PHACELIA TANACETIFOLIA (wild heliotrope)					●				●			●		●											
PHACELIA VISCIDA (sticky phacelia)					●				●			●		●											
* PHASEOLUS COCCINEUS (scarlet runner bean)				●					●		●	●										●	●		
* PHASEOLUS COCCINEUS ALBUS (white Dutch runner bean)	●								●		●	●										●	●		
PHLOX DRUMMONDII (annual phlox)	●	●	●	●	●	●		●	●			●	●		●			●						●	
* PORTULACA GRANDIFLORA (portulaca)	●	●	●	●		●		●				●	◎											●	
PRIMULA MALACOIDES (fairy primrose)	●		●	●					●						●		●								
PRIMULA OBCONICA (obconica primrose)	●		●	●	●				●						●		●								
PRIMULA POLYANTHA (polyanthus primrose)	●	●	●	●	●	●		●							●		●								
PROBOSCIDEA LOUISIANICA (unicorn plant)	●		●		●	●				●		●								●					
PUERARIA LOBATA (kudzu vine)					●						●	●	●	●								●	●		
* QUAMOCLIT COCCINEA (scarlet star glory)				●							●	●			●							●	●		
* QUAMOCLIT LOBATA (crimson star glory)				●							●	●			●		●					●	●		
* QUAMOCLIT PENNATA (cypress vine)	●	●		●							●	●	●									●	●		
* QUAMOCLIT SLOTERI (cardinal climber)				●							●	●	●									●	●		
RESEDA ODORATA (mignonette)		●		●					●			●			●			●	◎					●	

169

CHARACTERISTICS OF ANNUALS: CONTINUED

	Species	White	Yellow-orange	Pink-rose	Red	Blue-purple	Multicolor	Colored foliage	6 to 12 inches	1 to 2 feet	2 to 3 feet	Over 3 feet	Sun-average soil	Sun-dry soil	Sun-moist soil	Partial shade-average soil	Partial shade-dry soil	Partial shade-moist soil	Cut flowers	Fragrance	Dried flowers (everlastings)	Ornamental grasses	Climbing vines	Hedges, screens	Window boxes, planters	Hanging baskets
*	RICINUS COMMUNIS (castor bean)				●			●				●	●						●					●		
*	RUDBECKIA HIRTA GLORIOSA (gloriosa daisy)		●							●	●		●			●	●		●							
	SALPIGLOSSIS SINUATA (painted tongue)		●	●	●	●					●		●						●							
	SALVIA FARINACEA (mealycup sage)	●				●					●		●						●							
	SALVIA HORMINUM (clary)	●		●				●		●			●						●		●					
	SALVIA PATENS (gentian sage)					●				●			●						●							
	SALVIA SPLENDENS (scarlet sage)	●		●	●	●			●	●	●		●						●							
*	SANVITALIA PROCUMBENS (creeping zinnia)		●				●		●				●	●												●
*	SCABIOSA ATROPURPUREA (pincushion flower)	●		●	●	●				●	●		●						●	●						
	SCHIZANTHUS WISETONENSIS (butterfly flower)	●	●	●	●	●	●			●	●		●			●	●		●	●					●	●
	SENECIO CINERARIA (dusty miller)		●			●	●	●	●				●	●											●	●
	SENECIO CRUENTUS (cineraria)	●		●	●	●	●			●								●								
	SENECIO ELEGANS (purple groundsel)	●		●	●	●				●			●						●							
	SILENE ARMERIA (none-so-pretty)			●						●			●												●	
	SILENE OCULATA (rose-of-heaven)	●		●	●	●			●				●						●						●	
	SILENE PENDULA (drooping catchfly)	●		●	●				●				●												●	
*	TAGETES (African-French hybrid marigold)		●		●		●		●				●						●	●					●	
*	TAGETES ERECTA (African marigold)		●								●	●	●						●	●					●	
*	TAGETES PATULA (French marigold)		●		●		●		●	●			●						●	●					●	●
*	TAGETES TENUIFOLIA PUMILA (dwarf marigold)		●						●				●						●	●					●	●
	THUNBERGIA ALATA (black-eyed Susan vine)	●	●				●					●	●			●							●		●	●
	THUNBERGIA GIBSONII (orange clock vine)		●									●	●			●	●		●				●		●	●
	THYMOPHYLLA TENUILOBA (Dahlberg daisy)		●				●		●				●	●					●						●	
*	TITHONIA ROTUNDIFOLIA (tithonia)			●								●	●	●					●					●		
	TORENIA FOURNIERI (wishbone flower)	●	●			●	●		●							●		◎							●	●
	TRACHELIUM CAERULEUM (throatwort)					●				●			●		●				●	●						
	TRACHYMENE CAERULEA (blue lace flower)	●				●				●			●						●	●						
	TRICHOLAENA ROSEA (ruby grass)			●								●	●	●							●	●				
*	TROPAEOLUM MAJUS (common nasturtium)	●	●	●	●				●	●		●	◎						●	◎					●	●
	TROPAEOLUM PEREGRINUM (canary-bird flower)		●									●	●			●	●						●			
	TROPAEOLUM SPECIOSUM (flame flower)				●							●	●			●			●				●			
	URSINIA ANETHOIDES (dill-leaf ursinia)		●				●			●			●	●					●						●	
	VENIDIUM FASTUOSUM (monarch-of-the-veldt)	●	●				●			●			●	◎					●							
	VERBENA HORTENSIS (garden verbena)	●		●	●	●	●		●				●							◎					●	●
	VERBESINA ENCELIOIDES (golden crownbeard)		●								●	●	●	●					●							
	VINCA MAJOR VARIEGATA (variegated periwinkle)					●		●		●			●			●							●		●	
	VINCA ROSEA (Madagascar periwinkle)	●		●	●		●		●	●			●													
	VIOLA WILLIAMSII (tufted pansy)	●	●		●	●			●				●			●		●	●	●					●	
	VIOLA WITTROCKIANA (pansy)	●	●	●	●	●	●		●				●			●		●	●	●					●	
	XANTHISMA TEXANUM (star-of-Texas)		●								●	●	●	◎					●						●	
	XERANTHEMUM ANNUUM (common immortelle)			●	●					●			●						●		◎					
*	ZEA MAYS JAPONICA (rainbow corn)						●					●	●	●								●				
*	ZINNIA ELEGANS (zinnia)	●	●	●	●	●	●		●	●	●		●						●							

Indicates species that are relatively easy to grow from seed outdoors anywhere in the United States or southern Canada.

◎ *Indicates a characteristic for which the plant is especially noted.*

Credits

The sources for the illustrations that appear in this book are listed below. Credits for pictures from left to right are separated by semicolons, from top to bottom by dashes. Cover—Gottlieb Hampfler.
4—Keith Martin courtesy James Underwood Crockett; Leonard Wolfe. 6—Farrell Grehan (garden design by Matt Kearney, Superintendent of Grounds, Dumbarton Oaks, Washington, D.C.). 10 through 15—Drawings by Vincent Lewis. 17—Ralph Crane (plantings by John Chiappelone, Burlingame Garden Center, Burlingame, Calif.). 18, 19—Marjorie Pickens. 20, 21—Leonard McCombe (garden design by Jacques Cartier, Santa Fe, N.M.). 22, 23—Humphrey Sutton (Mr. & Mrs. Walter Dunnington, Southampton, N.Y., garden design by Umberto Innocenti, A.S.L.A.); Humphrey Sutton (Mr. & Mrs. Lloyd Hilton Smith, Southampton, N.Y., plantings by Henrik Andreasen). 24 through 27—Bill Ratcliffe. 28, 29—Dean Brown. 30, 31—Guy Burgess; Allan Grant (garden design by Harriet Wimmer, A.S.L.A., San Diego, Calif.). 32, 33—James Underwood Crockett (garden design by Waltham Field Station, University of Massachusetts). 34, 35—Leonard Wolfe. 36—Farrell Grehan. 38 through 45—Drawings by Vincent Lewis. 48 through 51—Chart by Rebecca Merrilees. 53—Dean Brown (garden design by Fairman Furness, Media, Pa.). 54, 55—Dean Brown. 56, 57—Fred Lyon from Rapho Guillumette (garden design by Thomas Church, A.S.L.A., San Francisco, Calif.). 58-59—Guy Burgess (garden design by Jane S. Ries); Ralph Crane (2) (plantings by John Chiappelone). 60—Nina Leen (garden design by Herbert L. Seigle, Pittsburgh, Pa.; plantings by Terrestris Greenhouses, New York City). 61—Marjorie Pickens. 62—Ralph Crane (plantings by John Chiappelone). 68, 69—Drawings by Vincent Lewis. 71—Molly Adams. 72 through 75—Pedro Guerrero (flower arrangements by Fleurette Guilloz). 76—Richard Meek (courtesy Howard Bodger Seeds, Ltd., Lompoc, Calif.). 80 through 87—Drawings by Vincent Lewis. 88 through 163—Illustrations by Allianora Rosse. 164-165—Maps by Adolph E. Brotman.

Acknowledgments

For their help in the preparation of this book, the editors wish to thank the following: Bachman's Florists & Nurserymen, Minneapolis, Minn.; Mrs. Ernesta Drinker Ballard, Director, Pennsylvania Horticultural Society, Philadelphia, Pa.; Mrs. Griffing Bancroft, La Jolla, Calif.; Behnke Nursery Co., Beltsville, Md.; Burkhart Landscape Co., Dallas, Texas; Mahlon R. Colborne, Horticulturist, Sterling Forest Gardens, Tuxedo, N.Y.; Mrs. L. N. Copeland, St. Louis, Mo.; Mrs. Edith Crockett, Librarian, Horticultural Society of New York, New York City; Mrs. Muriel C. Crossman, Librarian. Massachusetts Horticultural Society, Boston, Mass.; Robert J. Falasca, American Seed Trade Association, Washington, D.C.; Mrs. O'Neil Ford, San Antonio, Texas; Elizabeth C. Hall, Senior Librarian, Horticultural Society of New York, New York City; Mrs. Henderson Heyward, Charlottesville, Va.; Dr. Ray R. Kriner, Entomologist and Pesticide Specialist, Rutgers University, New Brunswick, N.J.; Lambert Landscape Co., Dallas, Texas; Carlton B. Lees, Executive Director, Massachusetts Horticultural Society, Boston, Mass.; Charles S. Lewis, Director, Sterling Forest Gardens, Tuxedo, N.Y.; Mrs. Lothian Lynas, Assistant Librarian, New York Botanical Gardens, New York City; The Manhattan Gardener, Ltd., New York City; Mrs. Edwin McCarty, Atlanta, Ga.; Richard B. Myrick & Associates, Dallas, Texas; Klaus Neubner, Chief Horticulturist, Park Seed Co., Greenwood, S.C.; Mrs. Edward J. Neuner, Chesterfield, Mo.; Albert P. Nordheden, Program Officer and Senior Horticulturist, Horticultural Society of New York, New York City; Dr. T. E. Pope, Horticulturist, Chamber of Commerce, New Orleans, La.; Carolyn Ramsey, New Orleans, La.; Charles Reid & Sons Nursery, Osterville, Mass.; Philip Tattersfield & Associates, Vancouver, B.C.; Dorothea Schnibben Thompson, Chapel Hill, N.C.; John Wassung, Westport, Conn.; Henry G. Wendler, Garden Information, Massachusetts Horticultural Society, Boston, Mass.; Mrs. Ola Word, Director, Longue Vue Gardens and Rosedown Plantation, New Orleans, La. Recipe for marigold chowder on page 78 is from *A Feast of Flowers* by Francesca Tillona and Cynthia Strowbridge, © 1969 by Francesca Tillona and Cynthia Strowbridge, reprinted by permission of the publishers, Funk & Wagnalls, New York City.

Regional consultants

Dr. Curtis H. Dearborn
Research Horticulturist
Palmer, Alaska

Professor A. F. DeWerth
Floriculture Section
Texas A&M University
College Station, Texas

Professor R. D. Dickey
Ornamental Horticulturist
University of Florida
Gainesville, Florida

Robert J. Dingwall
Chief Horticulturist
Missouri Botanical Garden
St. Louis, Missouri

Dr. C. G. Hard
Associate Professor,
Landscape Design and
Environmental Planning

University of Minnesota
St. Paul, Minnesota

Dr. A. C. Hildreth, Director Emeritus
Denver Botanic Gardens
Denver, Colorado

Leslie Laking
Director of the Royal
Botanical Gardens
Hamilton, Ontario, Canada

Dr. Joseph W. Love
Horticultural Science Department
North Carolina State University
Raleigh, North Carolina

Victor H. Ries
Garden Consultant
Columbus, Ohio

Dr. Roy L. Taylor
Director of the Botanical Garden
The University of British Columbia
Vancouver, Canada

John Walker
Professor of Horticulture (ret.)
University of Manitoba
Manitoba, Canada

Dr. Fred B. Widmoyer
Professor and Head of the
Department of Horticulture
New Mexico State University
Las Cruces, New Mexico

Jean A. Witt
Seattle, Washington

Joseph A. Witt
Assistant Director
University of Washington Arboretum
Seattle, Washington

Index

Numerals in italics indicate an illustration of the subject mentioned

PRINTED IN U.S.A.